Customer Satisfaction Research Management

Also available from ASQ Quality Press:

Analysis of Customer Satisfaction Data
Derek R. Allen and Tanniru R. Rao

Linking Customer and Employee Satisfaction to the Bottom Line
Derek R. Allen and Morris Wilburn

Customer Centered Six Sigma: Linking Customers, Process Improvement, and Financial Results
Earl Naumann and Steven H. Hoisington

Customer Satisfaction Measurement Simplified: A Step-by-Step Guide for ISO 9001:2000 Certification
Terry G. Vavra

Improving Your Measurement of Customer Satisfaction: A Guide to Creating, Conducting, Analyzing and Reporting Customer Satisfaction Measurement Programs
Terry G. Vavra

Measuring Customer Satisfaction: Survey Design, Use, and Statistical Analysis Methods, Second Edition
Bob E. Hayes

The Trust Imperative: Performance Improvement Through Productive Relationships
Stephen Hacker and Marsha Willard

Customer Satisfaction Measurement and Management
Earl Naumann and Kathleen Giel

Performance Measurement Explained: Designing and Implementing Your State-of-the-Art System
Bjørn Andersen and Tom Fagerhaug

Value Leadership: Winning Competitive Advantage in the Information Age
Michael C. Harris

To request a complimentary catalog of ASQ Quality Press publications, call 800-248-1946, or visit our Web site at http://qualitypress.asq.org.

Customer Satisfaction Research Management

A Comprehensive Guide to
Integrating Customer Loyalty and
Satisfaction Metrics in the Management
of Complex Organizations

Derek R. Allen

ASQ Quality Press
Milwaukee, Wisconsin

American Society for Quality, Quality Press, Milwaukee 53203
© 2004 by ASQ
All rights reserved. Published 2004
Printed in the United States of America

12 11 10 09 08 07 06 05 04 03   5 4 3 2 1

Library of Congress Cataloging-in-Publication Data
Allen, Derek R., 1959–
 Customer satisfaction research management : a comprehensive guide to
  integrating customer loyalty and satisfaction metrics in the management of
  complex organizations / Derek R. Allen.
   p. cm.
  "American Society for Quality."
  Includes bibliographical references and index.
  ISBN 0-87389-593-2 (hard cover, casebound)
  1. Consumer satisfaction—Research. 2. Customer loyalty—Research.
3. Customer services—Quality control—Research. 4. Customer services—
Management—Research. 5. Marketing research—Management. I. American
Society for Quality. II. Title.

 HF5415.335.A432 2004
 658.8'343—dc22   2004003921

ISBN 0-87389-593-2

Publisher: William A. Tony
Acquisitions Editor: Annemieke Hytinen
Project Editor: Paul O'Mara
Production Administrator: Randall Benson
Special Marketing Representative: David Luth

ASQ Mission: The American Society for Quality advances individual,
organizational, and community excellence worldwide through learning, quality
improvement, and knowledge exchange.

Attention Bookstores, Wholesalers, Schools, and Corporations: ASQ Quality Press
books, videotapes, audiotapes, and software are available at quantity discounts
with bulk purchases for business, educational, or instructional use. For
information, please contact ASQ Quality Press at 800-248-1946, or write to ASQ
Quality Press, P.O. Box 3005, Milwaukee, WI 53201-3005.

Quality Press
600 N. Plankinton Avenue
Milwaukee, Wisconsin 53203
Call toll free 800-248-1946
Fax 414-272-1734
www.asq.org
http://qualitypress.asq.org
http://standardsgroup.asq.org
E-mail: authors@asq.org

To place orders or to request a free copy
of the ASQ Quality Press Publications
Catalog, including ASQ membership
information, call 800-248-1946. Visit our
Web site at www.asq.org or
http://qualitypress.asq.org.

∞ Printed on acid-free paper

Contents

List of Figures

Preface

This book, intended for advanced service quality managers and marketing researchers who manage large-scale customer satisfaction programs, is the third and final title in a series that focuses on customer satisfaction measurement, analysis, and implementation. The first book, *Analysis of Customer Satisfaction Data* (Allen and Rao, 2000), examined how customer satisfaction data are analyzed using a wide variety of advanced statistical techniques. The second book, *Linking Customer and Employee Satisfaction Data to the Bottom Line* (Allen and Wilburn, 2002), provided a theoretical and empirical treatment of the linkage between customer and employee attitudes and corporate financial performance. This final book assumes you are at least minimally familiar with the psychometric aspects of customer satisfaction measurement, statistical analysis, and linkage research that attempts to establish a causal relationship between customer attitudes and business outcomes.

Although I cover some theoretical groundwork in the first chapter, the remainder focuses on a series of topics that will remain salient in customer satisfaction and loyalty research for many years. Among these are the challenges of conducting global customer satisfaction measurement (CSM) programs, linking performance metrics to management compensation systems and financial outcomes, and results deployment. I have also described reporting innovations and the more problematic aspects of implementing and tracking key-driver analyses.

I begin with the theoretical and empirical relationship between customer satisfaction and financial performance. In essence, the first chapter makes a case for the importance of customer satisfaction with respect to the bottom line. The next seven chapters all address applied business problems associated with managing large-scale customer satisfaction programs. Chapter 2 describes the increasingly varied roles enjoyed by customer satisfaction programs and considers CSM as one of the components of a broader business performance measurement system: the balanced scorecard.

A significant portion of the text is dedicated to programs that link customer feedback to management incentive systems. Chapter 3 and Chapter 4 both address this very important aspect of customer satisfaction program management. Chapter 3 provides a general theoretical discussion of human motivation in the workplace, which becomes increasingly focused and ends with a specific examination of the role of customer feedback in incentive systems. With a strong theoretical foundation set, Chapter 4 turns directly to quantitative applications involving customer feedback and management incentive systems. Several case studies are presented with references to Appendix B, which provides a host of statistical tests appropriate for different scenarios including the use of the finite population correction factor.

The use of multiple regression and various derivatives remains a cornerstone in the statistical derivation of importance in customer satisfaction programs. Chapter 5 reviews the differences between derived and stated importance, describes how key-driver analysis serves as a marginal resource allocation tool, and briefly introduces some exotic forms of multiple regression analysis. Of special interest is a discussion of the sometimes dynamic nature of key-driver results. In particular, longitudinal changes in key-driver status (or magnitude) are a source of considerable discourse in many of the hundreds of customer satisfaction programs I have encountered as a consultant.

CRM represents an important paradigm shift in business strategy— from a product-centric organization to a customer-focused enterprise. The nature of CRM and its abstruse connection with customer satisfaction measurement (CSM) is the focus of Chapter 6. The relationship between CRM and CSM is especially engaging because one of the ostensible benefits of CRM is greater customer satisfaction. As described in this chapter, customer feedback can be an input to a CRM system and also used to measure its efficacy.

Although an entire book in this series is dedicated to explicating the relationship between customer satisfaction and desirable business outcomes like profitability and market share, Chapter 7 presents the fundamental building blocks necessary to establish this link empirically. Those of you interested in a more comprehensive treatment of the topic may want to refer to the second book in this series.

Chapter 8 introduces management surrounding global customer satisfaction programs. A variety of practical topics relating to instrument design, data collection, and general program management are discussed. Of particular relevance is a treatment of the psychometric implications of cultural bias in global customer satisfaction programs. One of the most salient and perplexing topics in these programs involves comparisons of metrics across countries and the effects of cultural idiosyncrasies. A review of the literature and some approaches to this potentially troublesome topic are presented.

One particularly important aspect of customer satisfaction programs—the linkage to business processes—is reviewed in Chapter 9. Occasionally, companies become overly involved in measurement and tracking statistics, losing sight of the need to implement the results. Indeed, results deployment is often neglected by consultants for two reasons: (1) measurement and reporting are easier to accomplish, and (2) consultants may have little clout in the client's organization. Chapter 9 focuses on these very practical aspects of customer satisfaction program management.

The final chapter of this book presents an innovative approach to the treatment of customer satisfaction and loyalty data. In effect, the architecture introduced in Chapter 10 asserts that most customer satisfaction research fails to engage dissatisfied or moderately satisfied customers. Instead, a focus on the so-called top box(es) has shifted managerial attention away from customers whose upside profit potential may be very high. That is, the return from increasing the satisfaction of an already satisfied customer may actually be lower than similar increases among more disgruntled customers. Finally, the chapter describes a way to develop unique driver profiles for customers at various points in the cumulative loyalty distribution.

Throughout this book, I present a variety of case studies that involve numerous industries, ranging from financial services to manufacturing. Customer satisfaction and loyalty research has matured most rapidly within industries that enjoy a wealth of customer data. Financial services, in particular, have a tremendous amount of customer data available. As a result, the examples in this book tend to involve banks and manufacturers of high-involvement products where customer satisfaction is highly relevant. Such is often not the case in the consumer packaged goods arena in which brand awareness, equity, and shelf placement typically dictate low-involvement purchase decisions. A great deal of very interesting work has been conducted involving brand equity and aesthetics, but this book purposefully avoids this body of literature and instead focuses on high-involvement products and services where quality enhancements may yield significant gains in customer satisfaction.

Acknowledgments

This book would not have been possible without the theoretical and technical foundations laid by many applied and academic researchers over the past 25 years. The completion of this work was greatly facilitated by the administrative skills of Sandy Cummings at Market Probe, who produced all of the graphics and spent many hours ensuring that editorial changes were implemented.

Maya Hughes provided insightful editorial input and project management during the development of this book and to her I am extremely grateful. Bob White also contributed his editorial skills to ensure an accurate manuscript. Karen Garvin endured yet another technical proofing challenge, helped ensure bibliographic accuracy, and enhanced numerous portions of this book.

Karina Kortbein at the University of California-Northridge is responsible for the discussion of inferential statistics presented in Appendix B. She also conducted library research concerning various statistical techniques, facilitated the discussion concerning cross-cultural psychometrics, and provided technical proofing.

Clearly, the support of Dr. T. R. Rao, President of Market Probe, and his decision to cultivate an organizational culture focused on methodological and statistical innovation helped ensure this book's success.

Thanks also go to the anonymous ASQ reviewers whose insights and valuable comments enhanced this volume's contribution to the customer satisfaction and loyalty research literature. Finally, I would like to express my gratitude to Annemieke Hytinen, ASQ Quality Press acquisitions editor, and Paul O'Mara, project editor.

1

Customer Satisfaction, Retention, and Profitability

INTRODUCTION

Customer satisfaction has its roots in the global quality revolution. Formalizing customer satisfaction as a component in national quality competitions such as the Malcolm Baldrige National Quality Award has further validated the customer satisfaction research agenda. Indeed, customer satisfaction enjoys a high-profile role among the Baldrige Award criteria; customer focus and satisfaction count for more than 25% of the total points in the evaluation system.

This chapter provides a succinct history of customer satisfaction research and reviews more contemporary attempts to link satisfaction to retention, and ultimately, corporate profitability. The overall objective of this book is to facilitate the implementation of customer satisfaction data in the management of complex organizations. Thus we must first demonstrate both theoretical and empirical linkages between customer satisfaction and desirable business outcomes like profitability and market share.

Ultimately, it is the fundamental assumption reflected in Figure 1.1 that drives most customer satisfaction programs. The relationship between service and product quality and overall customer satisfaction has been repeatedly demonstrated. This chapter establishes the importance of customer satisfaction in business operations and describes systematic evidence that suggests companies with higher customer satisfaction ratings tend to be more successful.

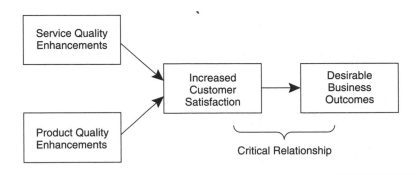

Figure 1.1   Fundamental assumption driving customer satisfaction measurement.

HISTORY OF CUSTOMER SATISFACTION RESEARCH

The first research involving the measurement of customer satisfaction occurred in the early 1980s. Works by Oliver (1980), Churchill and Surprenant (1982), and Bearden and Teel (1983) tended to focus on the operationalization of customer satisfaction and its antecedents. By the mid-1980s, the focus of both applied and academic research had shifted to construct refinement and the implementation of strategies designed to optimize customer satisfaction, according to Zeithaml, Berry, and Parasuraman (1996:31).

Rigorous scientific inquiry and the development of a general service quality theory can be attributed to Parasuraman, Berry, and Zeithaml (1985). Their discussion of customer satisfaction, service quality, and customer expectations represents one of the first attempts to operationalize satisfaction in a theoretical context. They proposed that the ratio of perceived performance to customer expectations was key to maintaining satisfied customers. Several years later, Parasuraman, Berry, and Zeithaml (1988) published a second, related discussion that focused more specifically on the psychometric aspects of service quality. Their multi-item SERVQUAL scale is considered one of the first attempts to operationalize the customer satisfaction construct. The SERVQUAL scale focused on the performance component of the service quality model in which quality was defined as the disparity between expectations and performance.

The battery of items used in the SERVQUAL multi-item scale is still used today as a foundation for instrument development. The primary areas considered in the scale involved tangibles, reliability, responsiveness, assurance, and empathy. For many years these dimensions were regarded as the basis for service quality measurement.

Throughout the 1980s, both applied and academic researchers focused on these (and other) issues and their effects on overall customer satisfaction, according to Zeithaml et al. (1996:31). That is, the primary research question involved which of the five areas was most important vis-à-vis customer expectations. Much of the earliest applied work involving the derivation of attribute importance involved stated importance measures. Surveys commonly sought both importance and performance measures for every item. The gap between these two measures was considered instrumental in resource allocation. Large gaps demanded the most attention. Note, however, that Parasuraman et al. (1988) employed regression analysis to assess the effect of each dimension relative to a dependent measure in their introduction of the SERVQUAL model. Using regression analysis and other dependency models to derive the importance of attributes relative to an outcome measure is now considered de rigueur.

CUSTOMER SATISFACTION AND BUSINESS OUTCOMES

That some businesses are interested in maximizing customer satisfaction does not necessarily reflect their corporate altruism. Indeed, an interest in customer satisfaction is almost always self-centered. After all, why should businesses measure, track, and attempt to improve customer satisfaction if there is no tangible benefit? The underlying premise, especially before the early 1990s, was that satisfied customers yield greater profits. Companies with more satisfied customers would be more successful and more profitable. And yet only limited empirical evidence supported this notion. Buzzell and Gale (1987), for example, produced evidence to link market share growth and service quality; however, the lack of more substantive evidence supporting the contention that customer satisfaction was instrumental in ensuring corporate profitability led the Council on Financial Competition to the following indictment in 1987: "Service quality as an issue is seriously overrated; service certainly is not as important as the mythic proportions it has taken on in industry trade publications and conferences."

This type of skepticism likely precipitated a flurry of academic and industry research aimed at linking customer satisfaction to corporate profitability and market share. Rust and Zahorik (1993), for example, focused on the retail banking industry. Their research related customer satisfaction, retention, and profitability. The authors concluded that retention rates drive market share and customer satisfaction is a primary determinant of retention.

Their model permitted Rust and Zahorik "to determine the spending levels of each satisfaction element which will maximize profitability, subject to the assumptions of the model and accuracy of parameter estimation" (1993:212).

Rust and Zahorik (1993:211) suggested a number of ways companies could improve customer satisfaction and thereby increase retention rates that drive profitability. Among these were "training programs to help personnel to be more responsive to customers, upgraded facilities, better data-handling systems, customer surveys and newsletters." The authors further suggested that companies with weak customer service cultures may need to change fundamentally the way they do business.

AN INTERVENING VARIABLE: CUSTOMER RETENTION

More recent efforts by authors like Zeithaml et al. (1996) have also attempted to refine the link between customer satisfaction and profitability by focusing on an intervening variable: retention. The authors presented four objectives associated with the study:

- A synthesis of existing research that links service quality and behavioral outcomes

- A hypothetical model that relates service quality to certain behaviors that precede defection

- Presentation of empirical evidence connecting service quality and behavioral intentions

- Development of a fundamental research agenda that will link individual-level behaviors to outcomes like sales and customer retention

Using a mail survey methodology, the authors achieved a 25% response rate and reported a total of 3069 returned surveys. The survey itself included several operationalizations of service quality. The first involved the SERVQUAL scale originally introduced by Parasuraman et al. in 1988. The second battery of items included a set of refined items intended to reveal five dimensions of service quality: reliability, responsiveness, assurance, empathy, and tangibles.

Behavioral intentions were developed in an effort to capture the full range of possible outcomes. A 13-item battery was developed and partially based on previous research by Cronin and Taylor (1992) and Boulding, Kalra, Staelin, and Zeithaml (1993) that presumably measured a wider range of behavioral intentions. Some of the unique survey content involved likelihood to pay a price premium and behavioral loyalty despite price increases.

The data were analyzed using a factor analytic approach. The 13-item battery was reduced using this method. Figure 1.2 summarizes the five-factor solution the authors presented. As shown, the five factors encompassed five dimensions of behavioral intent.

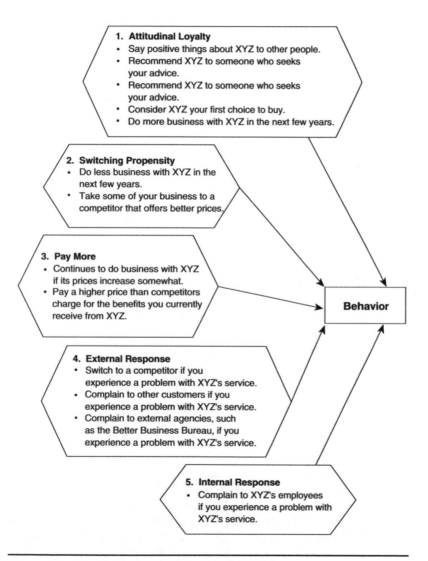

Figure 1.2   Five dimensions of behavioral intention.

When the behavioral intention measures were regressed on the SERVQUAL scale, the results strongly confirmed the authors' hypotheses. In short, the following propositions were supported:

- Customers who do not experience service problems have the best behavioral intention scores.

- Customers who do experience problems and have them favorably resolved have moderately favorable behavioral intention scores.

- Those with unresolved problems were associated with the least favorable behavioral intention scores.

Zeithaml et al. concluded that the relationship among service quality, retention, and profitability was anything but straightforward. Nonetheless, their study strongly confirmed the intuitively appealing notion that service quality significantly affects behavioral intentions.

CUSTOMER SATISFACTION, SHARE, AND PROFITABILITY

Anderson and Fornell (1994) studied a large data set of Swedish companies in their quest to produce empirical evidence that customer satisfaction pays off with greater profits. The authors presented five hypotheses relating customer satisfaction to attractive financial outcomes (see Figure 1.3).

The first hypothesis suggests that economic returns are one outcome of customer satisfaction. In short, higher levels of customer satisfaction are presumed to yield greater economic returns.

Despite its apparent simplicity, this first hypothesis captures myriad possible relationships between two key variables. For example, if increasing customer satisfaction yields a greater return on investment, at what point does this relationship begin to falter? Diminishing returns must come in to play at some point. Similarly, how much should a company invest in its effort to increase customer satisfaction in hopes of reaping bigger and bigger financial rewards?

The third hypothesis summarized in Figure 1.3 suggests that market-perceived quality has a positive effect on overall satisfaction. This is an intuitively palatable statement that accommodates the accumulation of sentiment (good or bad) relative to a company's goods or services. Past experiences with a company's product will be associated with a half-life of unknown duration. One *recent* bad experience, for example, may more strongly affect quality perceptions than a similarly negative experience in the distant past.

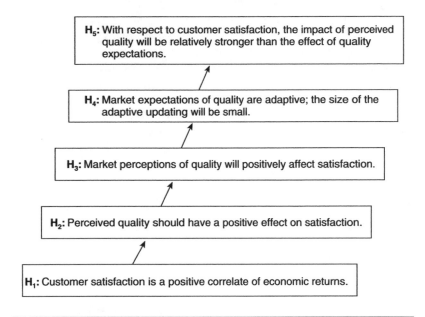

Figure 1.3   Hypotheses relating customer satisfaction to economic returns.

The fourth hypothesis links quality expectations in the market to customer satisfaction. Anderson and Fornell proposed that a customer's experience in period X_{t-1} would influence expectations in the current period X_t. In short, past experience will drive current expectations. The authors referred to this phenomenon as "adaptive expectations." This experiential information is constantly updated in the marketplace; its effects are felt on both the production and consumption sides of the equation.

Customers in mature, stable industries have more experience with suppliers' quality. The implication is that in more mature industries' adaptive expectations, the most recent (X_{t-1}) experiential information will have a lesser effect on current assessments of quality. In other words, recent experiences will have a smaller impact on marketplace quality judgments compared to the cumulative effect of past information. Again, customers in mature markets will have greater experience with quality, and, as a result, recent, perhaps anomalous, variations in quality will carry less weight. Adaptive expectations are at the core of Anderson and Fornell's final hypothesis. They suggested that the marketplace has adaptive expectations involving suppliers' goods. The relative weight given to the most recent information concerning quality will, they argued, be considerably less than the weight of all past historical information.

The study of Swedish industrial data (Anderson and Fornell, 1994) yielded some very interesting results. Both quality and expectations had a positive effect on customer satisfaction. Quality had a stronger effect on customer satisfaction. The authors concluded that a substantive "carryover effect" supported the proposition that customer satisfaction is cumulative. The effect of quality expectations on customer satisfaction was also statistically significant.

The financial outcome variables produced strong statistical models. In fact, return on investment (ROI) was strongly linked to customer satisfaction. Evidence also supported the contention that customer satisfaction is a cumulative phenomenon that develops over time. The implication is that short-term variations in quality will not necessarily affect overall customer satisfaction.

Interestingly, this study suggested that as market share increased, customer satisfaction declined. A modest ($r = -0.25$) but statistically significant correlation between the two variables was encountered. The authors found that an increase in market share from one year to the next was often associated with a *decrease* in customer satisfaction. One explanation for this phenomenon is that as companies grow they are less able to meet the idiosyncratic needs of certain customers. They are no longer able to focus on the individual customer and must instead make products that will appeal to a broader mass market.

In an effort to demonstrate the efficacy of the ROI model, the authors presented an empirical prediction of the value of a one-point increase in customer satisfaction. When projected for five years, the results were startling. Consider applying the Swedish industrial model to a sample of U.S. firms with average assets of $7.5 million and average ROI of 11%. The results would be considerable: "the cumulative incremental return associated with a continuous one-point increase in satisfaction over a five-year span would be $94 million, or 11.4% of current ROI" (p. 67).

Clearly, the Anderson and Fornell study represents a significant contribution to the growing literature linking customer satisfaction to business outcome variables. Their explicit illustration linking actual revenues to changes in customer satisfaction is noteworthy. As the body of research treating customer satisfaction as an antecedent of critical business outcome variables becomes more mature, some general heuristics likely will be developed. For example, these might be very general guidelines with respect to the impact that service versus product satisfaction variables have on profitability.

A RETURN ON QUALITY MODEL

That many companies have not yet quantified the financial benefits of their quality programs led Rust and Zahorik (1995) to focus specifically on linking service and product quality with financial outcome variables. The fact that many companies were disappointed with their quality programs precipitated Rust and Zahorik's focus on a quantitative measure they termed "return on quality," or ROQ.

The ROQ approach, according to the authors, makes four fundamental assumptions. The first of these is that quality is an investment not unlike other investments in plant production, human resources, or office equipment. Unfortunately, most companies do not take this tack. Instead, the modal approach to the quality investment equation is a leap of faith that it will produce returns at some point. Few companies explicitly link their quality investments to actual money earned or saved.

The second fundamental assumption of the ROQ approach is that quality efforts must be financially driven. This is consistent with the first assumption that quality is an investment.

A third assumption offered by the authors involves the possibility that *too much* money can be spent on quality initiatives. Implicit here is that not all quality improvement programs are valid. The authors' fourth ROQ assumption suggests that some quality initiatives may have questionable efficacy. Indeed, too often the so-called religion of quality has permitted programs of questionable value to flourish.

In their effort to quantify the impact of service quality improvements on profitability, Rust and Zahorik posited a chain of effects beginning with a hypothetical quality improvement effort. If effective, the quality improvement effort yields increases in perceived quality, customer satisfaction, and possibly reduced costs. Increased customer satisfaction then exerts a positive effect on customer retention and also word-of-mouth advertising. The latter is important because most authors have not explicitly acknowledged that word-of-mouth advertising is a benefit of service quality initiatives. Based on the increased customer retention and positive word-of-mouth advertising, revenues and market share are presumed to go up. The decreased marketing costs combined with the increase in the customer base lead to greater profitability, according to the Rust and Zahorik model.

Accountability is also a cornerstone of the ROQ quality improvement model. Rust and Zahorik outlined a series of five steps critical to the ROQ process (see Figure 1.4). The first step involves information gathering. Industry trends, competitive positioning, and customer satisfaction data should all be examined in the information-gathering stage. The second step in the ROQ quality improvement process involves the articulation of ROQ outcomes using the information gathered in the first step. This step should yield projections involving the financial implications of the quality improvement process. These might include, for example, estimates of market share.

The third stage in the ROQ quality improvement process involves limited testing of improvements. For example, if a national pizza chain was interested in the effects on customer satisfaction of a drive-through service,

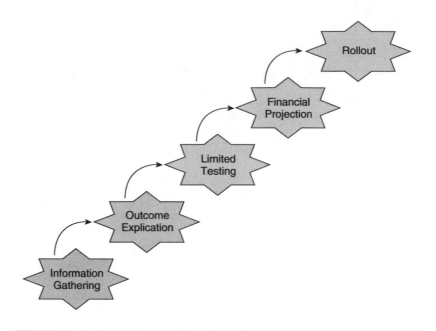

Figure 1.4   Five steps of the ROQ quality improvement process.

it would be prudent to test the enhancement in a limited number of stores. This testing process would permit management to predict with greater certainty the outcome of a national rollout.

The fourth step in the ROQ process involves financial projections based on empirical data. These might involve a cost-benefit analysis in which the costs of the drive-through service could be contrasted with the marginal increase in sales attributable to the new service. Finally, the fifth stage involves a full rollout of the quality improvement effort.

The link between customer retention and profitability appears unequivocal to some authors. Reichheld and Sasser (1990:105), for example, concluded that retention was a stronger predictor of corporate success than "scale, market share, unit costs, and many other factors usually associated with competitive advantage." By focusing on the link between customer satisfaction and an intervening variable (retention) known to affect profitability, Zeithaml et al. were able to build a strong case for the importance of service quality.

Danaher and Rust (1996) also focused on the financial benefits of service quality. Their study took a slightly different tack. Rather than focus on increased profitability as a result of lower attrition rates, they emphasized the utility of service quality in *attracting* new customers and increasing the usage rates of existing customers. Of particular importance was the benefit of word-of-mouth advertising attributable to high service quality levels.

The effect of customer satisfaction on profitability may be exerted through an intervening variable such as retention. Rust, Zahorik, and Keiningham's (1994) effort to establish a return on quality (ROQ) measure, for example, linked customer satisfaction to customer retention, which, in turn, was used as a predictor of market share. Based on a set of assumptions that included the possibility a company could spend too much on customer satisfaction, the authors developed a computer application that would permit users to forecast the profit implications of service quality improvement efforts.

Reichheld (1996:33–62) also discusses the relationship between customer retention and company revenue. Essentially, he argues that three relationships, paraphrased here, work together such that a small improvement in the customer retention rate can have a surprisingly large effect on company revenue:

- The customer *retention rate* has a strong effect on average customer *tenure*. (The other determinant is the customer acquisition rate.)

- In many product categories, there is a relationship between customer *tenure* and *purchase behavior*, with a customer who has more tenure spending more per year on average.

- A small change in the customer *retention rate* may, if maintained, have a substantial effect on the *number of customers* possessed by the company. This is an example of the phenomena of "compound interest." For example, if a company's customer attrition rate is five points lower than its customer acquisition rate, its customer base will by definition grow at 5% a year, thereby doubling in absolute size every 14 years.

An improvement in the customer retention rate has direct and indirect effects on company revenue, according to Reichheld. The direct effect is customer retention rate's effect on the number of customers possessed by the company. The indirect effect is customer retention rate's effect on average customer tenure, and average customer tenure's effect on yearly spending of the average customer.

THE ACSI STUDY

One of the most compelling empirical linkages between customer satisfaction and profitability involves the American Customer Satisfaction Index (ACSI), which was launched in 1994. The ACSI initiative has at least three primary objectives:

- *Measurement:* to quantify the quality of economic output based on subjective consumer input

- *Contribution:* to provide a conceptual framework for understanding how service and product quality relate to economic indicators

- *Forecasting:* to provide an indicator of future economic variability by measuring the intangible value of the buyer-seller relationship

This program, operated jointly by the National Quality Research Center at the University of Michigan and the American Society for Quality (ASQ), is based on quarterly data and over 50,000 interviews conducted annually with customers of measured companies. The ACSI measures customer satisfaction with 164 companies and 30 government agencies. The index relies on a 100-point scale. It is updated on a rolling basis with new measures for two economic sectors replacing data from the prior year.

The ACSI survey process involves collecting data at the individual customer level. Telephone surveys are conducted using random samples. Since its inception, the ACSI program has conducted more than 250,000 consumer interviews. Its database is immense and provides a wealth of information; thus far, the program has published 20 quarterly national indexes and less frequent annual indexes at the company, industry, and sector levels.

Each quarter, the ACSI data are aggregated to create company-level scores. Industry indixes are calculated as well and weighted by the sales of each company within a given industry. A further rollup is available at the sector level. Sector indexes subsume industry indexes and are also weighted by sales. The sectors are based on the one-digit Standard Industrial Code (SIC) classification.

The theoretical framework underlying the ACSI program is depicted in Figure 1.5. As shown, the causal sequence begins with customer expectations and perceived quality measures, which are presumed to affect, in order, perceived value and customer satisfaction (the ACSI metric). Customer satisfaction, as measured by the ACSI index, has two antecedents: customer complaints and, ultimately, customer loyalty. The latter is measured in terms of price tolerance and customer retention. One fundamental

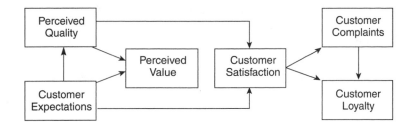

Figure 1.5   The ACSI model of customer loyalty.

assumption of the model is that for most companies repeat customers are a considerable profit source. Customer retention, estimated as *reported repurchase probability*, is a strong predictor of profitability. Using this structure, researchers at the University of Michigan are able to treat a company's customer base as an asset and calculate its net present value over time. This analytical approach has led to numerous papers relating customer satisfaction and financial performance.

The ACSI project has resulted in dozens of papers that confirm the relationship among quality, customer satisfaction, and financial performance. Anderson and Fornell (2000) provide a good background treatment of the ACSI program that facilitates an understanding of the types of data involved. An earlier work by Fornell, Johnson, Anderson, Cha, and Bryant (1996) also provides considerable detail with respect to the ACSI. Anderson and Fornell's collaboration with Rust (1977) represents an excellent treatment of the relationship among customer satisfaction, productivity, and profitability. The authors examine the relationship in both products and services. Although their focus is not the relationship between customer satisfaction and financial performance, Bryant and Cha (1996) discuss the expectation measures that are part of the ACSI questionnaire. Fornell's (1995) general discussion of the relationship between the quality of economic output and market share is also very enlightening.

The size of the ACSI database and the fact that 50,000 interviews are conducted annually has facilitated investigations of the relationship between customer satisfaction and financial performance at the industry level. For example, several researchers, including Johnson, Herrmann, Huber, and Gustafsson (1997), have focused specifically on the relationship among quality, satisfaction, and retention in the automotive industry. Auh and Johnson (1997) also focused on customer retention in the automotive industry. These authors also linked quality, satisfaction, and retention.

The ACSI program represents one of the few research projects to collect *longitudinal* data relating customer satisfaction, retention, and financial performance. Because the ACSI project involves quarterly data collection and has been running continuously since the fourth quarter of 1994, about 40 quarters of data will be available when the program celebrates its 10-year anniversary. This will permit even more robust inferences concerning the relationship between the index and key financial performance metrics by industry.

WHAT IS LOYALTY?

One shortcoming of many of the studies that operationalize customer retention based on respondent input is that the relationship between the respondent's assessment of his or her likelihood to repurchase a given product or service and the actual *behavior* is often tenuous. Frequently, three or four questionnaire items are used to measure repurchase intention or, more generally, loyalty:

- How likely are you to *purchase* this product/service again in the next three months?

- How likely are you to *recommend* this product/service to a friend or colleague?

- Overall, how *satisfied* are you with this product/service?

Often a composite of these three items is used as a general measure of loyalty or repurchase likelihood. In other cases, only the first item relating directly to repurchase likelihood is used. Some survey programs consider only those customers who score in the top 10% of each of these items to be likely repeat customers and, therefore, highly desirable. A score of a 9 or 10 on each of these items when measured on a 10-point scale is a reasonable reflection of repurchase intent.

Although repurchase behavior is a highly desirable outcome of customer satisfaction, the *behavior itself is not loyalty*. Rather, repurchase behavior manifests an attitudinal state we call loyalty, an attitude a consumer has about a service or product that leads to a long-term relationship and customer retention. Loyalty is not the purchase behavior itself. Just because a customer repurchases regularly from a supplier does not necessarily mean he or she is loyal per se. The customer may purchase repeatedly from a supplier for a wide variety of other reasons. Figure 1.6 confirms that repeat purchases can be the result of widely varying circumstances.

As shown in Figure 1.6, repeat customers—or more generally, customer retention—may be the result of any number of seemingly fortuitous circumstances. For example, a customer may lease a new car from the same dealer every two years over the course of a decade or more. The dealer per-

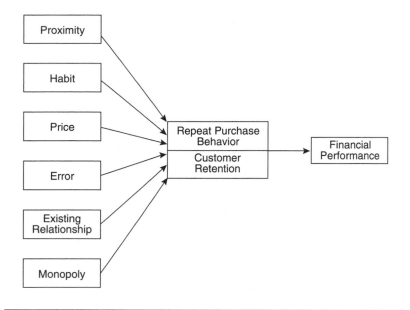

Figure 1.6   Reasons for repurchase behavior.

ceives this person as a loyal customer. It is quite possible, however, that the customer's repeat business is due only to the dealer's proximity to his or her home. Similarly, repeat purchases may be due to mere habit or be based solely on price. Other examples exist where the repeat purchase was made by mistake. Take, for example, the case of a purchasing agent who thought she had switched suppliers from Company A to Company B but was actually still buying from Company A because of a paperwork problem she was unaware of. In this case the buyer may appear to be loyal but in actuality is not even aware she is a customer. Finally, there are a host of transient, idiosyncratic reasons for repeat purchases. In some cases, a customer's relationship with an employee of the company may drive the purchase behavior. Similarly, a customer may frequent a given establishment because of its proximity to *another* business. In either case, if the situation changes, the repeat purchase behavior may suddenly and inexplicably stop.

Thus should circumstances change, many ostensibly loyal customers may defect. In the case of the proximate dealership, should a competitor move closer to the customer, he or she may switch allegiance based solely on proximity. Similarly, customers who repeatedly purchase a product or service based solely on price may quickly defect if a lower price alternative emerges. And, of course, the purchasing agent who erroneously concluded

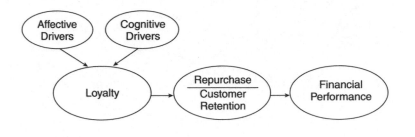

Figure 1.7   Affective and cognitive dimensions of loyalty.

she was purchasing from Company B may recognize her mistake and correct it.

As shown in Figure 1.7, the attitude we refer to as loyalty may be defined as having two distinct dimensions. The first is considered the *affective* dimension and reflects the emotional attachment a consumer may develop for a product or service provider. Emotional ties may interweave relationships with the brand, its image, or the company's employees.

A second dimension of loyalty may involve *cognitive* drivers. These are more rational and may involve the consumer's critical assessment of his or her relationship with the supplier. These evaluations may involve attitudes toward the supplier's product quality, price, problem resolution, or distribution structure. It seems reasonable to conclude that unlike customer satisfaction, attitudinal loyalty is much less dynamic. Customer satisfaction may rise and fall based on service or product quality experiences, but customer loyalty changes more slowly.

Of course, myriad other phenomena may affect an individual's decision to repurchase a product or service. Figure 1.8, for example, suggests a framework in which customer loyalty, customer satisfaction, customer value perceptions, and brand image all interact to affect behaviors such as repurchase, which, in turn, drives financial performance. All four of the key constructs in the figure are presumed to be affected by product and/or service quality. Note that these four constructs are considered interrelated; we have not explicitly linked them in the figure in the interest of clarity. Needless to say, loyalty, satisfaction, value, and image are strongly related.

As noted earlier, customer loyalty and brand image perceptions are probably not as dynamic as either customer satisfaction or value perceptions. In the latter case, a substantial increase in price could yield a precipitous decline in value perceptions. Similarly, if product quality begins to slip, customer satisfaction will likely decline accordingly. In both cases we would expect loyal customers—those with strong emotional and cognitive

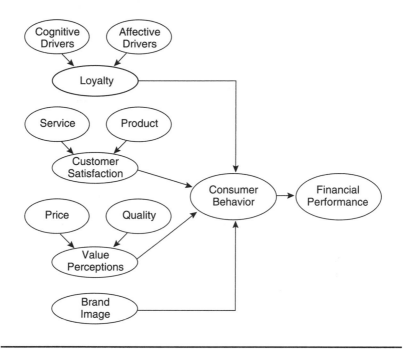

Figure 1.8 Quality and its effect on customer retention.

ties to the product or service—to continue repurchasing despite the adversities of increased price and lower product quality. Of course, even highly loyal customers as defined here will lose their patience if these problems are long term or particularly acute. The point is that customers who are strongly loyal in the attitudinal sense will be more likely to weather adversities than customers who are not, despite high levels of customer satisfaction and positive value perceptions.

2

Tracking and Reporting Customer Satisfaction Metrics

INTRODUCTION

This chapter first reviews the multidimensional role of customer satisfaction research, followed by an extensive discussion of the characteristics that define various program life stages. A complete and objective understanding of where a program stands relative to the full range of programs—from nascent to mature and highly sophisticated—will give you a good perspective for evaluating future directions. By their nature, customer satisfaction programs tend to evolve over time as internal audiences become more attuned to the data and to certain analyses and their implications.

A variety of reporting and data issues and innovations are also addressed, including approaches to processing customer comments, Internet surveys, and the role of quadrant charts. With respect to the latter, a slight variant of the traditional quadrant chart is introduced that is more consistent with the objectives of the Six Sigma quality improvement framework.

This chapter concludes with an introduction to loyalty segment formation, which is the basis for Chapter 10. Loyalty segments and an innovative approach to modeling disparate key-driver profiles across these groups has multiple benefits. First, it focuses managerial attention on the entire distribution of customers, not just those in the top-two boxes. The technique also recognizes that what drives loyalty among the most satisfied customers may not be relevant to their dissatisfied peers. Finally, from an analytical standpoint, the loyalty segment modeling technique appears partially to circumvent problematic collinearity in some data sets.

THE ROLES OF CUSTOMER SATISFACTION MEASUREMENT

Contemporary customer satisfaction programs enjoy many roles. They serve as feedback and input systems for numerous organizational functions as depicted in Figure 2.1. Aside from *behavioral feedback* such as purchase patterns and tenure, customer satisfaction measurement (CSM) programs provide organizations with a critical link to the people who buy their products or services.

Clearly, customer satisfaction programs may not enjoy a multiplicity of roles in all organizations. The optimized program, however, affects various organizational levels and functions. Such a customer satisfaction program has maximum benefit to organizations insightful enough to link consumer feedback to multiple systems. As shown in Figure 2.1, customer satisfaction programs can affect organizational processes in many ways:

Leadership tool: When used effectively by senior management, customer satisfaction can serve as a motivational tool for providing direction and objective feedback to employees. Many companies use customer satisfaction as a foundation in their mission or core value statements.

CRM program driver: The importance of CRM to customer satisfaction programs can not be understated. The CRM platform redefines how organizations interact with the world. It shifts the

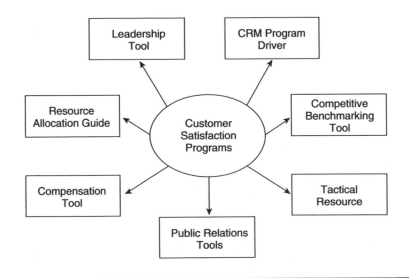

Figure 2.1   Multiple roles of customer satisfaction programs.

focus of key systems from products to customers. As a result, customer feedback often represents a critical input to CRM systems.

Competitive benchmarking tool: When customer satisfaction programs are expanded to include competitive benchmarking data, the results can have tremendous strategic implications. Knowing whether competitors are meeting customer expectations and what drives competitors' customer loyalty can help marketers formulate strategic plans.

Tactical resource: Transaction-oriented customer satisfaction programs focus on a recent customer interaction. These programs offer continuous feedback concerning key operations like problem resolution, accuracy, installation, and other processes. As a result, system changes can be implemented and the effects monitored.

Public relations tool: The very act of surveying customers implicitly communicates an interest in the relationship. Of course, a lack of follow-through with respect to unresolved problems may backfire and cause more misgivings. To be an effective public relations tool, a customer satisfaction program must be professionally executed and include mechanisms for addressing urgent customer problems.

Compensation tool: An explicit link between customer satisfaction feedback and employee compensation plans is in place in many organizations, particularly those with large branch or store networks. Linking compensation to a combination of growth, profitability, and customer feedback is widely practiced today and an effective way to reward employees.

Resource allocation guide: Key-driver (i.e., regression) analysis can help managers decide which service and product quality issues should be emphasized in an effort to maximize a key dependent measure such as overall satisfaction or loyalty.

THE CUSTOMER SATISFACTION PROGRAM LIFE CYCLE

Companies embarking on their first CSM and reporting program ponder questions that are very different from those asked at organizations with mature programs. In their infancy, customer satisfaction programs tend to be highly tactical and not infrequently are precipitated by a severe service or product quality problem. Alternatively, a realization of very little difference among competitors in terms of product quality shifts the focus to service quality and its measurement. In more extreme cases where it is difficult to differentiate among competitors based on either service or product quality, organizations tend to focus on brand and brand image issues. Thus, in commodity-like markets, brand imagery becomes considerably more salient. The ensuing discussion is relevant only for companies where there are opportunities to enhance the value proposition through superior service and product quality.

Figure 2.2 summarizes the customer satisfaction program life cycle for most organizations and synthesizes the main stages of customer satisfaction programs. Not all companies reach the pinnacle stage in which strategic and tactical issues are addressed in both the aggregate and unit levels. Indeed, many smaller companies are quite successful with a Stage 1 approach in which the customer satisfaction program is administered at the aggregate level and focuses on tactical issues. Many very successful customer problem resolution programs are Stage 1 customer satisfaction programs. Stage 2 programs tend to reflect a growing concern with relationship issues in addition to tactical applications. In many such programs there is a point at which the feedback instrument is split into two pieces: a transaction-oriented survey and a relationship survey. Finally, Stage 3 programs are characterized by the emergence of additional constructs such as brand image and loyalty in an effort to maximize the efficacy of models linking service and product quality issues to business outcomes.

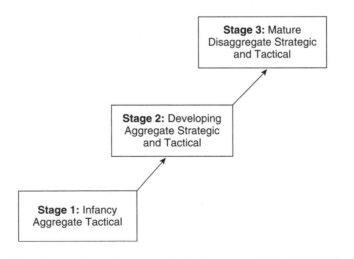

Figure 2.2 Customer satisfaction program life stages.

The three stages are profiled in greater detail in Table 2.1. The key differences across the stages involve strategic role, level of aggregation and reporting, and analytical sophistication. For example, Stage 1 programs tend to be annual with a focus on corporate-level goal setting coupled loosely with incentives, whereas more mature programs involve formal tracking and unit-level reporting with explicit performance–incentive links. Stage 1 programs tend to operate in a competitive vacuum, in contrast to Stage 3 systems that often include sophisticated best-in-class benchmarking. This elevates the role of Stage 3 customer satisfaction programs: they often play an integral part in strategic business strategy and planning.

Another characteristic that differentiates mature customer satisfaction programs from their nascent counterparts is the information used to guide performance improvement efforts. Stage 1 programs tend to be highly reactive and use frequency data related to problem incidence in this regard. In contrast, mature programs utilize derived importance metrics and performance levels. The most mature programs acknowledge that the cost of improving certain service or product quality issues may vary tremendously,

Table 2.1   Characteristics of customer satisfaction program life stages.

Stage 1: Infancy	Stage 2: Developing	Stage 3: Mature
• Tactical	• Tactical and strategic	• Tactical and strategic
• Aggregate	• Disaggregate	• Disaggregate
• Transaction survey	• Transaction and relationship surveys	• Transaction and relationship surveys
• Problem and process focus	• Strategic quality tool	• Business strategy tool
• Satisfaction is key DV	• Emergence of loyalty measures	• Loyalty link to ROI
• Univariate, aggregate reporting	• Multivariate, disaggregate reporting	• Multivariate, multilevel reporting
• Aggregate goal setting	• Performance link	• Unit-level incentives
• Focus on performance	• Performance importance maps	• Sophisticated derived importance
• Cost-effective process improvement	• Importance-based process improvement	• Cost and importance guide process improvement
• Annual baseline	• Tracking (quarterly or monthly)	• Tracking (quarterly or monthly)
• Competitively isolated metrics	• Limited benchmarking	• Best-of-class benchmarking
• Reactive implementation efforts	• Process champions	• Best practices database
• Focus on education	• Permeate organization culture	• Customer-centric culture

and as a result an optimized, cost-effective solution is sought through simulations or linear programming techniques. Thus, in Stage 1 programs, one data element is employed to guide enhancement: performance. In Stage 2 programs, both performance and importance are used. Finally, in Stage 3 systems, three data points are combined: performance, importance, and improvement cost. The nonlinearity of service or product quality improvement costs is discussed in greater detail in Chapter 9.

It would be misleading to suggest all customer satisfaction programs fall neatly into one of the three stages described in Table 2.1. The stages are by no means completely mutually exclusive, and it is possible, for example, to encounter a Stage 1 program that includes some of the characteristics of more mature systems. This is frequently the case when an organization with little or no customer satisfaction measurement experience hires an in-house expert who is charged with a fast-track program implementation. In this situation, the customer satisfaction program may simultaneously span all three life cycle stages or accelerate through them at an unusually fast pace.

Figure 2.3 illustrates the types of analytical challenges faced at various stages of the customer satisfaction program life cycle. Three axes are represented in the cube. The *x*-axis reflects aggregated versus disaggregated analysis. Aggregate analysis occurs at the overall corporate level. In contrast, disaggregated analysis involves replicating the same approach across numerous subunits such as districts, regions, states, or even customer groups. The benefit of disaggregated analysis is that it permits a unique

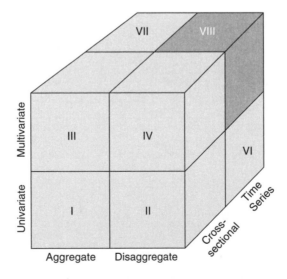

Figure 2.3   Program life cycle strategy-analytic implications.

service or product quality enhancement strategy to be developed and implemented at the subunit level. Conversely, the potential danger of excessive focus on disaggregated analysis is a lack of broad perspective.

The y-axis of the cube represents univariate versus multivariate analysis. The former addresses simple questions requiring percentages, means, or measures of dispersion such as variance. Multivariate techniques are used to determine key-driver status and a wide range of other more complex questions. Dimension-reducing techniques such as principal components analysis or factor analysis, for example, may be employed to reveal the underlying quality themes consumers rely on when evaluating services or products. A wide range of multivariate techniques have applications in customer satisfaction data analysis.

The z-axis of the cube in Figure 2.3 represents cross-sectional versus time series analysis. Cross-sectional analyses do not acknowledge changes in either univariate or multivariate measures over time. Organizations that embrace service or product quality improvement based on customer satisfaction measurement certainly should expect better scores from one year to the next. After all, underlying any customer satisfaction program is the assumption that improving specific service or product quality issues will yield enhanced overall satisfaction, which, in turn, will lead to desirable business outcomes such as enhanced market share and, ultimately, profitability. One of the most complex challenges in customer satisfaction programs involves disaggregated, multivariate time series problems. This type of analysis might, for example, address the dynamics of regression beta weights (key drivers) over time across a categorical variable such as sales district.

With respect to Figure 2.3, the most straightforward questions tend to occur in Block I, which is characterized by cross-sectional, aggregate-level univariate statistical analysis. The next step up from this level is encountered in Block II. Here univariate questions are posed at the subunit (e.g., district or customer segment) level rather than at the corporate level. Stage 1 customer satisfaction programs (Table 2.1) tend to focus on Block I and Block II analysis.

The next level of sophistication reflected in Figure 2.3 is encountered in Block III, which introduces multivariate analysis. Block III is characterized by aggregate-level multivariate problems such as key-driver analysis. The derivation of multivariate models at the subunit level is reflected in Block IV. Analysis within this block yields significant strategic value because it acknowledges that, for example, key drivers may differ across organizational units. Accordingly, strategy may be differentiated based on the idiosyncratic driver model of each district, region, or customer group.

Blocks V through VIII enhance the complexity of the preceding discussion by introducing a time factor. These four blocks consider everything just discussed across multiple time periods. For example, Block V (hidden from view in Figure 2.3) focuses on aggregate-level univariate measures over time. Similarly, Block VI considers the time implications of univariate metrics over multiple units such as districts. Block VII introduces multivariate time series at the aggregate analysis level; Block VIII adds another layer of complexity by considering changes in multivariate measures over time across multiple levels of a discrete variable such as sales district, state, or region.

The types of questions that may be addressed within the analytic structure presented in Figure 2.3 are presented in Table 2.2. Two illustrative questions for each analysis block are presented in the table. This demonstrates how the cubic structure can be used to facilitate an understanding of real-world applications. Virtually any question involving customer satisfaction data analysis may be subsumed within the three axes presented in the data analysis blocks.

REPORTING ISSUES

In customer satisfaction research, the strategic quadrant chart is frequently used to guide marginal resource allocation decisions. Typically, this entails plotting various service and product quality items in a two-dimensional space in which the x-axis reflects performance (satisfaction) and the y-axis denotes derived importance. Service or product quality issues characterized by low performance and high derived importance are often isolated as providing the best ROI in terms of maximizing either overall satisfaction or loyalty.

Interestingly, the covariation exploited in derived importance models is susceptible to a potential problem. Specifically, if the predictor variable (x_1) and outcome variable (y) have nearly zero variation, their covariation will be very high. Predictive power will be substantial, resulting in an item with high derived importance and little internal variance.

The role of variance in quadrant charts is often overlooked. From a Six Sigma perspective, it is desirable to reduce actual (or perceived) quality variation. Thus in quadrant charts it may be desirable additionally to display the variance associated with each service or product quality item that is plotted. Depicting the extent to which there is variation in quality can be instrumental in refining resource allocation decisions.

When actual quality variation is known to be extremely low, satisfaction data that reveal considerable variance would suggest measurement error or expectation differences among respondents. Conversely, if actual quality variation is considered high and satisfaction data reflect parallel variance, the implication is that quality improvements would yield superior returns.

Table 2.2   Strategic issues underlying analysis blocks.

CROSS-SECTIONAL ANALYSIS BLOCKS

Block I:	**Aggregate univariate problems**
	What is our current level of corporate satisfaction?
	In which service or product quality do we perform best as a corporation?
Block II:	**Disaggregate univariate problems**
	What is our current level of satisfaction in District 12?
	In which district is technical support service quality best?
Block III:	**Aggregate multivariate problems**
	As a corporation, which service quality issues drive satisfaction?
	How do we move our corporate CSM score up by 5 points?
Block IV:	**Disaggregate multivariate problems**
	Which districts will yield the greatest ROI from a 10% improvement in technical support?
	In which district(s) is invoicing a key driver of satisfaction?

TIME SERIES ANALYSIS BLOCKS

Block V:	**Aggregate univariate problems**
	Has our total service quality satisfaction index improved since last year?
	In which service or product quality issues did the corporation experience the greatest gains this quarter?
Block VI:	**Disaggregate univariate problems**
	In which districts did the total service quality satisfaction index improve since last year?
	Did District 14 improve in terms of invoicing satisfaction since last quarter?
Block VII:	**Aggregate multivariate problems**
	Has the status of invoicing as a key driver of overall satisfaction changed over the past three years?
	Has the relative importance of product delivery decreased since we increased the fleet size by 20%?
Block VIII:	**Disaggregate multivariate problems**
	Has the key-driver status of invoicing in District 18 changed since last year?
	In which districts has delivery emerged as a significant driver since last year?

Of course, variance (or the lack thereof) can occur anywhere across the satisfaction scale. Thus a quadrant chart that uses variance as the x-axis instead of satisfaction could be used as a supplement to the traditional performance-importance model. The variance-importance model would focus managerial attention on issues characterized by a strong impact on overall satisfaction or loyalty and high levels of perceived quality variation.

As implied earlier, this approach is most useful when the actual quality is known or may be estimated objectively.

At this point, it is unlikely many U.S. companies use this approach to depicting data in strategic quadrant charts. Overlaying variance data on existing performance-importance quadrants yields another dimension for evaluating future marginal resource allocation decisions. The standard deviation or variance may be plotted for each point on the quadrant as shown in Figure 2.4.

CUSTOMER COMMENT DATA

A focus on the quantitative data permeates this book. Not all customer satisfaction data are quantitative, however. Indeed, some extremely valuable information can be derived from customer comments, particularly when they are directed specifically at improving service or product quality. This brief discussion explores some meaningful ways that qualitative data can be incorporated into customer satisfaction programs.

From a derived importance modeling standpoint, the most valuable survey instrument structure involves a series of nested content areas, each defined by a series of predictor variables followed by a single overall

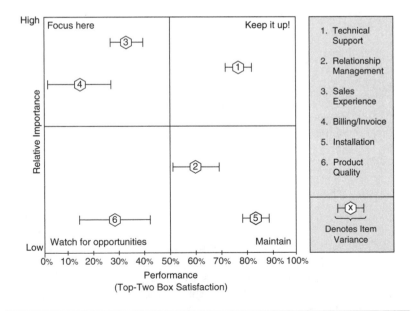

Figure 2.4   Performance-importance-variance quadrant chart.

dependent measure. For example, if we have three primary areas of interest—service quality, product quality, and technical support—there would be three corresponding questionnaire sections. Each would include a set of specific, actionable predictor variables followed by an overall assessment. Following these we typically place a set of overall dependent measures including overall satisfaction, willingness to recommend, and likelihood to continue using or repurchase. This represents the *minimum* content for establishing a causal sequence culminating in a loyalty index composed of the recommend and repurchase items.

The quantitative derived importance structure just described can be enhanced by accommodating a qualitative element. In the case of the section-dependent measures, comments can be elicited that address ways to enhance performance levels. For example, each comment related to a section summary evaluation may take the format shown on the next page. That is, after each key section-dependent measure, an open-ended question may be posed directing the respondent to indicate what specific actions the company could take to improve its quality.

By phrasing the questions in this fashion, we generate actionable comment data that can be used as an adjunct to the derived importance models. Textual data obtained in this way can help *prioritize tactical plans* aimed specifically at improving overall performance. This format is also more specific and increases the likelihood that customers will actually provide feedback because the request is very focused.

Managers who have orchestrated large-scale customer satisfaction programs with tens of thousands of surveys each year understand the problems associated with open-ended comment data. Initially, the idea of gathering supplementary qualitative data sounds very attractive. The reality of this situation, however, is driven home when we consider the amount of text that must be processed. A national customer satisfaction program with 80,000 interviews annually and four open-ended questions in the format illustrated earlier could produce several million words of text. This page contains about 500 words. A large-scale customer satisfaction program could easily generate 5000 full pages of text data.

Although it certainly would make sense to have unit managers process text data relating to their specific operations, this tack precludes an assessment of broad patterns in the qualitative data. That is, although branch managers will definitely find the comments of their customers very useful, corporate-level management cannot synthesize this much textual data and isolate meaningful patterns. One viable approach to this would be to have unit managers produce a one-page summary interpretation of comments produced by their customers. These summaries could be more reasonably assimilated by a single person or team at the corporate level. Still, the subjectivity and bias introduced by each unit manager when processing his or her own customers' comments may systematically bias the corporate team's interpretation of the summaries.

Interestingly, not a great deal of progress has been made over the past 20 years in terms of the quantitative treatment of textual data. The most primitive approaches employ simple word count algorithms. With the advent of artificial intelligence programming languages like LISP in the 1980s, one would have thought by the 21st century we would be enjoying significant improvements over the word count methodology. Although CPU speeds have increased by multiple orders of magnitude and the cost of volatile memory has dropped precipitously in the last 25 years, our ability to synthesize textual data remains awkward at best.

With respect to automated text processing, most of the major programs today still require significant human interaction. The most problematic aspect of processing huge volumes of customer comments is that even the most sophisticated programs have difficulty quantifying context, sarcasm, or irony. With human intervention aimed at clarification and coding, many

---

Teton Carabiners
Customer Satisfaction Survey

Your opinions and feedback are especially important to us at Teton Carabiners and we appreciate the time you take to complete this important survey each year. As an important Elite Tier Customer, your satisfaction is one of our primary concerns. Your patronage establishes you as a careful consumer of technical equipment and reflects the extent to which you value service and product quality.

1. Service Quality
Please evaluate Teton Carabiners in terms of the following service quality issues. In each case, please use a 10-point scale where 1 means Poor and 10 means Excellent.

	Poor									*Excellent*
a. Knowledge of sales staff	1	2	3	4	5	6	7	8	9	10
b. Courtesy of telephone reps	1	2	3	4	5	6	7	8	9	10
c. Invoicing accuracy	1	2	3	4	5	6	7	8	9	10
d. Problem solving	1	2	3	4	5	6	7	8	9	10
e. Guiding services	1	2	3	4	5	6	7	8	9	10
f. **Overall service quality evaluation**	1	2	3	4	5	6	7	8	9	10

What single thing could Teton Carabiners do to enhance its service quality in your opinion? Please use the space below to write in your answer.

_____

_____

continued

continued

2. Product Quality
Please evaluate Teton Carabiners in terms of the following product quality issues. Again, please use a 10-point scale where 1 means Poor and 10 means Excellent.

	Poor									*Excellent*
g. Closed strength Kn	1☐	2☐	3☐	4☐	5☐	6☐	7☐	8☐	9☐	10☐
h. Open strength Kn	1☐	2☐	3☐	4☐	5☐	6☐	7☐	8☐	9☐	10☐
i. Weight	1☐	2☐	3☐	4☐	5☐	6☐	7☐	8☐	9☐	10☐
j. Gate width	1☐	2☐	3☐	4☐	5☐	6☐	7☐	8☐	9☐	10☐
k. Wire gate quality	1☐	2☐	3☐	4☐	5☐	6☐	7☐	8☐	9☐	10☐
l. 6" Quickdraw quality	1☐	2☐	3☐	4☐	5☐	6☐	7☐	8☐	9☐	10☐
m. **Overall product quality evaluation**	1☐	2☐	3☐	4☐	5☐	6☐	7☐	8☐	9☐	10☐

What single thing could Teton Carabiners do to enhance its product quality in your opinion? Please use the space below to write in your answer.

_____

_____

3. Overall Evaluation
Considering Teton Carabiners, in terms of your overall reaction to our products and services, please rate us on the following issues.

	Never									*Definitely*
n. I would recommend Teton Carabiners	1☐	2☐	3☐	4☐	5☐	6☐	7☐	8☐	9☐	10☐
o. I will keep buying Teton Carabiners	1☐	2☐	3☐	4☐	5☐	6☐	7☐	8☐	9☐	10☐
p. Guides should always use Teton Carabiners	1☐	2☐	3☐	4☐	5☐	6☐	7☐	8☐	9☐	10☐
q. **Overall, I am very satisfied with Teton**	1☐	2☐	3☐	4☐	5☐	6☐	7☐	8☐	9☐	10☐

~Thank You~

text processing programs produce useful summaries of customer comment data.

When a survey instrument contains open-ended responses such as those elicited in the example presented in the Teton Carabiners example, it is possible to process the responses using an exhaustive set of summary codes. Of course, this requires significant human intervention but, in some cases, may be well worth the time and resources. Once every comment has been coded, it is possible to generate a frequency count matrix for each of the closed-ended numeric comments. This summarizes all the comments for each numeric question. As a result, researchers can provide comment code frequency distributions across current numeric satisfaction levels.

Table 2.3 provides an illustrative example of the type of matrix that can be developed when the coded comment data are integrated with numeric satisfaction data. Of course, possibly many more comment codes will be

Table 2.3   Comment code frequency matrix by current satisfaction level.

*(What single thing could we do to enhance our **service quality** in your opinion?)*

	Very dissatisfied				Very satisfied
Current satisfaction level:	**1–2**	**3–4**	**5–6**	**7–8**	**9–10**
Relationship issues					
R1:Relationship access	20%	30%	40%	8%	2%
R2:Relationship continuity	0%	25%	15%	50%	10%
R3:Relationship contract	5%	10%	65%	15%	5%*
Sales rep issues					
S1:Sales access	5%	20%	20%	10%	45%
S2:Sales presentation	60%	10%	10%	10%	10%*
S3:Sales courtesy	20%	40%	10%	10%	20%
S4:Sales callbacks	0%	10%	5%	5%	80%*
S5:Sales knowledge	10%	10%	20%	35%	25%
Problem resolution issues					
P1:Problem resolution	50%	20%	10%	10%	10%
P2:Problem documentation	5%	5%	5%	5%	80%*
P3:Problem solving Skills	10%	15%	15%	50%	10%
P4:Problem identification	60%	10%	5%	10%	15%
Documentation issues					
D1:Documentation accuracy	50%	20%	10%	5%	15%
D2:Documentation speed	10%	15%	15%	50%	10%
D3:Documentation on Web	10%	65%	5%	20%	0%*
D4:Documentation electronic	10%	15%	15%	40%	20%
Timing issues					
T1:Speed of callbacks	50%	20%	10%	5%	15%
T2:Faster confirmation	10%	15%	15%	50%	10%
T3:Faster response Overall	10%	55%	15%	20%	0%
T4:Turnaround time	10%	15%	15%	40%	20%
Technical support issues					
H1:TS Knowledge	5%	15%	50%	25%	5%
H2:TS Availability	10%	15%	15%	50%	10%
H3:TS Phone Center	60%	0%	0%	40%	0%
H4:TS Documentation	5%	20%	5%	50%	20%
H5:TS Hourly rate	60%	20%	5%	10%	5%*

* Statistically significant difference attributable to satisfaction level.
Highest percentile in each row has been highlighted.

developed—in all likelihood approximately 30 to 40 codes could be developed for each closed-ended question. A quantitative examination of textual data in this manner provides valuable insights into how managers can enhance performance ratings within specific content areas.

Once coded, the verbatim data may also be subjected to advanced multivariate dimension-reducing techniques such as correspondence analysis. This provides a way to leverage sophisticated *quantitative* analysis with inherently *qualitative* data. The results of this analysis can reveal the underlying dimensions of the qualitative feedback customers provide in an objective, quantitative fashion. Further explorations may facilitate inferences concerning differences in dimensionality across regions and other meaningful organizational classifications.

DEFINING LOYALTY SEGMENTS

It is becoming increasingly common for companies to track their customers in terms of a composite loyalty measure, not just overall satisfaction. As described in subsequent chapters, the key to a useful attitudinal measure is its ability to predict future customer behavior. It is now widely believed that measures including more than just overall satisfaction are better predictors of outcome variables such as repeat purchases, attrition, relationship breadth and depth, and a host of other company-level performance variables like market share and profitability.

The objective of defining loyalty segments is to track the size and composition of each segment rather than a single univariate statistic linked to overall satisfaction. By considering the distribution of all customers—even those who are disaffected—a more holistic view is achieved and strategies may be developed to address each segment. Chapter 10 presents an innovative means of developing unique key-driver models for each segment using multinomial logistic regression.

One of the most straightforward approaches to measuring loyalty involves a composite of overall satisfaction, willingness to recommend, and repurchase likelihood. Figure 2.5 summarizes this composite measure. Within each of the intersecting circles is the proportion of top-two box scores achieved (using a 10-point scale). The point at which all three circles overlap reflects the proportion of customers with a top-two box in *each* of the three individual measures. As shown, the illustration suggests that although roughly 60% of all customers were in the top-two boxes of each individual distribution, only 42% were associated with top-two box scores on all three measures. This core group is considered loyal, and it is this measure that is tracked across many organizations.

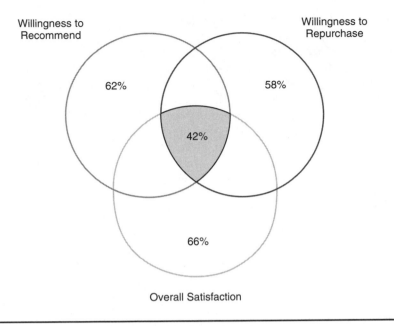

Willingness to Recommend

Willingness to Repurchase

62%

58%

42%

66%

Overall Satisfaction

Figure 2.5 Simple operational definition of loyalty.

Once the basic operational definition of loyalty has been completed, it is possible to decompose the overall distribution-based score ranges. Figure 2.6 demonstrates how the 30-point scale, created by summing the scores on the three items for each customer, can be broken into four distinct groups of customers. There are many approaches to this technique, of course. In the present case, only customers whose scores equal or exceed 28 on the 30-point scale are considered to be in the Loyal segment. The next segment (Satisfied) is composed of customers whose scores range from 25 to 27. Finally, the remainder of the distribution is allocated to the Ambivalent and Disaffected segments.

Considering the entire loyalty index distribution has substantive benefits. One of the most important involves the nature of tracking top-box scores as opposed to averages. The key is that top-box scores tend to focus management attention on the high end of the distribution. Little incentive exists to move customers at the bottom of the distribution to the middle. Particularly when management compensation is tied to loyalty scores, it is much easier and financially advantageous to focus on moving proximate customers into the top of the distribution. Thus, with respect to Figure 2.6, most managers motivated to increase their bonuses will seek to move Satisfied customers into the Loyal segment.

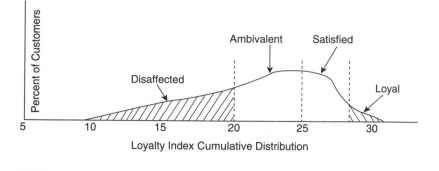

Figure 2.6   Loyalty distribution ranges and segments.

By focusing attention on the entire distribution, management incentives (described in Chapters 3 and 4) may be tied to statistically significant movement from one segment to the next. Thus a manager who moves a significant percentage of her Disaffected customers into the Ambivalent segment would receive the same recognition as one who moves a similar proportion of Ambivalent customers into the Satisfied segment. An alternative scenario could involve reduced points for movement at the low end of the distribution and a premium for moving customers into the Loyal segment. This approach naturally risks a focus on the Satisfied segment, however.

Without doubt any company engaging in this type of measurement system needs to create a longitudinal database that can be used to link inter-segment movement to behavioral outcomes. That is, the value of moving a customer from the Satisfied to Loyal segment should be quantified vis-à-vis the benefits of moving from the Disaffected segment to the Ambivalent segment or the Ambivalent segment to the Satisfied segment. The benefits of each jump are likely disparate and nonlinear. As demonstrated in the predecessor to this book (see Allen and Wilburn, 2002:117–20), customers whose satisfaction levels increased substantially over time were more profitable than those who experienced more modest increases. Similarly, customers whose satisfaction dropped were unequivocally linked to a precipitous decline in profitability.

With emprical evidence linking movement between each pair of segments to profit-based outcomes (or attrition levels), management attention may be prioritized based on the optimal segment shift profile. Consider the implications if movement across the segments was associated with decreasing profitability outcomes. In this case there would be a bigger benefit from shifting a Disaffected customer to the Ambivalent segment than moving a Satisfied customer into the Loyal segment. An optimized managerial strategy would place more emphasis on moving customers at the bottom of the scale into the next level segment. Of course, this is completely contrary to the conventional wisdom, which focuses management attention on movement into the top-two box category. Still, to the extent that Disaffected customers are profitable, they may yield the greatest overall benefit to the organization because they will invariably be associated with the greatest attrition risk. Replacing lost customers is expensive. Moving Disaffected customers into the Ambivalent segment may yield benefits measured in *avoided costs* rather than direct customer-level profits. That is, reducing attrition among even minimally profitable customers will be beneficial because the costs to replace them had they left are avoided.

Tracking customer feedback measures is more frequently associated with loyalty indexes similar to the composite presented in this section. One caveat with respect to indexes is that they are notoriously difficult to move. That is, it is hard to achieve statistically significant increases in indexes that contain numerous items. Further, regression-based models aimed at establishing the importance of individual service and product quality issues tend to produce modest results in terms of R^2 statistics. The latter is attributable to the variance canceling effect produced by adding a multitude of different survey items. In order to avoid this phenomenon, limiting the number of items in a loyalty index to three if at all possible is highly advisable.

The loyalty index and segmentation approach discussed in this section is revisited in Chapter 10, where an innovative approach to key-driver derivation is discussed. A technique that produces a separate key-driver solution for each segment is described and demonstrated relative to more traditional techniques. Of great interest is the finding that each segment is associated with a unique, idiosyncratic driver equation. Service and product quality enhancement strategies, therefore, must be matched to each segment.

As more empirical and theoretical evidence confirms that loyalty measures have greater predictive efficacy than overall satisfaction, we will see companies shift their tracking to indexes like the composite presented here. If loyalty indexes can predict future customer behavior more accurately, it is certainly worth exploring their use in a variety of situations. Certainly, the segment-based approach described earlier has some clear advantages, including a focus on all customers, not just those who can be most easily shifted into the top-box category.

3

Linking CSM to Management Incentives: Theoretical Foundation

INTRODUCTION

Chapters 3 and 4 are devoted to incentive systems and customer satisfaction results. Given the importance of the topic, this chapter focuses exclusively on the theory behind rewarding employees based on performance. A general discussion of human motivation is followed by a more focused treatment of motivation in the workplace and job satisfaction. The linkage between rewards and performance has some vocal detractors, and these concerns are presented to provide a balanced picture. Finally, the use of customer feedback to reward employees is considered. Readers with a background in organizational behavior may wish to move directly to Chapter 4, which introduces quantitative approaches to linking customer satisfaction to employee incentive systems.

Substantive anecdotal and empirical evidence clearly exists to support the notion that customer satisfaction yields desirable, objective business outcomes like increased market share and profitability. That this effect may be extended through customer retention appears a distinct possibility. It makes sense, then, to reward organizational behaviors associated with enhanced customer satisfaction. This chapter develops a theoretical foundation for linking customer feedback to employee rewards and recognition. The discussions concerning human motivation and the efficacy of extrinsic rewards underscores the notion that incentive systems may rely on a variety of employee rewards ranging from recognition and advancement to monetary payments. Chapter 4 builds on this material and focuses on specific quantitative approaches for linking management incentives to customer satisfaction results.

THE NATURE OF HUMAN MOTIVATION

The motivation to work remains an elusive topic, despite more than 50 years of theory development and empirical investigations by organizational psychologists, management consultants, and, more generally, corporations across the globe. Four classic theories of human motivation are based on the motivation to fulfill *needs*. These are relevant to managers interested in linking customer satisfaction scores to incentives because they address the most basic assumptions underlying the program. That is, employees can be motivated to perform based on rewards.

Establishing and sustaining employee motivation is important because of the clear advantages a motivated workforce yields: increased productivity, less supervision, process improvement feedback, less turnover, lower levels of absenteeism, and so on. The theories briefly addressed here have some important implications for managers. They fall into two broad categories: needs-based theories and process theories of motivation. The former collectively assumes that individuals possess the same set of basic needs and that meeting these needs is the basis for human motivation and, ultimately, behavior. Important needs-based theories of motivation include the following:

- Maslow's hierarchy of needs

- Herzberg's motivator-hygiene theory

- Need for achievement

- Expectancy theory of motivation

There are similarly several theories of motivation based on cognitive processes. Each of these posits a series of rational perceptions and decisions that underlie motivations and, ultimately, behaviors:

- Expectancy theory

- Equity theory

- Goal-setting theory

NEEDS-BASED THEORIES OF MOTIVATION

Maslow's hierarchy of needs (1954) is a broad theoretical framework for understanding human motivation. It was not developed to address workplace behavior specifically. It was rapidly adopted by organizational psychologists, however, and represents one of the cornerstone theories for understanding employee job satisfaction and motivation. In effect, Maslow proposed that human motivation progresses through a succession of increasingly complex needs, ending at a pinnacle deemed self-actualization as depicted in Figure 3.1. The theory suggests that, with respect to behaviors in complex organizations, employees will escalate their requirements as each step is met. For example, once physiological and security needs are met, employees will strive to fulfill social needs by developing supportive relationships with colleagues.

With the need for social affiliation met, employees will move to the next stratum, which involves self-esteem. Reward and recognition programs tend to focus on the need for self-esteem. Few individuals, according to Maslow and his contemporaries, ever reach the apex of this hierarchy: the fulfillment of the need for self-actualization. Maslow (1968:155) described the need for self-actualization as people's "pressure toward unity of personality, toward spontaneous expressiveness, toward full individuality and identity, toward seeing the truth rather than being blind, toward being creative, toward being good, and a lot else. That is, the human being is so constructed that he presses toward what most people would call good values, toward serenity, kindness, courage, honesty, love, unselfishness, and goodness."

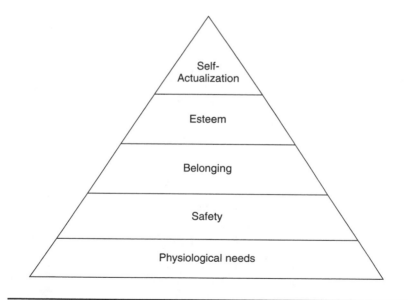

Figure 3.1　Maslow's hierarchy of needs.

Herzberg, Maunser, and Snyderman's (1959) motivator-hygiene theory was an explicit attempt to understand motivations in the workplace (see Table 3.1). Based on a largely qualitative methodology, Herzberg identified two distinct factors that affect job satisfaction: motivators and hygienes. Motivators involved factors intrinsic to the job such as recognition and growth. In contrast, hygienes were extrinsic job dimensions such as supervision and working conditions.

According to Herzberg's theory, motivators and hygienes exist as two separate and distinct continua. The difference between the two involves the amount of satisfaction/dissatisfaction inherent in each. Motivators elicit positive job attitudes because they tend to address self-actualization needs as described earlier. The presence of motivators has the potential to yield high levels of job satisfaction. The absence of motivators, however, does not necessarily cause dissatisfaction. Under this framework, the opposite of job satisfaction is not job dissatisfaction but simply a lack of satisfaction. Similarly, hygiene factors may cause varying levels of dissatisfaction, ranging, for example, from none to a great deal. For example, the presence of air conditioning on a hot day will generally not cause workers to be more satisfied because it is *expected*. If the air conditioning fails, however, dissatisfaction may result. Motivators and hygienes occur simultaneously to varying extents.

In a subsequent discussion of employee motivation, Herzberg (1968) introduced the acronym KITA ("kick in the —"). KITA can take three forms: negative physical KITA, negative psychological KITA, and positive KITA. Negative *physical* KITA as a motivator—although probably effective in the short run—could have serious consequences in today's litigious human resources environment. Of more interest are negative psychological KITA and positive KITA. The former occurs when we induce action through fear of what will happen if it is not done, whereas positive KITA involves *reward*. Although effective in the short term, positive KITA in the form of rewards or bonuses is not motivational, according to Herzberg. The

Table 3.1   Components of Herzberg's motivator-hygiene theory.

Motivators	Hygienes
Recognition	Supervision
Achievement	Company policy
Growth	Working conditions
Advancement	Status
Responsibility	Job security
Work itself	

implication is that to nurture long-term positive behaviors, rewards that involve motivator factors such as recognition, advancement, and responsibility should be emphasized.

The acquired needs theory of McClelland and colleagues (1953) suggested that three human needs drive behavior:

- Need for achievement (*n-ach*)

- Need for affiliation (*n-affil*)

- Need for power (*n-pow*)

The three needs have different implications in terms of human motivation. For example, the need for achievement (n-ach) involves seeking personal responsibility and attainable but challenging goals and feedback on performance. In contrast, the need for affiliation (n-affil) involves people's desire for friendly relationships and preference for roles with human interaction. Finally, the need for power (n-pow) involves the desire to make an impact and be influential and effective.

Clearly, employees differ considerably in terms of these three primary needs. Those with high need for achievement scores, however, tend to make the best managers. These individuals, according to Beck (2000:327), tend to be more persistent and work harder. Apparently, people with high n-ach tend to report family backgrounds characterized by rewards linked to achievement striving. Interestingly, Beck suggests that "young adults with high n-ach often report that their parents were not particularly warm individuals, and that they emphasized achievement rather than affiliation."

Of greatest importance are McClelland's (1985) subsequent findings that suggested individuals with high n-ach scores make the best managers. They are determined to be moderate risk takers, in need of immediate feedback. Indeed, McClelland concluded this type of employee may not be content unless in an environment characterized by rewards linked to achievements. This has significant implications for programs that link customer satisfaction scores to management incentives (discussed later). McClelland's research also suggested that individuals with high n-ach tended to attribute successful completion of a task to *ability*. These individuals also appeared to attribute failure to a *lack of effort*. This, too, has implications for linking customer satisfaction to extrinsic rewards.

Expectancy theory (Atkinson, 1958, 1964) extended achievement theory by assuming individuals weigh the probability of success and the value of the reward. It explicitly acknowledges the likelihood that people may be motivated simply by the reward of success itself, regardless of extrinsic incentives. One fundamental assumption is that more incentive value is attached to achieving a difficult goal than an easy one. According to expectancy theory, the probability that an individual will engage in achievement-oriented behaviors is a function of these three factors:

1. The motivation (M_s) for success

2. The probability (P_s) of success

3. The incentive value of success (I_s)

Accordingly, the tendency (T_s) to engage in achievement-oriented behaviors is depicted in Equation 3.1. Note that the incentive value of success (I_s) is equal to $1-P_s$. The implication of this relationship is that if M_s, P_s, or I_s is zero, the likelihood of the behavior (T_s) will be zero.

$$T_s = M_s \times P_s \times I_s \qquad (3.1)$$

This formula is consistent with the achievement theory assertion that high n-ach people are moderate risk takers. Because the incentive value of success (I_s) is equal to $1-P_s$, the maximum value of $P_s \times (1-P_s)$ occurs when the probability (P_s) is 50%. As Beck (2000:331) notes, when the task is too difficult there is little probability of success, and if it is too easy there is no incentive to succeed.

Expectancy theory also accommodates the inverse of T_s, which is the motivation to *avoid failure*. The tendency to avoid failure (T_{af}) is a mixture of the motivation to avoid failure (M_{af}), the probability of failure (P_f), and the negative incentive value of failure (I_f). Equation 3.2 summarizes the tendency to avoid failure:

$$T_{af} = M_{af} \times P_f \times I_f \qquad (3.2)$$

The tendency to avoid failure (T_{af}) and the tendency to success can be combined now to produce a single equation (3.3) that is predictive of behavior:

$$T_s + T_{af} = (M_s \times P_s \times I_s) + (M_{af} \times P_f \times I_f) \qquad (3.3)$$

As described by Beck (2000:333), if M_s exceeds M_{af}, an individual will favor tasks with a medium probability of success. However, if M_{af} exceeds M_s, the individual will tend to avoid tasks with a medium probability of success. Research by Atkinson and Litwin (1960) confirmed these predictions, suggesting that individuals with high M_s and low M_{af} scores would favor tasks with a medium chance of success.

McClelland's need for achievement theory and Atkinson's extensions have been criticized as too simplistic. Motivation, other researchers have reasoned, is probably more complex than the simple difference between one's motivation for success and avoidance of failure. Other researchers like Spence and Helmreich (1983) suggested that satisfaction with the work itself, a sense of completion, and competitiveness underlie achievement motivation.

Alderfer (1972) also built on Maslow's need for achievement theory. In effect, the author suggested that individual needs could be classified into three groupings:

- Existence needs

- Relatedness needs

- Growth needs

Existence needs involve nutritional and material requirements; relatedness needs revolve around relationships within family and work contexts. Finally, growth needs reflect a desire for personal psychological development. Alderfer's approach is distinguished from Maslow's achievement theory primarily based on the suggestion that these needs exist on a continuum rather than a hierarchy with discrete levels.

Weiner's (1985) *attributional theory of achievement* acknowledges that individuals may attribute their success (or failure) to a variety of causes. There are, the author maintained, both internal and external attributions. Individuals typically attribute their success to internal factors such as ability and their failure to external factors. Task success or failure may also be attributed to stable factors such as intelligence or unstable factors such as luck. It may also be attributed to controllable factors such as effort or uncontrollable factors such as an illness. Weiner's approach to understanding the nature of motivation revolves around *the emotional consequences of each attribution.*

PROCESS THEORIES OF MOTIVATION

Unlike the needs-based theories, process-oriented theories of motivation emphasize cognitions and their relationship to behaviors. The process theories of motivation described here are more specific to work behaviors than the more generally applicable needs-based theories described earlier (with the exception of the motivator-hygiene theory of job satisfaction).

Perhaps the most well known of the process architectures is Vroom's (1964) valence, instrumentality, and expectancy (VIE) theory. Central to Vroom's reasoning was the assertion that motivation at work is based on the employee's perception of the link between effort and reward. Specifically, *expectancy* is considered the perceived probability that an effort will be *instrumental* in achieving a *valued* objective. Valence refers to the value of the outcome for an individual. For example, this theory suggests that an employee will consider the benefits of a given level of effort. If that effort is perceived as instrumental in yielding valued results, the effort will be made. Quite simply, if an employee does not believe effort leads to improved importance or that the enhanced performance will yield a valued outcome like a promotion, achievement, or recognition, he or she will not engage in the behavior.

Figure 3.2 summarizes the relationship among motivation, effort, performance, and rewards. As shown, motivation leads to effort, which, in turn, affects performance and, ultimately, an outcome such as a reward. Note that motivation itself is driven by three important factors: (1) the effort–performance expectation, (2) the performance–reward expectation, (3) and the perceived value (valence) of the outcome.

Adams's equity theory (1975) extends Vroom's framework by incorporating a broader context. In effect, Adams argued that people consider the equity of a relationship with respect to both internal and external criteria. Of special interest is the comparison to *external* relationships. Equity theory suggests that people compare their effort–reward ratios with those of others in similar situations. For example, if employees believe their effort is equivalent to that of their co-workers and yet their pay rate is lower, this perception of inequity will affect their behavior. In order to establish a sense of equity they may lower their effort level, seek to have their pay rate increased, or otherwise display their displeasure with the situation.

Interestingly, equity theory has implications for situations in which the reward is perceived to exceed effort. This situation, although much less common than the reverse, yields interesting behavioral outcomes. According to Beck (2000:405) evidence suggests that people who believe a reward exceeds the value of their effort will increase their effort in an attempt to restore a sense of equity. Interestingly, it appears this sense of inequity is short lived.

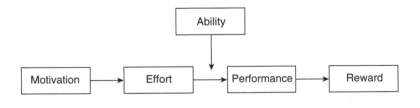

Figure 3.2 Expectancy theory of motivation.

Process theories of motivation have important implications for managers. In particular, they suggest that employee perceptions surrounding two main points should be considered. First, it is important to focus on expectancy values—the link between effort and performance. Employees must believe their effort will yield the desired results. In this vein, managers must also determine what rewards employees value, and these must be linked to performance.

Nadler and Lawler (1977) suggested a number of process theory implications for managing motivation in complex organizations. Of key importance to managers seeking to motivate employees by linking rewards to performance are the following points:

- Tailor rewards to individual employee values.

- Ensure that rewards are valued.

- Define performance objectives clearly based on desired behaviors.

- Make goals attainable.

- Link outcomes explicitly to goals.

- Verify system equity.

Of these prescriptions, the last is of particular importance. It advocates checking the entire performance–reward system to ensure it is equitable. This really means ensuring it is *perceived* as equitable. Top performers must feel they are rewarded for their enhanced performance levels. Further, the reward should be considered appropriate for the increased effort top performers put forth to achieve their high levels of performance.

Process theories of motivation also have broader implications for complex organizations. First, it is well known that reward systems can lead to self-fulfilling prophecies. That is, organizations get what they reward. For example, when reward is linked explicitly to performance rather than seniority, very different results may emerge. Organizations that traditionally reward tenure with little regard for performance often provide employees with a focus on long-term job security and the status quo.

Kerr's (1975) critique on management incentive programs in a variety of organizational settings suggests that organizations often inadvertently reward the wrong behaviors. He cites, for example, universities that frequently tout the quality of teaching in their institutions while only explicitly rewarding a successful publication track record. Similarly, Kerr suggested that orphanages often surround themselves with multiple layers of intractable bureaucracy aimed, ostensibly, at ensuring children are adopted by the most ideal families. We would hope the orphanage's goal would be to maximize the number of children placed in homes. However, Kerr noted that (at the time) this type of organization was typically rewarded by the state based on the number of children in the system. Total organization size (number of children) was typically a measure of status among orphanage directors. Those with the biggest institutions were considered to have the most status and the largest budgets and staffs. Clearly, this system rewarded organizations for *not* doing what they were set up to do in the first place.

When pay-for-performance systems are in place, the reward must be public. When it is acknowledged but hidden, the result, although not dysfunctional, is not optimal. Only by demonstrating to all relevant members of the organization the unequivocal link between performance and *meaningful* reward—and the magnitude of each—will motivation be maximized.

Because one critical management objective is the cognitive control of motivation through reward, Nadler and Lawler (1977:33–34) argued that *measurement* should play a central role in the process. That is, the measurement of motivation through employee surveys, they contended, should be used to assess the effectiveness of reward systems. Of course, employee commitment measurement systems are ubiquitous in large organizations today. Commitment to the organization rather than "job satisfaction" is typically the critical dependent measure in contemporary employee attitude measurement programs.

One substantive issue that Nadler and Lawler (1977:33) developed that has received considerable attention more recently involves the role of group structures in organizations. In effect, Nadler and Lawler suggested that small groups in organizations represent powerful tools for controlling motivation. Indeed, the authors indicated that rewards should be tied to group performance in addition to individual performance. The current salience of this issue in human resource management is evidenced by a variety of new books and articles on the subject. These are discussed later in this chapter.

REWARD AND RECOGNITION PROGRAMS

Before discussing specifically the linkage between customer satisfaction performance and reward program participation, let's consider some contemporary thought regarding incentive programs in organizations generally. Of considerable importance to this discussion is the efficacy of reward and recognition incentive programs. Do these programs work? The implicit objective of incentive programs—whether based on customer satisfaction, sales goals, or other measures—is that the reward will serve to motivate further employees who meet corporate objectives. The notion that employees will work harder to meet targets for which they will be rewarded is certainly intuitively palatable. However, there is considerable debate regarding how effective incentive programs actually are.

Incentive systems that link monetary rewards to performance are pervasive in contemporary organizations. Much of the theoretical literature discussed earlier suggests, however, that extrinsic rewards like bonuses and pay increases do not serve the overall organization well. One of the most vocal critics of incentive systems that reward performance is Kohn (1993a, 1993b). His contention that incentive plans linking performance to rewards are dysfunctional criticized the reliance on a carrot-and-stick mentality. Kohn emphasized the *short-term* effects of monetary inducements to perform. The result is temporary compliance, not long-term motivation. Kohn (1993a:59) rhetorically asked if rewards motivate employees. His conclusion was that yes, rewards motivate people—to get rewards!

Kohn (1993b) offered a six-point framework for understanding why incentive plans linking performance and rewards do not work. Figure 3.3 summarizes the six bases for Kohn's indictment of incentive systems. The first point is clearly consistent with Herzberg's motivator-hygiene theory, which proposed that pay represents a dissatisfier, not an intrinsic motivational tool.

Kohn's suggestion that rewards can punish involves the coercive nature of incentive systems. The manipulative nature of performance-based rewards, he argued, has undesirable long-term effects. Employees who perceive they are being coerced to behave in a certain fashion will likely revolt eventually.

The ostensibly ruinous effect of rewards on workplace relationships was cited as another reason that incentive systems are doomed to failure. Kohn (1993a:58) concluded that "the surest way to destroy cooperation and, therefore, organizational excellence, is to force people to compete for rewards or

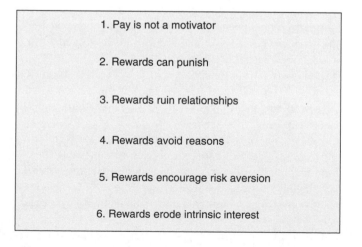

1. Pay is not a motivator

2. Rewards can punish

3. Rewards ruin relationships

4. Rewards avoid reasons

5. Rewards encourage risk aversion

6. Rewards erode intrinsic interest

Figure 3.3 Kohn's six-point indictment of incentive systems.

recognition or to rank them against each other." Further, relationships between staff and managers can be strained. As Kohn (1993a:58) warned, "Very few things threaten an organization as much as a hoard of incentive-driven individuals trying to curry favor with the incentive dispenser."

Reliance on incentive programs to solve productivity issues does little to address underlying problems, according to Kohn. It is much easier for managers to entice employees with rewards than it is to address fundamental performance obstacles. In the worst case, incentive systems displace meaningful solutions and the tools employees need to do their work effectively. As a result, Kohn argued, organizational change and growth are impeded.

Of particular interest in Kohn's criticism of incentive programs is his declaration that they produce risk-averse employees. When significant rewards are linked to performance, the result is that employees will be less willing to explore alternative avenues. Their behavior will be directed at maximizing the probability of achieving the reward. As Kohn concluded, the result is the *loss of creativity*.

Kohn's final objection to incentive programs involved their tendency to undermine intrinsic interest in behaviors that are linked to performance measurement and, ultimately, rewards. Recall from the discussions of both needs-based and process-oriented motivation theories that intrinsic interest and rewards appear to be particularly important determinants of behavior. Thus Kohn's (1993a:59) suggestion that incentive programs actually reduce intrinsic interest is especially damning. His reasoning is based on work by Deci and Ryan (1985) and "scores of experiments across the country" that have reached similar conclusions. Specifically, the evidence Kohn cites suggests that contingent pay systems (i.e., rewards) reduce interest in tasks. And, more importantly, extrinsic rewards linked to complex or interesting task performance are especially damaging. The explanation for this phenomenon is that people assume that if a reward is offered for a task, the behavior associated with it must be unpleasant.

Kohn summarized his perspective in a *CFO* interview (1994:17) in which he provided a one-sentence synopsis of his advice to companies: "Pay people well, pay them fairly—and then do everything you can to take their minds off money."

Kohn (1994:17) conceded that his radical message is not always well received by companies. Still, some companies have heeded his warnings and excised incentive programs from their compensation systems. Nashua Tape and Marshall Industries were cited as examples of companies that banished incentive systems and enjoyed more satisfied employees and productivity gains.

Given the nature of Kohn's arguments, it should be no surprise that a rebuttal including opinions from nine industry human resources experts

(Stewart et al., 1993) was published in the very next issue of *Harvard Business Review*. A wide range of concerns with Kohn's views were aired by the contributors. Some of the critics were particularly incensed, equating Kohn's perspective with communism and admonishing him that he "can't have it both ways . . . you simply can't have the equality of outcome you desire with the robust, dynamic economy we all want" (1993:38).

Although conceding that managers in both the United States and other countries often use incentive systems as a crutch, one critic countered it would be highly problematic if all employees were paid the same regardless of performance. Kohn neglected, according to one academic critic, to address the fundamental monetary incentive system dilemma: if pay is not tied to performance, a company risks losing its best employees. But, by rewarding performance, the company risks implicitly "encouraging self-interest instead of organizational commitment" (1993:40). This conundrum is not solved by Kohn's argument.

Others agreed that Kohn was on the right track with respect to the deleterious effect rewards can have on commitment and creativity. But at least one critic admonished Kohn for distorting this relationship by equating "bribes" with equitable compensation. Intrinsic motivation is clearly important, but several critics of Kohn's reasoning argued that extrinsic rewards like money and recognition are not unilaterally detrimental. Certainly, they agreed, if an employee feels completely controlled by an incentive system there can be negative effects. But they reasonably countered that extrinsic rewards can be beneficial and cited some interesting research. One study of some interest to his line of reasoning involved artists and commissioned works. This presumably unpublished experiment suggested that artists perceived commissioned pieces to involve more creativity (than uncommissioned work) when there were few constraints on their interpretation. As this contributor (Amabile) concluded, "it would be a mistake to believe that reward and recognition must always have a negative effect on performance or that creative people cannot be motivated by both money and interest in the work itself" (1993:42). Another contributor to the 1993 rebuttal to Kohn was the chairman and CEO of Tyco Laboratories. His response to Kohn's condemnation of incentive systems was unequivocal (1993:43):

> I'll accept that elephants cannot fly and that fish cannot walk, but Kohn's argument that incentive plans cannot work defies the laws of nature at Tyco Laboratories. Tyco provides a compelling case study that incentives can and do work for both managers and shareholders. In fact, we believe our incentive compensation program is at the heart of our company's success.

Further citing Tyco's apparently successful incentive plan, this Kohn detractor suggested that to be successful, incentive programs should be linked to *controllable* business unit performance variables. Tyco's program also included *uncapped* incentives, which ostensibly further fostered an entrepreneurial spirit among employees. Rather than yield dysfunctional competition, the result was apparently greater productivity and an esprit de corps.

Yet another contributor to the rebuttal to Kuhn's denunciation of incentive systems insisted that the problem with extrinsic rewards is not that they do not work but that they work too well. This academician conceded that rewards can and often do have unintended side effects, particularly when they are linked to the wrong behaviors. The author fully agreed with Kohn's assertion that incentive systems rewarding *individual* performance are not likely to yield teamwork and cooperation. He argued that an incentive plan explicitly rewarding *team* performance can be effective and avoid the pitfalls Kuhn cited as inescapable.

Kohn's position on incentive systems is controversial and, as we would expect, has detractors. Blanchard (1994:17), for example, suggested that Kohn's criticisms reflect a "lack of understanding about the principles and practices of good management." He argued that rewards need not undermine intrinsic interest and motivation if incentives are tailored to the individual's needs. Blanchard also maintained that Kohn focused excessively on the dysfunction of *monetary* rewards. When other forms of reward such as recognition are used, Blanchard reasoned, intrinsic motivation is not necessarily negatively affected.

Subsequent discussions of Kohn's position further expanded many of the points made in the first rebuttal. For example, whereas Kohn perceived rewards as manipulative, Blanchard regarded them as a form of partnering. Blanchard (1994:17) responded to Kohn's criticism by suggesting that "If you help employees obtain skills and provide opportunities to reach their goals, they will be motivated." The author also countered Kohn's suggestion that rewards create dysfunctional competition. When team-based rewards are used, Blanchard maintained, there is a reinforcement of individual and group objectives. And, whereas Kohn condemned incentive systems for producing risk-averse employees and smothering creativity, Blanchard (1994:17) argued that instead, poor goal setting was responsible: "If it is important to get people to take risks, be creative, or work together to solve problems, you need to clearly focus employee attention on those goals."

Clearly, Kohn's remarks in 1993 were incendiary and caused a great deal of debate. Perhaps that was what they were intended to do in the first place. At least one of the nine authors who joined the initial rebuttal expressed gratitude to Kohn for precipitating such an intense level of discourse. As is often the case, the answer probably lies somewhere in between the two extreme camps. That is, it seems reasonable to conclude that extrinsic rewards can be dysfunctional in certain cases, but a wide range of factors at the *individual*, *work team*, and *organization* levels affect this outcome.

CUSTOMER FEEDBACK IN INCENTIVE SYSTEMS

Most of the incentive system examples discussed in this chapter have linked productivity or revenue outcomes to rewards. It is extremely common in both midsize and large corporations to link customer feedback explicitly to management incentives. This is particularly true in organizations with disaggregated distribution systems. Fast-food chains, multibranch financial services providers, automotive services providers, and a wide variety of organizations characterized by multiple branches or stores use—to some extent—customer feedback metrics in determining bonus levels for store managers. Organizations with a distribution system that is ostensibly uniform at the customer level in terms of service and product quality will likely have some form of customer feedback system linked to incentives.

In franchise-like organizations typified by uniformity in signage, store-level architecture, service quality, and product offerings, consumers clearly perceive benefit. In particular, they have a reduced sense of risk. This is attributable to the consistency of service and products associated with the chain. Consumers know that if they buy lunch at one of the well-known fast-food chains, product and service quality will be very predictable. At many of the largest chains, the level of product quality variance across stores is presumably extremely small. This is because little autonomy is afforded at the store or branch level in terms of purchasing the raw materials required to produce the final product and its ultimate preparation. Branch managers in fast-food chains may really only be able to affect service quality because the product is highly constrained in terms of raw materials and processing.

In financial services, too, customers of large multibranch banks can expect little variation in terms of access to their accounts, service levels, and product offerings. Branch managers at banks cannot typically control the rate of interest paid for deposit products or the types of products offered. These are corporate-level issues over which the branch manager has little control. In banking, branch managers are probably constrained to affect customer satisfaction and loyalty through the in-person service they provide. Thus issues relating to the tellers and personal bankers may realistically be the only factors fully controlled by bank branch managers.

In the automotive industry it would be ridiculous to hold dealership managers responsible for overall product quality (excluding vehicle sales preparation issues). Instead, their real effect is limited to sales and service issues. This situation is actually somewhat problematic. It is typified by a manufacturer, which distributes its products through a network of independent dealerships. Dealerships are quick to recognize that product quality and reliability problems should be attributed to the manufacturer, not them. Consumers, however, do not necessarily perceive a chasm between the manufacturer and dealership and often blame the latter for any problems. Holding dealerships responsible for product quality and reliability in this context would be an egregious mistake, ultimately leading to dealer dissatisfaction and attrition.

Any organization selling centrally manufactured products through a dealership or store network cannot expect *actual* product quality variance at the dealer level. However, *perceived* product quality variance is a real possibility in this instance. It may be attributed to how *customer expectations* are shaped by salespeople at the dealership, as illustrated in Figure 3.4. If, for example, during the initial sales interaction, consumers are told the product will perform better than it is actually designed to, the gap between expected and actual performance may yield product dissatisfaction. In the event that substantive product quality variance is encountered across dealerships or stores, a review of the sales process may be warranted. The bottom line is that when it comes to consumer satisfaction, perception is reality. If customer expectations are unrealistically inflated, they may be dissatisfied with a product despite the fact that it is performing at the level it was intended to.

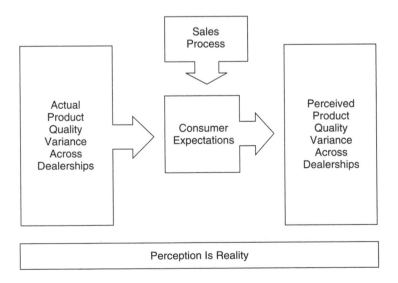

Figure 3.4   Actual versus perceived product quality variance.

RELATIONSHIP AND TRANSACTION SURVEYS

Given that customer satisfaction data have been—and will continue to be—linked to management rewards, it is surprising there is relatively little information concerning appropriate content. Specifically, if managers' compensation will be tied to customer feedback, the feedback should be related to service and product quality issues that managers can control. Accordingly, it would not be appropriate to provide branch managers incentives based on issues such as image and reputation. Branch managers and line staff members have little control over many things that affect consumer satisfaction and loyalty. In large fast-food franchises, prices, menus, and preparation are set at the corporate level. Similarly, corporate decisions regarding advertising and marketing communications content may shape brand image.

Thus it is appropriate to link compensation systems only to issues that may be affected at different organizational levels. It is highly problematic and dysfunctional to withhold rewards from employees based on performance on issues over which they have no control. So negative feedback concerning corporate image should not be linked to branch manager incentives. If possible, specific survey sections or individual items should be identified a priori as affecting various types of employees in terms of reward systems. The focus and content of customer satisfaction surveys varies tremendously.

Two types of surveys typically are encountered in customer satisfaction studies: *transaction surveys* and *relationship surveys*. Virtually all customer satisfaction programs can be characterized as belonging to one of these two categories. In certain cases, a hybrid that integrates the two is possible (discussed later). Distinguishing between these two types of customer feedback mechanisms is vital in the development of incentive systems because they typically contain very different items. If defensible linkages to employee rewards are desired, the content of these two survey instrument types is very important.

Transaction Surveys

Transaction surveys solicit customer feedback regarding a specific service or product quality interaction. This could involve a new car purchase experience, repair work, problem resolution, account opening or closure, new service, product installation, delivery, a hotel stay, airline flight, Web-based product purchase, theme park visit, dinner, or any other interaction. Transaction surveys typically focus on a very specific, discrete set of events that define the interaction. In the case of a dinner, the transaction includes initially being seated, menu selections, ordering, consuming the food, waiting for a bill, and finally paying and exiting. Other transactions may include fewer components. An ATM visit, for example, includes a much less lengthy interaction. Similarly, a visit to your local bank branch to deposit a check has relatively few subtransactions.

Transaction satisfaction is highly dynamic and may vary within respondents over time. The sum of all transaction interactions probably shapes a great deal of a customer's overall satisfaction and loyalty. It is important, however, not to confuse transaction satisfaction with overall relationship satisfaction. Transaction satisfaction relates to a specific interaction, whereas relationship transaction—as described in greater detail later—subsumes a wide variety of experiences, image perceptions, and other phenomena.

Mount Whitney National Bank

Hand Delivered by Courier for Your Convenience

Branch: Beverly Hills Mall Branch

Dear Mr. Smith:

Our records indicate you **opened a Global Access Account at our Beverly Hills Mall Branch on May 23**. The Mount Whitney National Bank private banking staff tries to monitor and improve our customers' satisfaction continuously. Please spend a few minutes filling out the brief survey below. Note that the postcard is already stamped and addressed so all you have to do upon completion is drop it in the mail.

As an incentive to complete the survey, we have reserved a special gift in your name at the **Beverly Hills Mall Branch**. Please see private banking representative **Tom Smith** to arrange shipment of your gift the next time you visit the branch.

For the question below, please use the 10-point scale to indicate your satisfaction. The scale range from 1, Poor, to 10, Excellent. Thinking about your visit and your Global Access Account opening, please evaluate the **Beverly Hills Mall Branch** in terms of the issues presented below:

Account Opening: Private Banker

	Poor									Excellent
1. Waiting time to see private banker	1□	2□	3□	4□	5□	6□	7□	8□	9□	10□
2. Ability of private banker to answer questions	1□	2□	3□	4□	5□	6□	7□	8□	9□	10□
3. Private banker's recommendations	1□	2□	3□	4□	5□	6□	7□	8□	9□	10□
4. Ability of private banker to answer questions	1□	2□	3□	4□	5□	6□	7□	8□	9□	10□
5. All paperwork available at visit	1□	2□	3□	4□	5□	6□	7□	8□	9□	10□
6. Private banker explained benefits	1□	2□	3□	4□	5□	6□	7□	8□	9□	10□
7. Overall satisfaction with private banker	1□	2□	3□	4□	5□	6□	7□	8□	9□	10□

---

continued

continued

Account Opening: Paperwork Required

	Poor									Excellent

8. Forms available quickly   1☐ 2☐ 3☐ 4☐ 5☐ 6☐ 7☐ 8☐ 9☐ 10☐

9. Deposit forms were easy to understand   1☐ 2☐ 3☐ 4☐ 5☐ 6☐ 7☐ 8☐ 9☐ 10☐

10. Application form was easy to
    understand   1☐ 2☐ 3☐ 4☐ 5☐ 6☐ 7☐ 8☐ 9☐ 10☐

11. International forms available   1☐ 2☐ 3☐ 4☐ 5☐ 6☐ 7☐ 8☐ 9☐ 10☐

12. Asian partnership bank forms available   1☐ 2☐ 3☐ 4☐ 5☐ 6☐ 7☐ 8☐ 9☐ 10☐

13. European sponsorship exit form   1☐ 2☐ 3☐ 4☐ 5☐ 6☐ 7☐ 8☐ 9☐ 10☐

14. Overall satisfaction with paperwork   1☐ 2☐ 3☐ 4☐ 5☐ 6☐ 7☐ 8☐ 9☐ 10☐

Considering your experience opening a **Global Access Account** at our **Beverly Hills Mall Branch**, overall how satisfied are you with the entire experience, including the private banking representative and the required forms?

	Poor									Excellent

15. **Overall satisfaction with account
    opening**   1☐ 2☐ 3☐ 4☐ 5☐ 6☐ 7☐ 8☐ 9☐ 10☐

Transaction satisfaction must be measured soon after the interaction. In the case of a bank deposit, this may be within 72 hours. For a fast-food purchase, it is best to obtain feedback within 24 hours. Generally speaking, the magnitude of the interaction in terms of time and money determines the transaction satisfaction half-life. Consumers recall every nuance of a major transaction like a home or auto purchase for several days. In contrast, an event like a fast-food lunch or a CD purchase decays rapidly in consumers' minds.

The important aspect of transaction surveys is that they represent a good measurement platform for relating consumer feedback to line employees and their managers. Typically, virtually all of the items in a transaction survey involve various aspects of the specific interaction. The structure of this type of survey instrument most often parallels the various transaction touchpoints in chronological order, decomposing it in sometimes excruciating detail. The objective is to isolate problematic aspects of the transaction and improve them.

A typical transaction survey for a bank branch visit is shown on pages 54–55. In this case, the transaction survey focuses on a specific account opening experience, and two primary subprocesses are identified structurally. The first involves the private banker; the latter half of the survey focuses on forms. Clearly, the latter issues are beyond the control of branch-level private bankers. The first section of the survey, however, focuses exclusively on issues that directly reflect the service quality delivered by the private banker. If quarterly (or other) bonus or reward systems are to be linked to these data, it would be prudent to include only the first section content in the compensation system. Again, linking rewards to factors that cannot be controlled by employees yields frustration and, ultimately, negative results.

In the case of the survey linking employee rewards to the content presented in the first half of the survey would be sensible. However, this is simply one transaction of many that any individual customer may experience over the course of a year. If a series of transaction surveys were in place, managers and other line staff could be linked explicitly to various feedback types. Further, these transactions may be differentially weighted in terms of their impact on the employee's bonus compensation. The problem resolution process, for example, may affect the quarterly bonus more substantially than a simple inquiry or account opening.

Finally, note that the survey is intended to be hand delivered by courier. This reflects the important role of timing in transaction surveys. In the present example, customers are high net worth individuals whose feedback is critical to the private banking function at this financial services provider. In this case, the cost of hand delivery is far outweighed by the very high response rate and public relations impact of this unusual channel. It would not be prudent to use this approach among a mass market customer base, of course!

Mass market transaction satisfaction surveys may be executed economically using telephone, Web, or IVR (interactive voice response) technologies. The latter involves an inbound architecture in which respondents call a computerized survey system and provide quality ratings using their telephone keypad numbers. Many IVR systems also permit respondents to provide verbatim comments, which are digitally recorded and may be accessed from virtually anywhere in the world by telephone. As the transaction magnitude increases, the data collection methodology should be changed accordingly. For example, an IVR survey would not be an appropriate survey platform for gathering data about a recently acquired yacht.

Assuming an organization can isolate customers by transaction and produce a sample file containing all those who, for example, visited a given store in the last 48 hours, these respondents may be contacted before the attitudes about their experience decay. IVR is being used successfully in retail and fast-food markets with great success. Although limited to usually less than three to five minutes, the IVR data collection methodology represents an excellent way to execute transaction satisfaction surveys. IVR systems often incorporate a respondent incentive and fulfillment function as well.

Relationship Surveys

Relationship surveys tend to be much more general and avoid feedback related to a specific service or product experience. Instead, relationship surveys may focus on satisfaction with products, service culture, image issues, and channels or access types. There is a substantial difference between transaction and relationship surveys in terms of employee accountability.

Transaction surveys are highly focused and permit valid inferences concerning the relationship between unit-level service or product quality and managerial performance. In contrast, the more general nature of relationship surveys tends to preclude this type of linkage. Relationship survey content tends to avoid the specificity that defines transaction surveys. Rather than focus on well-defined processes and their subcomponents, relationship surveys have a broader mission. They are aimed at an exhaustive measurement of the union between customer and provider. This involves topics such as access channels, general perceptions of service culture, product variety and quality and image-related topics such as social responsibility, pricing, and value perceptions. Combined, all of these issues define the totality of the relationship.

Because relationship surveys do not explicitly gauge feedback with respect to specific processes or employees, it is difficult to base reward systems on their results. When relationship survey data are linked at a unit (e.g., store, branch, or district) level to employee reward systems, the results can be worse than no bonus system at all. When employees feel they have no control over the measurements against which their performance is measured, their motivation will suffer. Motivation theorists would predict such a scenario would yield employees with virtually no incentive to provide high levels of service or product quality.

If unit-level managers have little or no motivation, turnover will increase, service quality will drop, and customer satisfaction with key processes may plummet. If permitted to continue, this trend will snowball and eventually erode overall relationship satisfaction. This phenomenon may seem counterintuitive, but is quite probable, especially in the absence of a parallel transaction satisfaction survey designed to provide continuous diagnostics.

Most relationship surveys are conducted annually or quarterly, and transaction satisfaction studies are typically continuous. As a result, it is very possible for significant relationship erosion to occur due to process exceptions if a continuous monitor (i.e., transaction survey) is not in place. Organizations that only measure relationship satisfaction and make the mistake of linking this feedback to unit-level incentives could encounter the problematic situation described earlier.

Of course, the preceding discussion assumes that performance-based rewards actually do motivate employees. As described earlier in this chapter, substantive empirical and theoretical evidence make suspect the relationship between monetary rewards and motivation. Still, one need not reward employees financially for exceeding customer satisfaction standards. A wide variety of alternate forms of recognition is possible.

HYBRID SURVEYS

In order to link customer feedback metrics to employee rewards—whether monetary or not—the metrics must relate to factors that can be controlled by the employees. Often it is not possible to have an annual relationship survey and a continuous transaction survey. In this case, a hybrid instrument may be developed. The hybrid satisfaction survey is composed of elements from relationship and transaction surveys. As such, the hybrid instrument is rarely administered on a truly continuous basis. Instead, data are typically reported on a quarterly basis, and no effort is made to link the feedback to a specific transaction.

The typical hybrid satisfaction survey attempts to shift the respondents' attention to their last transaction, but it does not reference a specific interaction by type and date. The hybrid satisfaction survey permits relatively defensible linkages between customer feedback and employee rewards. Of course, it sacrifices the specificity of a pure transaction survey and some of the holistic properties associated with a true relationship survey. Its benefits, however, probably outweigh these costs.

SUMMARY

Linking customer feedback data to employee rewards represents quite a minefield for the uninitiated. Aside from the controversy surrounding the efficacy of monetary performance rewards in motivation enhancement, the problem associated with using relationship survey data in reward systems is crystal clear. There is little doubt that when employees perceive their rewards to be linked to issues beyond their control, the results will not be desirable.

The next chapter offers an *atheoretic* treatment of using customer feedback in employee reward systems. A variety of approaches to developing performance metrics are presented. Further, the importance of statistical significance testing to the reward system is underscored. It is critical to establish mathematically defensible performance gauges because employees can be very creative in their attempts to shed doubt on the validity of this type of system, particularly when they fail to meet the standards for bonus participation.

4

Linking CSM to Management Incentives: Quantitative Approaches

INTRODUCTION

This chapter builds on the theoretical foundation presented in Chapter 3 and focuses specifically on quantitative approaches to linking customer satisfaction metrics to management incentives. Although an understanding of the material presented in the preceding chapter is not imperative for effective application of the quantitative strategies described here, a recognition that extrinsic rewards *may* yield unintended consequences will help you keep the examples presented here in perspective. Of particular concern is the inclusion of service and product quality issues that are controllable at the reporting unit level, as described in Chapter 3.

INCENTIVE SYSTEMS AND CUSTOMER SATISFACTION

Incentive systems that use customer satisfaction results almost always incorporate other additional measures. Of particular interest is financial performance. If provided incentives are exclusively based on customer satisfaction, a manager clearly may make decisions that could jeopardize profitability. For example, drastically reducing the cost of products would yield higher customer satisfaction levels—particularly with respect to price—but would also negatively affect profitability. Conversely, incentives based exclusively on financial performance can yield dysfunctional results such as those experienced by Washington Mutual. Kadet (2002:119–22) suggested that this financial services provider rewarded branch managers based on the ratio of net income to number of employees. As one past employee conceded, the easiest way for managers to ensure a healthy monthly bonus was to reduce staffing levels at the branch. Of course, the result was myriad customer service problems.

Incentive systems must incorporate both customer satisfaction and objective business measures such as profitability. Other components to consider include market share growth, customer retention levels, and so-called share-of-wallet measures. The latter quantify share at the level of a specific customer's business. An average share-of-wallet score of 50%, for example, suggests that customers spend half of their available dollars with a particular business unit. This is an individual-level measure of business penetration that is typically available only through competitive intelligence sources or primary data collection efforts.

ACCOMMODATING MEASUREMENT ERROR

Exactly which metrics should be tracked and linked to incentives, the frequency and nature of the reward, and how performance is quantified are all important issues that deserve elaboration. Of special concern is the measurement of various performance goals. Unlike objectives such as sales targets or market share growth, customer satisfaction is typically associated with *measurement error* due to sampling. As a result, sampling error should be addressed when setting customer satisfaction performance goals.

A critical aspect of psychometric-based targets in incentive systems involves index development. Indexes are appealing from both intuitive and managerial perspectives. Combining several questions into a single measure may better reflect the extent to which a high level of service and product quality has been achieved. For example, the composite of three key items—overall satisfaction, willingness to recommend, and likelihood to continue—is a very popular loyalty index. Evidence suggests this index is a better predictor of future behavior than any one of its three components individually.

When combining psychometric measures to create a new composite index, it is critical to concede that each component is associated with measurement error. Unlike other more objective business measures such as profitability, revenue, customer head counts, or units sold, sample-based survey data may be associated with significant measurement error. Thus combining too many survey items into a grand composite measure is likely to yield undesirable results. The reality is that an index composed of more than three survey items becomes difficult to move; the components' errors offset one another, and the resultant index becomes less and less sensitive to management action. A static measure that appears to move only grudgingly will not engender much support among a population of branch managers whose bonus compensation is linked to the apparently immobile metric.

A final note on index creation involves weighting. This is a very popular approach that presumably reflects managerial priorities across the index components. One way this is achieved is by employing a weighting variable that sums to 1.00 across the inputs such as those depicted in Table 4.1.

Table 4.1 presents the weighted index calculation for two observations (R_1 and R_2) to illustrate the effects of this approach. As shown, there are three index components, each associated with a weight that, when averaged, equal 1.0. The first component weight is 1.0; the second variables (courtesy and food quality) have weights of 0.7 and 1.3, respectively. In this case, it is clear that management places much more value on the food quality component than the other issues.

Data for two customers using a 10-point scale are presented under the score headings. As shown, the two observations yield parallel scores when the inputs are simply summed to a total of 25. When the weights are applied, however, the first customer's (R_1) index score drops while the second customer's (R_2) index score is enhanced. Use of the weights clearly changes the outcome of this situation; when raw data are manipulated in this fashion, a number of questions arise. It is prudent to approach the weighting issue very cautiously because in the final analysis, the data are literally being altered.

Keep in mind that the measurement error described earlier is also subject to the weighting factor. The extent to which this error is not uniformly distributed across the index components may further complicate matters. An index component associated with greater measurement error and a high weight value will yield a compounded measurement term in the overall index. The result, of course, is reduced index sensitivity.

If possible, weighting should be empirically based and defensible. A variety of rationales for weights have been explored. Some are purely subjective; others appear more quantitative. One frequently encountered weighting criterion involves derived importance, as described in Chapter 5 and elsewhere in this book. Under this framework, service or product quality issues that are strong covariates of a dependent measure are given greater

Table 4.1 Weighted index creation.

Index component	Weight	R_1 Score	R_2 Score	R_1 Wt	R_2 Wt
Waiting time	1.0	8	8	8.0	8.0
Courtesy	0.7	9	8	6.3	5.6
Food quality	1.3	8	9	10.4	11.7
Index score		25	25	24.7	25.3

weight in the index calculation. With respect to the data presented in Table 4.1, for example, the weights could be construed as indicators of the extent to which each component covaries with a measure such as loyalty or overall satisfaction. Weighting the strongest covariate is intuitively palatable because it effectively rewards exceptional performance in areas known to yield loyalty.

CASE STUDY: SUPERCAM DEALER BONUS PROGRAM

This case study involves SuperCam Technologies, a manufacturer of mechanical camming units for use in industrial applications. In total, 25 SuperCam branches service the needs of manufacturers throughout North America. An integral component of the SuperCam corporate mission involves customer satisfaction. Not surprisingly, the company has a mature customer satisfaction measurement and tracking program in place. More importantly, customer satisfaction represents a cornerstone of the company's branch manager bonus incentive program.

The SuperCam customer satisfaction survey is shown on the next page. It is characteristically brief and includes six key service and product quality issues and three dependent measures: overall satisfaction, propensity to recommend, and intent to continue the relationship. The latter three items are of particular importance in the tracking program. Note that the scale anchor points involve satisfaction level for the first of these items and agreement level for the last two. Although it is useful to differentiate between the first six and last three items in the survey, this delineation largely reflects a model building (i.e., key-driver analysis) strategy. This example is not concerned with establishing dependence between the set of three dependent measures and the six service and product quality items. Key-driver analysis is used at SuperCam, but it is not the focus of this case study.

Rather than track only overall customer satisfaction, SuperCam tracks the proportion of customers who provide a top-two box rating (6 or 7 on the 7-point scale) on all three of the critical outcome measures. The SuperCam tracking metric focuses on customers who assign a rating of 6 or 7 on all three variables. It is SuperCam management's contention that only when customers provide top-two box ratings on all three measures can we be certain their expectations are being met.

In an effort to evaluate its 25 branches objectively, SuperCam management set a target level of 50% based on the top-two box rating just described. The annual bonus system's customer satisfaction component

Dear Valued Customer:

At SuperCam, we try continuously to monitor and improve our customers' satisfaction. You have been randomly selected to participate in our study. Our records indicate you took delivery of a D-13W Digital Cam in September 2002. Please spend a few minutes filling out the brief survey below. Note that we have included a self-addressed stamped envelope so all you have to do upon completion is drop it in the mail. We have also included $10 to compensate you for your time and prompt attention.

For the questions below, please use a 7-point scale to indicate your satisfaction. The scale ranges from 1, Very Dissatisfied, to 7, Very Satisfied.

	Very Dissatisfied					Very Satisfied	
1. Sales process	$_1\square$	$_2\square$	$_3\square$	$_4\square$	$_5\square$	$_6\square$	$_7\square$
2. Value for price paid	$_1\square$	$_2\square$	$_3\square$	$_4\square$	$_5\square$	$_6\square$	$_7\square$
3. Delivery time	$_1\square$	$_2\square$	$_3\square$	$_4\square$	$_5\square$	$_6\square$	$_7\square$
4. Setup and installation	$_1\square$	$_2\square$	$_3\square$	$_4\square$	$_5\square$	$_6\square$	$_7\square$
5. Installation instructions	$_1\square$	$_2\square$	$_3\square$	$_4\square$	$_5\square$	$_6\square$	$_7\square$
6. Product quality	$_1\square$	$_2\square$	$_3\square$	$_4\square$	$_5\square$	$_6\square$	$_7\square$
7. Considering all these aspects of your last SuperCam product purchase, how satisfied are you with us?	$_1\square$	$_2\square$	$_3\square$	$_4\square$	$_5\square$	$_6\square$	$_7\square$

	Strongly Disagree					Strongly Agree	
8. I would recommend SuperCam to a colleague	$_1\square$	$_2\square$	$_3\square$	$_4\square$	$_5\square$	$_6\square$	$_7\square$
9. I will continue to do business with SuperCam in the future	$_1\square$	$_2\square$	$_3\square$	$_4\square$	$_5\square$	$_6\square$	$_7\square$

~ Thank You ~

required a branch to post a top-two box score that was *statistically* higher than the 50% target level. This is an important distinction and deserves further clarification. If SuperCam management were to set a cutoff top-two box level of 50%, it could reasonably be argued that a score of 48% could not be statistically differentiated from the cutoff level. Indeed, a 95% confidence interval around the 50% level might suggest that scores between 45%

and 55% are within the 95% confidence interval, given a sample size of about 150. As a result, it is necessary to adjust the upper and lower bounds around the 50% cutoff to reflect *statistically significant* differences above or below the objective.

Based on establishing a 95% confidence interval around the 50% objective, SuperCam management was able to determine whether a given branch was performing significantly above or below the 50% target level. Equation 4.1 presents one way to calculate the z-score necessary to assess the significant difference between a branch score and the 50% objective level. As shown, p_1 is the branch top-two box score, 0.50 is the 50% target, and n is the sample size. Using this formula, SuperCam management was able to calculate z and assess its *two-tailed* significance. We are interested in the two-tailed significance because we are not positing the direction of the difference. Assuming a 95% confidence level, a statistically significant difference is presumed when the absolute value of z exceeds 1.96. If we relax the 95% confidence level to 90%, a z-score exceeding 1.64 would confirm statistical significance. Accordingly, it will be easier to demonstrate a significant difference using the relaxed 90% confidence level than the 95% confidence level. For a more detailed discussion, see Appendix A.

$$z = p_1 - 0.50/\sqrt{((p_1 \times (1-p_1))/n)} \qquad (4.1)$$

Assuming a sample size of 125 and a target level of 50%, a top-two box score greater than 58.7% or less than 41.3% would be necessary to demonstrate that a branch's score is statistically above or below the target. Using the relaxed 90% confidence level, a top-two box score greater than 57.3% or lower than 42.7% would be statistically significant. So dropping the confidence level from 95% to 90% narrows the interval around the target level from ±8.7 percentage points to ±7.3 percentage points. This action would in all likelihood increase the number of branches that are characterized as significantly above or below the target level. Similarly, we could decrease the number of branches significantly above or below the target level by implementing an even more stringent 99% confidence level.

Table 4.2 presents the scores for each of the 25 SuperCam branches across the four quarters in 2003. For each quarter, three key statistics are provided. First, the top-two box score for each branch is shown; it reflects the percentage of customers in a given branch area that provided a 6 or 7 rating on each of the three key survey items. The second column reflects the number of respondents providing completed surveys each quarter. This number typically ranges between 100 and 150 across the four quarters. Finally, the z-score column is of particular interest. It is important to understand that

Table 4.2 SuperCam branch incentives by quarter: comparison to 50% performance target.

Branch	Q1-2003 Results		Q2-2003 Results		Q3-2003 Results		Q4-2003 Results		Bonus Points
	T2-Box	n	z-score*	T2-Box	n	z-score*	T2-Box	n	z-score*	T2-Box	n	z-score*	

Branch	T2-Box	n	z-score*	T2-Box	n	z-score*	T2-Box	n	z-score*	T2-Box	n	z-score*	Bonus Points
Donner	65%	123	3.49	60%	142	2.43	54%	138	0.94	49%	135	−0.23	2
Sun City	55%	154	1.25	52%	125	0.45	48%	135	−0.47	51%	126	0.22	0
Elbrus	46%	128	−0.91	41%	132	−2.10	42%	152	−2.00	46%	143	−0.96	−2
Vinson	62%	135	2.87	65%	128	3.56	62%	146	2.99	62%	128	2.80	4
Elm Grove	55%	142	1.20	51%	145	0.24	55%	161	1.28	61%	137	2.64	1
Elkville	44%	129	−1.37	48%	138	−0.47	51%	152	0.25	61%	125	2.52	1
Sommers	39%	136	−2.63	44%	135	−1.40	48%	143	−0.48	52%	131	0.46	−1
Franklin	64%	124	3.25	61%	152	2.78	59%	113	1.95	58%	126	1.82	2
Rock Isle	54%	132	0.92	53%	146	0.73	52%	125	0.45	51%	135	0.23	0
Shelby	57%	148	1.72	52%	148	0.49	59%	146	2.21	61%	154	2.80	2
Smithville	59%	146	2.21	54%	138	0.94	59%	125	2.05	62%	149	3.02	3
Hunterton	46%	132	−0.92	55%	129	1.14	45%	135	−1.17	51%	152	0.25	0
Newport	43%	129	−1.61	48%	127	−0.45	42%	137	−1.90	48%	133	−0.46	0
Napa	47%	132	−0.69	41%	151	−2.25	42%	129	−1.84	39%	128	−2.55	−2
Janesville	56%	136	1.41	51%	146	0.24	48%	142	−0.48	55%	142	1.20	0

*The z-score reflects a test to determine whether the current quarter's score is significantly higher/lower than the target level of 50%.

continued

continued

Table 4.2 SuperCam branch incentives by quarter: comparison to 50% performance target.

Branch	Q1-2003 Results			Q2-2003 Results			Q3-2003 Results			Q4-2003 Results			Bonus Points
	T2-Box	n	z-score*	T2-Box	n	z-score*	T2-Box	n	z-score*	T2-Box	n	z-score*	
Sun Valley	61%	134	2.61	59%	128	2.07	54%	135	0.93	58%	149	1.98	3
Big Bend	59%	111	1.93	57%	135	1.64	52%	129	0.45	59%	125	2.05	1
Estes Park	58%	128	1.83	61%	142	2.69	62%	123	2.74	61%	137	2.64	3
Norway	43%	153	-1.75	49%	152	-0.25	59%	121	2.01	60%	129	2.32	2
Elger	52%	145	0.48	47%	123	-0.67	53%	139	0.71	59%	143	2.19	1
Ranier	59%	133	2.11	52%	128	0.45	52%	132	0.46	53%	121	0.66	1
Ouray	45%	156	-1.26	51%	128	0.23	59%	145	2.20	62%	135	2.87	2
Mt. Whitney	39%	145	-2.72	38%	129	-2.81	38%	126	-2.78	42%	134	-1.88	-3
Winnetka	56%	138	1.42	59%	137	2.14	54%	137	0.94	57%	152	1.74	1
Lake Forest	41%	149	-2.23	41%	145	-2.20	51%	122	0.22	56%	145	1.46	-2

*The z-score reflects a test to determine whether the current quarter's score is significantly higher/lower than the target level of 50%.

in the present context we are interested in a *two-sided* test. That is, we want to know if a given branch's score is significantly higher or lower than the 50% target level. Either finding is noteworthy from a management perspective.

Statistically significant deviations from the 50% target level have been highlighted in Table 4.2. Specifically, z-scores greater than ± 1.96 have been highlighted. For example, the first row presents performance summaries for the Donner branch. As shown, scores for this branch were significantly higher than the target level in the first and second quarters. The last row in the table presents summary data for the Lake Forest branch, which performed significantly below the target level in three of the four quarters.

The final column in Table 4.2 summarizes the quarterly performance for each branch in terms of bonus points. For each quarter, SuperCam has elected to add one point for every quarterly performance score that is significantly higher than the 50% target level. Scores significantly below the target subtract one point; scores that do not represent statistically significant departures from the target have no effect on the bonus total. As a result, branches with four consecutive performance ratings that are significantly above the target get +4 bonus points for the year. Branches that consistently perform significantly below the 50% level may end the year with up to -4 bonus points. The potential range of this distribution is $+4$ to -4. One quarter significantly below the 50% level can offset a quarter associated with a score significantly above the threshold. As a result, a branch with one score significantly above the threshold and one significantly below the threshold may end the year with no bonus points—essentially the same score as a branch with scores that hovered around the 50% level.

A summary of the 25 branch bonus point scores is presented in Figure 4.1. As shown, the modal annual score involved $+1$ bonus point. None of the

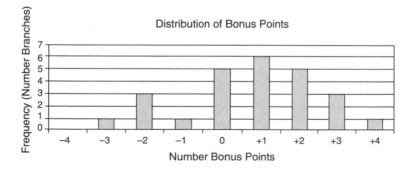

Figure 4.1 SuperCam branch bonus points distribution. *(Comparison to 50% threshold level at 95% confidence.)*

branches received a final score of -4 points, but one branch ended the year with $+4$ points. Five branches had no points, and six branches had $+1$ point at the end of the year. Nine branches—more than one-third—had $+2$ or more bonus points.

A different approach to calculating incentive bonus points is presented in Table 4.3. In this case the test for significance is based on a comparison with a given branch's last year composite top-two box performance score. Instead of using a single threshold value of 50%, this approach recognizes 2003 quarterly performance levels relative to a branch's 2002 performance. An increase or decrease relative to each branch's 2002 performance level affects the 2003 bonus calculations. Statistically significant increases or decreases (at the 95% confidence level) relative to the 2002 baseline affect the bonus point calculation. We are interested in a two-tailed significance test again because performance levels below or above the baseline are of importance. To test the difference between two proportions, we relied on Equation 4.2.

$$
p_1 - p_2 \left/ \sqrt{\left(\frac{p_1(1-p_1)}{n_1} \right) + \left(\frac{p_2(1-p_2)}{n_2} \right)} \right.
$$

$$(4.2)$$

The costs and benefits of this approach relates to individual branch manager motivation. Those performing at particularly low levels in 2002 are rewarded for significant improvements, even if those improvements involve scores that are low relative to the other branches. In contrast, branches with high scores in 2002 are only rewarded if their 2003 scores are significantly higher. In both cases, quarterly scores in 2003 that are significantly lower than the 2002 baseline yield negative points.

Table 4.3 confirms that the two bonus point award systems yield quite different results. Some of the branches with high scores based on exceeding the 50% top-two box criterion do not perform as well under the standards reflected in Table 4.3. The first branch in the table (Donner), for example, was associated with +2 bonus points under the 50% threshold framework. The system reflected in Table 4.3, however, yields a very different story: the Donner branch receives -1 bonus points. Despite performing at relatively high levels in the first two quarters of 2003, these scores were not recognized in the bonus point formula because they were not significantly higher than the 2002 baseline score of 60%.

Figure 4.2 presents the distribution of branches by number of bonus points based on the new participation criterion. As shown, only one branch consistently outperformed its 2002 scores across the four quarters of 2003.

Table 4.3 SuperCam branch incentives by quarter: comparison to 2002 performance level.

Branch	2002 Summary		Q1–2003 Results			Q2–2003 Results			Q3–2003 Results			Q4–2003 Results			Bonus Points
	T–2 Box	n	T2–Box	n	z–score*	T2–Box	n	z–score*	T2–Box	n	z–score*	T2–Box	n	z–score*	
Donner	60%	545	65%	123	1.04	60%	142	0.00	54%	138	−1.27	49%	135	−2.30	−1
Sun City	54%	622	55%	154	0.22	52%	125	−0.41	48%	135	−1.27	51%	126	−0.61	0
Elbrus	44%	589	46%	128	0.41	41%	132	−0.63	42%	152	−0.44	46%	143	0.43	0
Vinson	52%	547	62%	135	2.13	65%	128	2.75	62%	146	2.20	62%	128	2.09	4
Elm Grove	51%	522	55%	142	0.85	51%	145	0.00	55%	161	0.89	61%	137	2.12	1
Elkville	39%	579	44%	129	1.04	48%	138	1.91	51%	152	2.65	61%	125	4.57	2
Sommers	37%	611	39%	136	0.43	44%	135	1.49	48%	143	2.39	52%	131	3.14	2
Franklin	61%	612	64%	124	0.63	61%	152	0.00	59%	113	−0.4	58%	126	−0.62	0
Rock Isle	51%	579	54%	132	0.62	53%	146	0.43	52%	125	0.20	51%	135	0.00	0
Shelby	48%	543	57%	148	1.96	52%	148	0.86	59%	146	2.39	61%	154	2.90	3
Smithville	53%	489	59%	146	1.29	54%	138	0.21	59%	125	1.21	62%	149	1.97	1
Hunterton	45%	490	46%	132	0.20	55%	129	2.03	45%	135	0.00	51%	152	1.29	1
Newport	49%	566	43%	129	−1.24	48%	127	−0.20	42%	137	−1.49	48%	133	−0.21	0
Napa	44%	513	47%	132	0.62	41%	151	−0.66	42%	129	−0.41	39%	128	−1.03	0
Janesville	62%	490	56%	136	−1.25	51%	146	−2.35	48%	142	−2.96	55%	142	−1.48	−2

*The z-score reflects a test to determine whether the current quarter's score is significantly higher/lower than 2002 performance level.

continued

continued

Table 4.3 SuperCam branch incentives by quarter: comparison to 2002 performance level.

Branch	2002 Summary		Q1–2003 Results			Q2–2003 Results			Q3–2003 Results			Q4–2003 Results			Bonus Points
	T-2 Box	n	T2-Box	n	z-score*	T2-Box	n	z-score*	T2-Box	n	z-score*	T2-Box	n	z-score*	
Sun Valley	60%	548	61%	134	0.21	59%	128	−0.21	54%	135	−1.26	58%	149	−0.44	0
Big Bend	49%	579	59%	111	1.96	57%	135	1.69	52%	129	0.62	59%	125	2.06	2
Estes Park	56%	622	58%	128	0.42	61%	142	1.10	62%	123	1.25	61%	137	1.08	0
Norway	52%	567	43%	153	−1.99	49%	152	−0.66	59%	121	1.42	60%	129	1.67	−1
Elger	62%	579	52%	145	−2.17	47%	123	−3.04	53%	139	−1.92	59%	143	−0.65	−2
Ranier	49%	571	59%	133	2.11	52%	128	0.61	52%	132	0.62	53%	121	0.80	1
Ouray	41%	622	45%	156	0.90	51%	128	2.07	59%	145	3.97	62%	135	4.55	3
Mt. Whitney	45%	601	39%	145	−1.32	38%	129	−1.48	38%	126	−1.47	42%	134	−0.64	0
Winnetka	49%	600	56%	138	1.49	59%	137	2.14	54%	137	1.06	57%	152	1.78	1
Lake Forest	50%	588	41%	149	−1.99	41%	145	−1.97	51%	122	0.20	59%	145	1.97	−1

*The z-score reflects a test to determine whether the current quarter's score is significantly higher/lower than 2002 performance level.

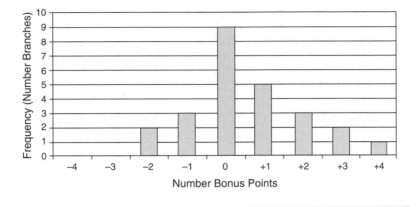

Figure 4.2   SuperCam branch bonus points distribution. *(Comparison to 2002 performance level at 95% confidence.)*

This same branch was the only one to score +4 bonus points using the 50% performance threshold level in Table 4.2. Nonetheless, fewer branches enjoyed positive bonus points under the system in which performance levels in 2003 were compared to the 2002 baseline numbers.

As implied earlier, the biggest difference between the two alternate SuperCam customer satisfaction incentive systems may involve employee motivation. In particular, the system that involves a comparison to 2002 recognizes increases in customer satisfaction regardless of the absolute performance level. A branch that improves its performance, regardless of whether its last year levels were stellar or abysmal, is rewarded. Thus managers who are performing poorly might have more motivation to increase satisfaction because their target may appear more attainable. For example, given a 50% performance threshold, a branch would have to have a score of roughly 59% (based on 125 observations) to be eligible for bonus points. For a branch with chronically low performance levels, the 59% target may seem impossibly high.

Clearly, a variety of approaches to the calculation of bonus points is possible. Alternatives include relying on a single, annual composite, a weighted average, a rolling three- or four-quarter average, comparisons to competitors, and so on. In global programs where cultural bias may affect customer satisfaction scores, it is often necessary to avoid comparisons with absolute targets such as a 50% performance level. Instead, comparisons to each branch's past performance or a key competitor's performance may be more appropriate. Although this makes establishing a normative corporate target level problematic, it helps circumvent criticism that, for example, certain cultures tend to avoid providing negative feedback.

The SuperCam branch incentive program subsumed three types of data: customer satisfaction, profitability, and market share growth. This is quite typical. As noted earlier, it would be quite possible for a branch to enjoy very high customer satisfaction scores simply by giving away its products. To avoid this, most branch incentive programs require that customer satisfaction goals be married to objective business performance metrics. Thus, in the SuperCam case, only branches that had more than $+2$ bonus points *and* met profitability and market share targets would be eligible for the bonus pool.

SUMMARY

One potential shortcoming of the approach outlined in this chapter is its focus on the most satisfied customers—those in the top-two boxes. Rarely do incentive systems accommodate the remainder of the distribution. And yet a comprehensive program should at least acknowledge customers who are not on the verge of top-two box status. There is such a tremendous emphasis on "delighted" or "loyal" customers, it is little wonder attrition levels are so high among the least satisfied dregs. Indeed, it almost appears to be a self-fulfilling prophecy.

Consider the potential return associated with a 20% enhancement to the loyalty levels of two customers: one who is very satisfied and another who is on the verge of switching to a new supplier. In the former case, two issues are at play. The first involves the increasing resources necessary to affect a 20% enhancement at various loyalty levels. The second issue involves the likely return in terms of consumer behaviors that the 20% enhancement will precipitate. In both cases, a focus on the less satisfied customer may be the most effective strategy. For example, it typically requires less effort to enhance the loyalty of a moderately satisfied customer than one who is already ecstatic. Further, the potential return in terms of desirable behaviors may be much lower for the already satisfied customer. If he or she is already fully vested in the relationship, little marginal value may be associated with further loyalty enhancements. In contrast, the least satisfied customers may have the greatest potential returns requiring the least resources.

Why, then, do we focus on the "delighted" or "committed" customers whose loyalty makes them practically disciples? One reason for this bias is semantic. After all, customer satisfaction programs focus on *satisfaction*. They are not called customer *dissatisfaction* programs. Of course, it is also much more uplifting for companies to discuss customer dynamics in terms of those who are product or service disciples rather than those who are disgruntled and on the verge of abandoning the relationship.

In Chapter 10, a potential solution to this quandary is introduced. The approach leverages the entire loyalty distribution and focuses management attention on moving customers at each discrete stratum up to the next level. In each case, a unique driver equation is developed to address specifically the movement from one layer to the next. When coupled with an organizational structure that links managers to loyalty segments, this approach may emerge as substantively more successful than traditional methods aimed exclusively on the top-two boxes.

5

Implementing
Key-Driver Results

INTRODUCTION

This chapter discusses the implementation of key-driver analyses. In order to treat this subject effectively, we first examine some critical issues relating to regression-based procedures aimed at deriving the importance of various service and product quality variables. Then we articulate the strategic differences between stated and derived importance, describe how to interpret regression-based key-driver results, and look at implementation issues. Of particular interest is a vexing problem frequently encountered in customer satisfaction research: volatile key-driver results.

DERIVED VERSUS STATED IMPORTANCE: MANAGERIAL IMPLICATIONS

Derived importance models represent a cornerstone of customer satisfaction research. The *statistical derivation* of attribute importance currently represents the norm in the customer satisfaction research industry. The difference between the stated and derived importance approaches can be illustrated using a simple example. Consider the case of Gemini Automotive. Gemini autos are considered the safest in the industry, a characteristic that qualitative research has revealed is especially important to these customers. For the purposes of this example, assume Gemini Automotive can only control five variables relating to the passenger cars it manufactures.

As depicted in Table 5.1, Gemini Automotive has collected survey data relating to both the importance and performance (i.e., customer satisfaction) for five business variables. The stated importance gap analysis approach involves assessing the importance and performance for each variable.

Ostensibly, those variables characterized by large gaps should receive priority in business planning. In fact, we can plot the position of each of the five variables in a quadrant chart as shown in Figure 5.1.

When *asked* which of these issues is most important to them, a large proportion of consumers indicate that safety is of great concern. After all, with some exceptions, most consumers will not indicate that comfort is more important to them than their safety. Thus, under the stated importance measurement framework, we would expect occupant safety to emerge as

Table 5.1   Performance–importance gap analysis.

Controllable variable	Stated importance[1]	Stated performance[2]	Gap score[3]
Passenger comfort	8.9	8.5	−0.4
Engine power	8.4	8.9	0.5
Occupant safety	9.0	9.2	0.2
Interior options	8.5	8.6	0.1
Navigation (GPS) options	8.4	8.0	−0.4

[1] Mean score on 10-point scale where 1 is Very Unimportant and 10 is Very Important.
[2] Mean score on 10-point scale where 1 is Very Dissatisfied and 10 is Very Satisfied.
[3] Difference between stated importance and performance scores.

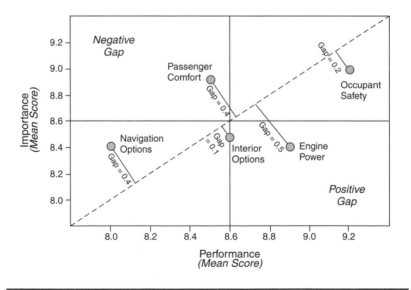

Figure 5.1   Gemini Automotive gap chart.

one of the most critical design features. This phenomenon was expected to be even more pronounced among Gemini owners because they are known to focus on safety features.

The quadrant chart presented in Figure 5.1 is defined by the performance x-axis and importance y-axis. Items that appear at the top half of the quadrant were rated as important by customers. The x-axis reflects current customer satisfaction levels. The line drawn diagonally through the quadrant indicates parity between performance and importance. That is, a variable depicted on the line would be characterized by equal levels of performance and importance. In contrast, those that appear above or below the diagonal line reflect negative and positive importance gaps. In particular, items that appear in the top-left triangle are characterized by importance ratings that exceed the performance ratings. The converse is true for the bottom-right triangle.

From a managerial standpoint, the stated importance quadrant map is quite unequivocal. It suggests the most important automobile feature to Gemini owners is occupant safety. The manufacturer enjoys a positive gap with respect to occupant safety as well. The most glaring negative gap involves passenger comfort; importance exceeds performance by a significant margin for this variable. Based on Figure 5.1, Gemini management would probably continue to allocate design, research, and engineering dollars into safety systems and, to a lesser extent, passenger comfort. After all, it is these two areas that customers indicated were most important to them.

In contrast to the stated importance measurement approach, the derived importance framework employs multiple regression to determine mathematically the impact of each issue on a single outcome variable that we are attempting to maximize: typically overall customer satisfaction. This approach leverages the statistical covariation that occurs between each predictor variable and the single outcome measure.

Some confusion surrounds the implication of the word *importance* in the dependence model (e.g., multiple regression) context. Take, for example, the reaction of product managers at a world-class manufacturing company when told that product quality was not important. Their initial inclination was to dismiss the results and walk out! The simple fact is that the use of the term *importance* tends to cloud the true meaning of what we are trying to convey. In the regression context, an important variable covaries strongly with the dependent measure. Once they understood this, the managers and engineers at the manufacturing company just described were actually quite pleased. Their products were—and still are—considered best in class and enjoy stellar customer satisfaction scores. That product quality was not a strong driver of overall satisfaction suggests there was little real or perceived variation in product quality, and it was therefore not able to covary with the dependent measure.

When we reconsider the Gemini Automotive case using a derived importance methodology, we encounter very different strategic implications. In particular, a regression-based procedure was used to derive the importance of the five key business variables relative to a single, dependent measure: overall satisfaction with the vehicle. As shown in Table 5.2, the derived importance data provide a very different perspective. Because the data confirmed there was only a very modest level of covariation between occupant safety and overall satisfaction, this variable emerged as the weakest driver. In contrast, the derived importance data suggest that satisfaction with interior options tended to be a very strong driver of overall satisfaction.

The Gemini Automotive data can now be reconsidered in a performance–importance framework as shown in Figure 5.2. In this case, the derived importance metrics from Table 5.2 have been used to define the y-axis. Clearly, the two quadrants provide data with significantly different strategic implications. The stated importance model in Figure 5.1 would suggest focusing on the two issues associated with the largest gap scores: passenger comfort and navigation options. In contrast, the derived importance framework depicted in Figure 5.2 suggests a completely different tack is appropriate. The five issues remain similarly positioned with respect to the x-axis (performance), but their positions on the y-axis have changed drastically.

Figure 5.2 suggests that interior options and passenger comfort are the most important product issues for Gemini Automotive to address because these variables tend to covary most strongly with the dependent variable: overall satisfaction with the car. If Gemini wants to maximize this outcome (overall satisfaction), the best way to proceed involves enhancements to passenger comfort and interior options.

Occupant safety was not important in this context because it did not correlate substantively correlate with the outcome measure. This is probably because consumers did not perceive variance with respect to occupant

Table 5.2   Stated versus derived importance: Gemini Automotive.

Controllable variable	Stated importance[1]	Derived importance[2]	Stated performance[3]	Gap score[4]
Passenger comfort	8.9	0.77	8.5	−0.4
Engine power	8.4	0.64	8.9	0.5
Occupant safety	9.0	0.12	9.2	0.2
Interior options	8.5	0.87	8.6	0.1
Navigation (GPS) options	8.4	0.56	8.0	−0.4

[1] Mean score on 10-point scale where 1 is Very Unimportant and 10 is Very Important.
[2] Averaged squared partial correlation calculated over all permutations of predictor variables.
[3] Mean score on 10-point scale where 1 is Very Dissatisfied and 10 is Very Satisfied.
[4] Difference between stated importance and performance scores.

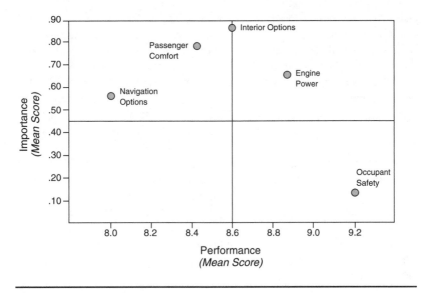

Figure 5.2   Gemini Automotive: derived importance quadrant chart.

safety. In order for there to have been strong covariation between satisfaction with occupant safety and overall satisfaction, there would have to be respondents who perceived low levels of occupant safety and, as a result, also rated their overall satisfaction with the automobile quite unfavorably. It is this type of covariation that is needed to determine that a given service or product quality issue is a significant predictor of overall satisfaction—or any other dependent measure. Had a fair proportion of respondents experienced safety failures, it is likely occupant safety would have emerged as more important in this context.

MARGINAL RESOURCE ALLOCATION MODELS

So exactly what are we conveying when we say something is important in a dependence model context? Derived importance results provide managers with road maps for *maximizing* an outcome variable such as overall satisfaction. In order to achieve the greatest increase in overall satisfaction (or any other outcome variable), we focus on the predictor variable(s) that have the greatest effect on it. More accurately, we isolate predictor variables that *covary* most strongly with the outcome variable. This covariation is at the heart of derived importance models.

Derived importance models are probably erroneously labeled. A more appropriate name might be *marginal resource allocation* models. Note that we must consider only marginal resources because *reallocating* existing resources based on a derived importance model will not necessarily yield the desired results. Consider again the example of Gemini Automotive, which blindly reallocates existing resources based on its key-driver analysis. Assume the following, simplified set of key drivers in Table 5.3.

If Gemini Automotive management erroneously decides to reallocate resources based on this set of 2002 baseline key drivers, they may choose to reduce the number (and quality) of navigation system options in order to free research and development funds for passenger comfort enhancements. This reallocation of resources yields a completely different set of drivers in the next year (2003) baseline. The new drivers reflect the effects of management's decision to reallocate existing rather than *marginal dollars*. Because navigation system options were cut back, customers became less satisfied with this product feature. In fact, it appears from these data that the dissatisfaction was sufficiently acute to affect overall satisfaction. Such a turn of events underscores the *dynamic nature of key drivers*. It also illustrates why key-driver analysis should really be considered a marginal resource allocation tool.

Because it plays such a major role in the derivation of attribute importance in customer satisfaction research, the next portion of this chapter describes various forms of derived importance analysis. Although the primary focus is on *multivariate techniques*, we review the pitfalls of less sophisticated *bivariate* approaches first. Before describing some competing methods for deriving service and product quality importance, let's consider what type of survey structures are necessary to yield data of the appropriate format.

KEY-DRIVER QUANTIFICATION

The vertical placement of items in a quadrant chart as described earlier clearly depends on how importance was derived statistically. The technique employed can have significant managerial implications and should be carefully considered. The following discussion reviews a series of increasingly

Table 5.3   Gemini Automotive: hypothetical key drivers over time.

Service/Product satisfaction	2002 baseline Key-driver Status*	2003 baseline Key-driver Status*
Passenger comfort	Yes	Yes
Engine power	No	No
Occupant safety	No	No
Interior options	Yes	Yes
Navigation (GPS) options	No	Yes

*Key-driver status based on derived importance metric greater than 0.70.

sophisticated ways to derive statistically the importance of a service or product quality issue relative to a single dependent measure like overall satisfaction or loyalty. The discussion begins with a review of bivariate measures of importance and proceeds to multivariate techniques such as multiple regression. Following a review of regression techniques, a variety of more exotic derivatives are introduced. Finally, the value of structural equation modeling to depict causal sequences is discussed.

BIVARIATE MEASURES OF IMPORTANCE

The simple bivariate correlation coefficient is a very useful tool when embarking on a data exploration. Its implications, however, are frequently misinterpreted, and the overzealous researcher may jump to erroneous conclusions about the relative importance of the predictor variables. Its failure to accommodate multivariate data, of course, makes it largely inadequate for applied customer satisfaction research.

Using the correlation coefficient to make inferences concerning the relationship between each predictor variable and dependent variable frequently involves ranking the correlation coefficients. Although simple, this way of determining attribute importance can be misleading, as implied earlier. We cannot make valid inferences concerning the relative magnitude of correlation coefficients. It is not appropriate to conclude that $r_{x1y} = .74$ is more than three times stronger than $r_{x3y} = .23$. What is frequently overlooked, however, is that when *squared* the correlation coefficient is interpreted as the *proportion of variance shared by two variables.*

When squared, the relationship between overall satisfaction and product reliability ($r_{x1y} = .74$) suggests the two variables have about 55% of their variance in common. In contrast, the relationship between overall satisfaction and price ($r_{x4y} = .28$) suggests these two variables share only 5% of their variance. The difference in linear relationship between these two variables and overall satisfaction is much greater than would have been suggested by a simple comparison of the correlation coefficients.

It is easy to forget that the correlation coefficient r has a multivariate relative: the multiple correlation coefficient. It is most frequently encountered in multiple regression analyses as the R^2—a summary statistic that reflects the amount of variation in the dependent variable accounted for by the predictor variables. All researchers who evaluate or conduct multiple regression analyses are familiar with the R^2 statistic. That R^2 is the multivariate equivalent of r^2 is sometimes overlooked, however. The multiple correlation coefficient (R) is addressed later.

It should be clear now that the squared correlation coefficient is quite a good bivariate measure of relative importance. Of special note is its ratio-level property. This permits inferences concerning *relative* importance. It would be reasonable to conclude based on the squared correlation, for example, that one variable shares *twice as much* variance with the outcome as another. This aspect of the correlation coefficient —that its square has some especially useful properties—is leveraged later in this discussion when we introduce Kruskal's approach to the optimum relative importance metric.

Simple linear regression involves a single outcome variable being regressed on *one predictor variable.* It is a *bivariate* statistical technique as shown in Equation 5.1, which consists of just one predictor variable and one outcome variable. Remember that the term β_0 is simply the intercept term and can be considered to be the value of *y* when all the predictor variables are equal to zero.

$$y = \beta_0 + \beta_{\pm 1} \tag{5.1}$$

MULTIVARIATE MEASURES OF IMPORTANCE

The term *multivariate correlation analysis* may seem like an oxymoron to some. After all, most of us are familiar with the bivariate correlation and generally do not extend this family of techniques to multivariate settings. The *partial correlation,* for example, is not frequently encountered in applied customer satisfaction research settings. Unlike the Pearson correlation coefficient, the partial correlation can tell us a great deal about the relationships underlying a set of predictor variables. In brief, the partial correlation provides us with a measure of linear relationship between two variables *once the effects of the remaining variables have been taken into account.* The symbol for the partial correlation (Equation 5.2) is slightly different because we must convey both the relationship being measured and the variables we are holding constant. For example, the term $r_{x1y.x2}$ indicates we are measuring the relationship between x_1 and *y* after the relationship between *y* and x_2 has been taken into account. This term, when *squared,* provides us the unique variance common to the two primary variables (i.e., *y* and x_1) once the effects of x_2 have been accommodated.

$$r_{12.3} = \frac{r_{12} - r_{13}r_{23}}{\sqrt{(1 - r_{13}^2)(1 - r_{23}^2)}} \tag{5.2}$$

Equation 5.2 illustrates how the partial correlation takes into account the effects of a third variable (Nunnally, 1978:168–70). The partial correlation offers an excellent alternative or supplement to a simple bivariate correlation. Its most desirable property involves its ability to take into account the effects of other variables. It is by definition, therefore, a multivariate technique.

A very useful cousin of the partial correlation is the *semipartial correlation* (Nunnally, 1978:171–75). Although it plays an important role in both multiple correlation analysis and common factor analysis, the semipartial correlation is not encountered frequently in exploratory customer satisfaction research. It is useful, however, to understand how the partial and semipartial correlations differ. Equation 5.3 presents the formula for the semipartial correlation.

$$r_{1(2.3)} = \frac{r_{12} - r_{13}r_{23}}{\sqrt{1 - r_{23}^2}} \tag{5.3}$$

In Equation 5.3 we're interested in controlling x_3 only for x_2, not x_1. The semipartial correlation lets us hold a variable constant for only one of the two variables involved in the correlation. Why, you might ask, would we possibly want to do this? The principal reason involves the relationship between the variable we are holding constant (x_3) and the variables we are interested in (x_1 and x_2). If, for some reason, we feel x_3 should legitimately covary with x_1, we may want to hold x_1 constant only for x_2. Again, this rarely occurs; the real reason for introducing it involves the semipartial correlation's role in factor analysis and multiple correlation analysis.

The multiple correlation coefficient is most frequently encountered in a slightly different form in multiple regression analysis. In applied customer satisfaction research, reporting the R^2 statistic associated with a key-driver analysis is practically de rigueur. Nonetheless, few practitioners remember this key metric is really the squared multiple correlation coefficient. In a key-driver analysis context, the multiple correlation coefficient has an important diagnostic role. When it is low ($R^2 < 0.70$), the implication is that the predictor variable set is not strongly predictive of the dependent variable. Typically, this results in additional qualitative research aimed at generating additional items for the survey instrument.

The multiple correlation has some desirable properties, as noted by Nunnally (1978:176–85). Of greatest interest may be the fact that R will always be equal to, or exceed, the highest pairwise correlation involving the outcome and predictor variables. From Table 5.2 we know the multiple correlation between y and the five predictor variables must be at least .74 (because $r_{x1y} = .74$) and will likely be higher barring any strong relationships among the predictor variables. It should be clear that if the predictor variables are *orthogonal* (i.e., have zero correlations with one another) that R^2 will be equal to the sum of the squared bivariate correlations. This is illustrated in Equation 5.4.

$$R^2_{y.123} = r^2_{yx1} + r^2_{yx2} + r^2_{yx3} \text{ when } r_{x1x2} = 0; \ r_{x1x3} = 0; \ r_{x2x3} = 0 \quad (5.4)$$

Again, Equation 5.4 is valid *only when the predictor variables are orthogonal.* When strong dependencies exist among the predictor variables, we turn to a different means of determining the total shared variance among the outcome and predictor variables. Equation 5.5 employs the semipartial correlation as just described and can be used to calculate the R^2 value. In effect, Equation 5.5 confirms that the R^2 is equal to the squared correlation between y and x_1 (r^2_{yx1}) plus the squared correlation between y and x_2 holding x_1 constant for x_2 ($r^2_{y(x2.x1)}$) plus the squared correlation between y and x_3 with both x_1 and x_2 held constant for x_3.

$$R^2_{y.123} = r^2_{yx1} + r^2_{y(x2.x1)} + r^2_{y(x3.x1x2)} \quad (5.5)$$

Although not immediately obvious, a closer inspection of the sequence in Equation 5.5 reveals that after the first term (which is a simple correlation), each is a successively higher order squared semipartial correlation. Each term in Equation 5.5 is contributing *unique* variance with respect to y. The reason semipartial and not *partial* correlations are used in this calculation is illustrated by considering the second term in Equation 5.5, which is contributing variance unique to x_2 once x_1 has been taken into account. In short, we use semipartial correlations because although we are interested in partialing variance on the predictor variable side, we do not want to partial this variance from the *dependent* variable.

MULTIVARIATE REGRESSION MODELS

The most frequently encountered multivariate approach to key-driver analysis involves ordinary least squares (OLS) multiple regression. In this context, there is a series of predictor variables and a single dependent variable as illustrated in Equation 5.6. The power of multiple regression analysis is that it considers the simultaneous effect of the k predictor variables ($x_1 - x_k$) on the single dependent measure (y). Typically, this equates to a set of specific service or product quality issues on the predictor side of the equation and a single summary measure of overall satisfaction on the outcome side. The magnitude of the beta (β) coefficients reflects the statistically derived variable importance. To read a detailed treatment of multiple regression models, turn to a classic source such as Draper and Smith (1998).

$$y = \beta_0 + \beta_1 x_1 + \ldots + \beta_k x_k + e \tag{5.6}$$

Multiple regression and its numerous cousins represent the primary approach to the statistical derivation of attribute importance in customer satisfaction research. Dependence models take a variety of other forms. For example, whereas multiple regression can accommodate a variety of predictor variable types (e.g., binary predictor variables), the dependence model can take other forms. Most notably, these involve alternative *outcome variable* forms. Dichotomous outcome variables such as group membership or purchase status flagrantly violate critical assumptions underlying multiple regression analysis—namely, that the dependent variable is normally distributed. Logistic regression is the alternative to multiple regression when the outcome variable is dichotomous. When the dependent measure is categorical, *multinomial* logistic regression or multiple discriminant analysis are appropriate analytical tacks. For a definitive review of logistic regression, refer to Hosmer and Lemeshow (1989).

INTERACTION TERMS

In customer satisfaction and loyalty research, our interest is typically focused on isolating the individual contributions of a series of service and product quality variables vis-à-vis a dependent measure. More often than not, testing interaction effects are overlooked. And yet, the possibility that interactions occur—particularly in customer feedback data—is very real. In the case of service or product quality interaction effects, the sum of the parts is greater than the whole.

Conceptually, an interaction effect may involve two or more variables. Consider an illustrative example in which a bank customer visits a local branch. If he or she encounters two (or more) instances of poor service—for example, a hostile teller followed by an accounting error—the effect may be *greater* than the sum effects of the two lapses. Conversely, a guest at a world-class hospitality provider such as Fairmont Hotels who encounters both superlative service and product quality may experience greatly enhanced satisfaction and loyalty. Again, the effect of experiencing both of these *simultaneously* is greater than the individual contributions of the inputs.

From a statistical or mathematical standpoint, interaction effects are very easy to test. Typically, a simple interaction involving two variables x_1 and x_2 is defined as the product of these two. The new variable is included with the originals in a dependence model framework, and the significance of its contribution to the dependent measure is examined. If the interaction term is statistically significant, the implications are clear: by improving both components, a greater yield in the outcome measure will be enjoyed.

Interaction effects are not frequently considered in applied customer satisfaction and loyalty research. Testing for interactions is not a complex or difficult task and if at all possible should be included in exploratory analyses. Neglecting a significant interaction effect is analogous to "leaving money on the table" in many cases. Service or product quality issues that have only modest driver status individually may yield a significant interaction effect when considered simultaneously.

HIERARCHICAL BAYES REGRESSION

Hierarchical Bayes (HB) regression has recently emerged as a viable alternative to ordinary least squares (OLS) multiple regression. The method is computationally intensive and, until recently, tended to preclude widespread acceptance among applied researchers. Hierarchical Bayes regression is different from many of the multivariate techniques discussed in this book because it subsumes two levels of parameter estimates: the individual and aggregate. This approach is used in conjoint analysis in which individual-level part-worths are calculated for every observation. This profile represents the individual's unique combination of preferences.

HB regression assumes that individual-level parameters (i.e., betas) can be estimated and are distributed in a multivariate normal fashion (Orme, 2000:58). Interestingly, these individual-level importance weights—or more precisely, beta coefficients—shape a given consumer's behaviors and attitudes. Individual-level betas may be used to segment consumers based on the derived importance of a series of service or product quality issues. The aggregate-level HB coefficients are parallel to those derived using more traditional least squares approaches to multiple regression analysis.

HB regression is particularly useful when derived importance metrics are desired for heterogeneous populations. Typically, it is advantageous to conduct derived importance analysis at the lowest meaningful organizational or geographic subunit, such as a branch or state. In certain situations, however, aggregate analysis must be conducted using data that span numerous disparate groups. This heterogeneity can confound OLS regression, which is incapable of isolating and identifying latent subgroups. Latent class solutions based on HB regression can identify homogenous clusters of respondents based on the similarity of their individual-level beta profiles. The problematic situation occurs when two distinct groups of respondents exist, one for which a given service quality issue is a strong positive driver of satisfaction and the other for which the same issue is either not a driver or a negative driver. Under these conditions, an aggregate-level OLS regression will produce derived importance metrics that underestimate the impact of this particular predictor variable. This is because aggregate-level OLS permits the strong driver status of the variable among one group to be offset by the lack of (or negative) covariance associated with the other.

A full discussion of the benefits of HB regression is beyond the scope of this book. Increases in CPU processing speeds and the availability of commercial software for conducting this type of analysis have made the technique increasingly popular among applied researchers focused on producing stable and robust estimates of derived importance. HB regression provides some attractive benefits, including good performance under severe collinearity and the ability to identify latent groups based on homogeneous driver profiles. Although only a few specialized software programs are currently available, it may only be a matter of time before the major statistical analysis packages include HB regression procedures.

EFFECTS OF COLLINEARITY

The two derived importance issues that are most problematic from a management perspective involve collinearity and the ability to make ratio-level inferences regarding the importance of key predictors. The former condition, discussed in greater detail later, occurs when substantive relationships exist among two (or more) predictor variables. Unfortunately, this is almost always the case in customer satisfaction research specifically and attitudinal research generally. Unless the predictors are perfectly uncorrelated with one another, in fact, this condition is always present. The ability to diagnose situations in which collinearity degrades the regression model will help avoid making erroneous conclusions concerning the importance of key variables. Because attribute importance has direct managerial implications in terms of how key service and product quality issues are depicted in quadrant charts, a discussion of a common problem that may yield erroneous results should be of great interest to those who manage customer satisfaction programs.

A comprehensive discussion of the mathematical diagnosis of harmful collinearity is beyond the scope of this book. Belsley (1991) provides the definitive treatment of the subject. Rather than focus on the mathematical foundations of collinearity, it will be helpful for managers to recognize some of its manifestations:

- Reversed signs

- Large errors around betas

- Hypersensitivity

Of these symptoms, perhaps the most classic involves reversed beta coefficient signs. For example, when a regression model suggests that increasing satisfaction with technical support will *decrease* overall satisfaction, managers should proceed very cautiously. This is not a result that should simply be overlooked and the reversed sign ignored! If the bivariate analysis does not support this relationship (i.e., the correlation between overall satisfaction and technical support satisfaction is *positive*), the model is highly suspect. Other possible signs of harmful collinearity involve hypersensitivity of the model to the removal of variables or alternate random samples. In the former case, a model that yields wildly different results when a single variable is removed may also be of concern depending on the magnitude of its relationship with the dependent measure. Similarly, if a sample is randomly split and the two subsamples yield very different driver profiles, collinearity should be suspected. Situations in which key drivers substantively differ over time are of special concern and addressed at greater length later.

Two metrics are commonly used to diagnose the level of collinearity in a data set. The first is the variance inflation factor (VIF). A more desirable approach (Belsley, 1991:57) involves the condition index. Both diagnostics are provided by the most common statistical packages. Belsley (1991:129) suggested that condition index values approaching 100 are indicative of degrading levels of collinearity. Individuals who manage programs that involve strategy development based on derived importance results would be advised to check the condition index routinely.

Ordinary least squares regression and other multivariate procedures that involve the inversion of the predictor variable matrix are particularly susceptible to collinear data. Reversed signs and highly sensitive volatile models due to collinearity are commonplace in applied customer satisfaction research. Situations in which analysts simply ignore the reversed sign problem by taking the absolute value of the beta coefficients are not uncommon. Clearly, the decision to ignore the manifestations of highly collinear data can have substantive managerial implications. When a degrading level of collinearity is present, numerous strategies are available to circumvent the problem, as summarized in Table 5.4.

Table 5.4 Analytical approaches to harmful collinearity.

Technique	Description	Strengths	Weaknesses	References
Ridge regression	Add a ridge estimator (k) to the least squares equation so $\mathbf{B}_R = (\mathbf{X'X} + k\mathbf{I})^{-1}\mathbf{X'y}$	This mathematical ploy can reduce the level of collinearity in the data.	Explicit manipulation of primary data may be challenged.	Belsley (1991:299–300) Birkes and Dodge (1993:180–83)
Principal components regression	Reduce dimensionality and regress dependent variable on orthogonal principal components.	Orthogonality makes collinearity issue moot because the predictor variables are perfectly uncorrelated with one another	PCs are sometimes difficult to decipher mathematically and intuitively.	Jackson (1991:263–81) Jolliffe (1986:129–55)
Dominance analysis	Unique contribution of each variable to R^2 statistic over multiple permutations.	Collinearity effects are averaged out over numerous equations.	Computationally intensive; not available in any statistical package.	Budescu (1993:542–51)
Kruskal's RI algorithm	Average squared partial correlation over all permutations of equations.	Collinearity effects are averaged out over numerous equations, ratio-level importance metric.	Computationally intensive; not available in any statistical package.	Kruskal (1987:6–10)
Bivariate techniques	Abandon multivariate approach and use a bivariate metric, thereby making the collinearity problem immaterial.	Collinearity not a problem because the importance metric relates only two variables: the dependent variable and a single predictor.	Does not summarize the simultaneous effects of the combined predictor variables.	

continued

continued

Table 5.4 Analytical approaches to harmful collinearity.

Technique	Description	Strengths	Weaknesses	References
Introduce new data	Collect additional data.	Simplicity.	Expense and no guarantee that collinearity will be lessened.	Belsley (1991:297)
Bayesian techniques such as Hierarchical Bayes (HB) Regression	Use the introduction of prior information about the predictor variables' relationship with the dependent measure to guide model development.	Prior knowledge can be leveraged.	Prior knowledge may be faulty, and statistical theory is not well known among users.	Belsley (1991:297–98) Orme (2000:16–63)
Combine/exclude variables	Exclude a variable with strong pairwise association with other variables or combine two strongly related variables into an index.	Removing a single, problematic variable or combining two that strongly covary may substantially reduce collinearity.	Removing a variable may be hard to justify politically. Combining two may be more appealing but if they are not intuitively related, the index may be challenged.	Naes and Martens (1985:545–85)
Partial least squares	Similar to principal components regression in that dimension reduction and dependence are established.	Predictors are orthogonal linear combinations of original variables so collinearity is not present.	Linear combinations may be difficult to communicate to users; technique is not well known.	Naes and Martens (1985:545–75)

STRATEGIES FOR DYNAMIC KEY DRIVERS

One of the most troublesome aspects of regression-based key driver analysis occurs when importance appears highly dynamic over time. If you manage a customer satisfaction program that produces performance and importance results quarterly, you will likely encounter the following situation. In one quarter, results for a particular organizational unit suggest a specific service or product quality issue is highly important, but in the next quarter the variable emerges as trivial. When field managers complain they have not made any changes that would have affected this issue, the derivation of importance specifically and the customer satisfaction program generally become suspect. This situation occurs frequently and is a source of understandable frustration among those who manage customer satisfaction programs.

Initially, collinearity should be excluded as a source of the dynamism. As described earlier, collinearity can produce volatile key-driver results both in a cross-sectional framework (when randomly split samples are used) and from a longitudinal perspective. Assuming there are not *degrading* levels of collinearity, the best place to obtain stable baseline estimates of the extent to which each variable is related to the dependent measure is the correlation coefficient. Both beta and correlation coefficients are associated with confidence bands affected by sample size. Thus, when comparing importance metrics across two reporting periods, it is possible to conduct tests to determine whether the differences are statistically significant at, for example, the 95% confidence level. Crow, Davis, and Maxfield (1960:159) provide a means for constructing a confidence band around a correlation coefficient. Kleinbaum and Kupper (1978:107) suggested Equation 5.7 as one means of testing the difference between two correlation coefficients:

$$Z = \frac{\frac{1}{2}\log_e \frac{1+r_1}{1-r_1} - \frac{1}{2}\log_e \frac{1+r_2}{1-r_2}}{\sqrt{\frac{1}{n_1-3}+\frac{1}{n_2-3}}} \qquad (5.7)$$

The null hypothesis that r_1 equals r_2 is rejected when Z exceeds the critical value associated with either a one-sided or two-sided significance test. Our efforts to diagnose problems associated with dynamic key drivers would typically involve a two-sided test. The direction of the difference is of little consequence.

Of course, the broader context is multivariate. Our primary interest in this case is whether two beta coefficients differ across either two reporting periods or a randomly split sample. Again, of concern is the reason for the driver status of a particular variable varying across the two conditions (i.e., time periods or samples) when there have been no concomitant managerial changes. A typical, incredulous query from the field might be "Why has the importance of technical support changed from last quarter—we haven't done anything to affect it—last quarter it was important and this quarter it isn't. What should we do?"

This scenario is not at all uncommon and the source of a lot of frustration when managing large-scale customer satisfaction tracking programs. Assuming the volatility is not attributable to collinearity, our first tack should involve an objective test of the change. In this case, we are interested in whether the beta (β) coefficient associated with an item is significantly different across the two time periods. If the difference is statistically significant, the program manager may want to adopt one of the strategies discussed later in this chapter.

Kleinbaum and Kupper (1978:99–102) provide methods for testing the null hypothesis $H_o: \beta_{11} = \beta_{12}$ for both small samples (t-test) and large samples (Z-test). The large sample approach to testing H_o is provided in Equation 5.8:

$$Z = \frac{\hat{\beta}_{11} - \hat{\beta}_{12}}{\sqrt{S_{\hat{\beta}_{11}}^2 + S_{\hat{\beta}_{12}}^2}} \tag{5.8}$$

where the slope variances are estimated as shown in Equation 5.9 and Equation 5.10:

$$S_{\hat{\beta}_{11}}^2 = S_{Y|X_1}^2 / (n_1 - 1) S_{X_1}^2 \tag{5.9}$$

$$S_{\hat{\beta}_{12}}^2 = S_{Y|X_2}^2 / (n_2 - 1) S_{X_1}^2 \tag{5.10}$$

The tests in Equations 5.7 and 5.8 permit managers to test the equivalence of a single beta (β) coefficient across two groups or time periods. A more complex question involves differences across multiple beta coefficients and multiple groups. This situation might arise if unique regression models are developed for each of, for example, six customer segments. A general hypothesis involving structural equivalence can be addressed using covariance structure analysis and is described by Bollen (1989:356–58) and McArdle and Hamagami (1996:89–124). A series of increasingly restrictive hypotheses concerning structural invariance can be tested using structural equation modeling (SEM) techniques. In fact, covariance structure analysis permits tests of both structural and factorial congruence across groups. The latter involves the extent to which the dimensionality of key constructs like *service quality* are consistent across multiple groups. This is equivalent to testing simultaneously whether factor analyses and regression analyses are invariant across multiple groups. A more sophisticated approach to assessing structural and factorial changes over time is provided by Willet and Sayer (1996:125–57).

Note that the tests for parameter equivalence across regression models described here are also appropriate in different situations. In particular, when separate key-driver models are developed for different customer groups and there is an interest in the relevance of differences, the Z-test presented in Equation 5.8 (or its small sample equivalent) are appropriate. Similarly, the more sophisticated covariance structure approach to parameter differences may be used to test hypotheses involving equivalence across two or more groups.

Based on the preceding, if the difference in a particular beta coefficient across two time periods (or randomly split samples) is not statistically significant, the trivial nature of the change must be communicated to users. In effect, the program manager must tell users that although there was a change in the driver status of a given variable, it was not statistically meaningful. Large swings in importance metrics that are not statistically significant suggest the sample size is small. Regression-based key-driver analyses should be based on several hundred observations if stable estimates are desired. Programs that report key-driver status on a quarterly basis based on a sample size of 100 may yield volatile results over time. If this is the case, it would be sensible to base the quarterly key-driver analyses on a weighted rolling data frame that subsumes a total of, optimally, 400 or more observations. Weighting should be based on quarters so the most recent quarter has the greatest influence in the model development. In short: *Small sample sizes are often responsible for volatile key-driver results.*

If the study is annual or even less frequently executed and it is not feasible to combine several years of data for each reporting unit, reporting units should be meaningfully combined based on relevant organization structure or geography to generate adequate sample sizes. Key drivers should then be developed for the combined rolled-up data. The results must then be communicated in a fashion that emphasizes the stability and geographic or organizational relevance. From a cost-benefit standpoint, the downside of this approach (key drivers that are not unique at the lowest reporting level) is far outweighed by not having to defend highly dynamic, perhaps erroneous importance metrics.

A more frustrating situation occurs when large sample sizes yield dynamic, statistically significant key-driver variation and field users report they have not made operational or managerial changes that would yield the effect. When this occurs (and collinearity has been excluded as a source of the volatility), several explanations should be considered:

- Perceived managerial/operational changes

- Systematic sampling bias

- Nonresponse bias

- Dramatic changes in performance levels that reduce/inflate variance

- Effects of missing values and/or missing value imputation technique

Reality is in the mind of the *consumer,* and if customers believe there have been service or product quality changes, their survey responses may be affected. Another possible reason for statistically significant changes that cannot be linked to managerial actions involves the presence of systematic sampling bias. Program managers should consider carefully the manner in which a sample is generated for the customer satisfaction program. Tests for significance across key demographic or behavioral variables can reveal whether samples are being drawn in a nonrandom fashion. Similarly, the response rate associated with each survey administration should be evaluated. If very low response rates (less than 50%) are present in one or both reporting periods, nonresponse bias may be responsible for key-driver volatility. Significant changes in the distribution of key variables (on either the predictor or outcome side) can affect key-driver results. A statistically significant reduction in the variance of a given predictor variable (as determined by the F-test) across two reporting periods can affect its covariance with the outcome measure. Finally, the effects of missing values should be considered. The astute program manager should investigate the proportion of missing values for a given variable across the reporting periods. If missing value imputation is performed before the key-driver analysis, it would be helpful to know how this procedure affected the variable's relationship with the outcome measure and the other predictor variables. Missing value imputation procedures vary considerably in terms of their ability to preserve the original covariance structure of the data. Mean imputation, in particular, can affect these relationships so an examination of the pre- and postimputation means and correlations across the two reporting periods represents one area of possibly fruitful exploration.

SUMMARY

Collinearity and dynamic key drivers will remain salient topics in customer loyalty and satisfaction research for some time. Indeed, until there is a fundamental paradigm shift in the way *importance* is measured, the strong interrelationships on the predictor side of dependence models will continue to frustrate researchers. There are, as described earlier, a number of approaches that circumvent the harmful effects of collinear data with varying degrees of success. Techniques such as Kruskal's are very effective; however, they preclude the development of forecasting models because the importance metrics are based on a measure of covariation. Chapter 10 continues a discussion first presented in Chapter 2 concerning the development of loyalty segments and the use of multinomial logistic regression to develop equations for multiple groups simultaneously. Limited empirical evidence suggests this could be a very useful strategy. It appears to be less susceptible to the effects of collinearity and also recognizes that what drives loyalty in the low end of the distribution may not emerge as a driver at the high end. As a result, different strategies may be developed to improve the loyalty of highly dissatisfied versus more loyal customers.

6

CRM and Customer Satisfaction

INTRODUCTION

This chapter focuses on the link between customer relationship management (CRM) and marketing research generally and customer satisfaction specifically. The CRM promise has fallen short of expectations in many areas, according to various experts. First, this chapter considers industry expectations with respect to CRM. The discussion then shifts to what CRM has actually delivered. Those of you familiar with salient topics in CRM already know a substantive gap is associated with the CRM promise. Indeed, at this writing CRM has been criticized for falling short in a number of areas. The numerous reasons for this involve unrealistic expectations, inadequate funding, inappropriate evaluation metrics, and staffing problems.

CRM represents a complex business strategy—it is not simply a tool or technique. Accordingly, many exhaustive treatments of the subject exist. This chapter cannot reasonably provide a comprehensive discussion of CRM; many books address the technical and strategic implications of the CRM architecture. Interested readers should consider books by Berson, Thearling, and Smith (1999); Bergeron (2002); Goldenberg (2002); Gulycz and Brown (2002); or Dyche (2001). These resources stress different aspects of CRM ranging from general strategic issues to more technical data mining discussions.

CRM AS A BUSINESS STRATEGY

Customer relationship management (CRM) proposed a fundamental change in how businesses should interact with customers. This paradigm shift occurred gradually but was most distinct during the late 1990s. From a historical perspective, the development of CRM clearly reflects an orientation that moved from products to customers. Figure 6.1 illustrates the change in marketing strategy and communications from the 1960s to the present. As

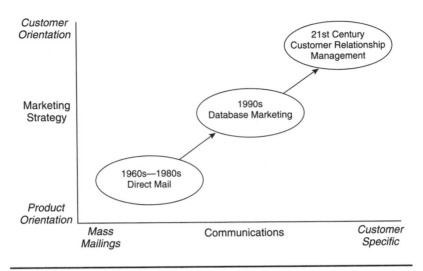

Figure 6.1   Gradual paradigm shift to CRM.

shown, businesses in the 1960s tended to focus on product-oriented mass mailings. As information technologies matured in the 1980s and 1990s, database marketing emerged. An increasing emphasis on the customer and concomitant information technology advances led to CRM.

Note that CRM emerged as a result of both strategic and technological innovations. Arguably, until the mid-1980s, disk-based computer storage space was quite expensive and applications development was restricted to second- and third-generation languages like FORTRAN, RPG, and COBOL accessing data in complex, hierarchical databases. Indeed, the Y2K fiasco in which year was recorded as a two-position field can be traced to the high cost of disk space in the late 1970s in addition to a lack of foresight. The emergence of relational database technology, fourth-generation programming languages, cheaper data storage and retrieval options, and increasingly powerful computing power made possible the data-intense CRM applications available today.

Not surprisingly, the most defining characteristic of the CRM approach to business management involves its shift from a product-centric organization to a focus on the customer. This shift dictates both structural organizational changes and a parallel development of management information systems that reflect a focus on the customer relationship rather than the product. In the latter case, for example, data structures that emphasize the customer must accommodate historical aspects of the transactional relationship.

The key to CRM is that it relies heavily on technology and should include organizational structure changes that mirror the customer focus of management information systems. One potentially troublesome aspect of structural changes in the organization is the necessity for marketing and information technologies (IT) departments to work closely. As Yu (2001:18–19) noted, in many companies these groups often have very different cultures.

In an effort to improve customer service, CRM integrates "customer touch points" such as call centers, sales teams, retail stores, websites, and problem resolution processes. The integrated operation yields a much richer customer data repository and provides the organization a better, more complete picture of their interactions with customers. More importantly, the integrated customer touch points result in better customer service because, for example, retail store operations, sales teams, and call centers all share customer information. That a customer recently had a problem resolved by a specific call center, for example, is shared across the various touch points. This knowledge can be leveraged by other parts of the company to enhance service or product quality issues affecting the customer relationship. In the final analysis, once CRM has been adopted as part of a business strategy, consumers should perceive a more integrated organization that is in touch with its customers.

The earliest efforts to establish CRM tended to focus on the operational issues surrounding touch-point integration. As these systems became more congruous, it became clear that measuring the customer relationship involved collecting and storing voluminous amounts of data. Transaction-based data involving purchases, returns, inquiries, website visits, and other interactions yielded a rich longitudinal database for industries characterized by high levels of customer contact. Financial services companies, in particular, enjoyed an enviable depth and breadth of customer data.

It is easy to understand why CRM depends so heavily on technology when we consider the amount of data that must be stored. Davenport, Harris, and Kohli (2001:63) cited two illustrative cases. Fingerhut, a direct-marketing company, maintains 4 million customer names with up to 1000 profile variables per household. Understandably, its data warehouse can store nearly 5 trillion bytes! A very successful Internet portal (Yahoo!) was also cited as a company with huge amounts of customer data. Because Yahoo! records each visitor's navigation history, 400 billion bytes of data *per day* are stored. The need for readily accessible data storage space, efficient relational database technologies, and computing power at these companies reflects the role technology has played in the development of CRM.

CRM: THE PROMISE

In the 1990s, CRM emerged as a critically important paradigm shift that appeared ready to change business strategy radically. Its premise was simple. Getting in touch with customers by presenting them with an integrated organization and developing a better understanding of individual customers through data shared across functional departments would yield more satisfied, loyal customers. The bottom-line effect of the CRM promise was improved service and product quality, which would yield more satisfied customers. The effects of enhanced satisfaction involve increased retention, scale economies, market share, and, ultimately, profitability. Empirical linkages between enhanced customer satisfaction and desirable business outcomes were well documented in the 1990s by authors like Reichheld (1996), Rust and Zahorik (1993, 1995), and Zeithaml et al. (1996). As a result, the CRM promise clearly appeared valid and was especially appealing because the road to success appeared to be paved with computer technology.

Almquist, Heaton, and Hall (2002:17) underscored the importance of CRM as a customer retention strategy. As these authors asserted, the costs of acquiring new customers have steadily increased and, as a result, retaining existing customers has become more salient. They noted, for example, that whereas credit card mailings have increased by 12% annually, response rates have fallen steadily and now are around 0.6%. Similar difficulties were observed in terms of Internet advertising and telemarketing. The notion that CRM could reduce customer attrition, therefore, represented a very attractive possibility given the increasing cost of acquiring new customers.

Keep in mind that CRM, no matter how well executed, is problematic in situations characterized by low-involvement purchases and customer anonymity. Thus CRM was most enthusiastically received in the financial services, travel, telecommunications, and insurance industries. The bottom line is that if you do not even know who your customers are, CRM may not be a realistic objective! Although retailers, notably, have made progress recording relationships by issuing various credit options or frequent buyer programs, many remain relatively isolated from their customers. Other strategies such as warranty cards appear to have yielded modest results, with participation rates rarely exceeding 40% even for expensive high-involvement consumer durables.

The CRM promise of the 1990s tended to focus on technological solutions, operational integration, and transaction-based data. Many proponents lost sight of the fact that CRM is not an IT platform. As noted earlier, it represents a fundamental shift in the way companies interact with customers. A failure to recognize that CRM is a business strategy, not a tactic, led to disillusionment in some circles, described in the following section.

CRM: THE REALITY

A 1998 *Harvard Business Review* article titled "Preventing the Premature Death of Relationship Marketing" reflected a growing corporate disillusionment with CRM. Bernstel (2001:14) reported that in the financial services industry, CRM accounted for annual spending of $6.8 billion and had yielded questionable results. The author cited a survey among bank executives that confirmed CRM had one of the lowest satisfaction rates among executives of any of the 10 most popular management tools. Even more recently, Cirillo and Silverstein (2002:53), in an article titled "Can CRM Be Saved?" confirmed that customer satisfaction rates for CRM initiatives were disappointing. Almquist et al. (2002:18–19) cited a 2001 Data Warehousing Institute study that suggested only 16% of companies with CRM implementations say the systems have exceeded their expectations. Indeed, 41% of the 1200 respondents indicated they believed CRM was "a potential flop."

Cirillo and Silverstein (2002:53) suggested that by the turn of the century CRM was practically devoid of content. It could mean practically anything and was used as a label for software products involving sales force automation, call center technologies, and a variety of other applications. Indeed, CRM had become synonymous with the technology; in many instances, business strategy had not appreciably changed. The only real business management implication of CRM for many organizations was the necessity to amortize the cost of very expensive software over various functional departments. According to Yu (2001:19), the median annual CRM budget now exceeds $1 million. Almquist et al. (2002:18) noted that in 2000 spending on CRM was $23 billion, which was expected to rise at a 27% rate. By 2005, the level of U.S. spending would exceed $75 billion.

Successful CRM clearly requires robust technology. But more importantly, it requires changes in fundamental business strategy. Technology alone will not guarantee a significant return on investment for CSM programs. As Crosby and Johnson (2002a:10) noted, successful CRM programs require "adhering to an integrated business strategy that goes well beyond single-point solutions in areas such as branding, customer service, or CRM technology." This is consistent with Pettit's (2002:3) conclusion that overall "CRM has not yet delivered on its ultimate promise—the transformed and improved customer experience." The author attributed this to an emphasis on technology that resulted in huge volumes of data and powerful analytical tools but little, if any, strategic direction.

Citing a 2001 Data Warehousing Institute study involving 1200 business executives and IT managers, Almquist et al. (2002:19) noted that the primary threats to CRM initiatives were a lack of cross-functional planning, no coherent CRM business strategy, and a failure for sales and marketing functions to changes processes. Other risk factors included a lack of senior-level support, inadequate project representation, and poor IT choices.

Gordon (2001:6) suggested that the absence of a strategic plan could be the reason many companies have had only modestly successful CRM programs. The author proposed that "If there are differences of opinion as to whether the company's CRM initiative is creating new, mutual, enduring and competitively superior customer value, then it is quite possible that the implementation has been tactical rather than strategic." Gordon charged the close link between CRM and technology as responsible for this lack of strategic focus.

Strategic clarity and collaboration across traditional organizational boundaries must accompany technological innovation. Indeed, the technological hurdles seem to pale in the face of management and marketing challenges. It is important to concede that people—not companies and technology—maintain customer relationships. This simple notion dramatically affects the success of CRM programs. Integrating data across disparate organizational functions was relatively easy from a technological standpoint, but getting *people* to collaborate across departments was a much more complicated job. As noted earlier, at least one author (Yu, 2001:18) has cited the troublesome aspects of requiring departments with very different cultures to communicate more effectively.

The critics cited here do not represent a unilateral indictment of CRM. Despite a number of dissenters, there are also many experts who cite successful CRM experiences. Ingold (2002), for example, suggests CRM has yielded fruitful results in the insurance industry by improving service and distribution options to customers and providing powerful analytical tools to researchers. Similarly, Songini (2001) cites the case of FleetBoston Financial Corporation, which has reported tremendous success with CRM. Adams (2001) provided evidence that in the hotel industry CRM is considered to have three components:

- Incentives

- Customized communications

- Rewards and recognitions

Adams's description of CRM at Radisson and Wyndham International presents examples that exemplify how customer transaction and profile data can be used to increase loyalty and revenues. Finally, Galimi (2001) suggested that among HMOs there has been a recognition that CRM—although costly—can yield significant benefits.

Almquist et al. (2002:19) cited the case of a European credit card company that enjoyed more that $30 million in incremental income attributable to a well-executed CRM strategy. Key considerations in this successful project involved a realignment of organizational processes, flexible customer management processes, accelerated test cycles, and a more modest role for technology. The company's ability to differentiate service levels based on potential value helped it retain profitable customers and successfully attract prospects.

Other success stories deliver a consistent message. Davenport et al. (2001:63) interviewed executives at 24 companies considered to be "standouts in customer-knowledge management," such as Harley-Davidson, Procter & Gamble, and Wachovia Bank. Qualitative findings confirmed their suspicion: recording vast amounts of transaction (and other) data does not necessarily lead to successful CRM implementation and ROI. Many of the study participants suggested that they maximized the value of customer data by considering "the person behind the transaction—recording what customers do during sales and service interactions." The emphasis in these companies on the human side of the data appeared to let them "better understand and predict customers' behaviors" and as a result, "they can rely less on technologies to collect, distribute, and use transaction-driven knowledge."

MARKETING RESEARCH DATA AND CRM

As Nichols (2000:28) noted, the earliest CRM endeavors focused on increasing operational integration across multiple customer touchpoints. In the 21st century, the emphasis has been on CRM analytics. To a great extent this interest has been reflected in the introduction of numerous data mining tools. Indeed, the producers of two of the most respected statistical analysis packages in the United States sell highly sophisticated self-contained tools to aid in the analysis of CRM data.

One very big difference between marketing research data and CRM data is that the former is typically incomplete, based on a *sample* of customers (or noncustomers). The cost of primary data collection typically precludes a census approach for marketing research projects. Sampling theory, of course, confirms it would be very wasteful to survey all customers when a sufficiently large randomly selected sample will yield estimates that are very accurate measures of the population. Nonetheless, marketing research projects typically deal with samples of customers, whereas CRM data mining analytics may easily involve the entire customer database. Efforts to relate CRM data to marketing research data, therefore, are restricted to the samples.

CRM systems generate an unusually large amount of data, hence the introduction of data mining tools designed to find patterns, isolate outliers, and provide multiple data reduction facilities. Data mining, however, is not marketing research in the traditional sense. Certainly, many of the techniques employed to synthesize CRM data—exotic forms of multivariate techniques and neural networks—are often used in marketing research. But data mining is typically not associated with the collection of primary psychometric data. Of course, marketing research projects can feed CRM systems and subsequent data mining efforts can leverage attitudinal data where available. This relationship is described in greater detail later.

One great benefit of the CRM strategy is that transactional and behavioral data captured as part of the customer relationship can be linked with psychometric data obtained through traditional survey methodologies. The benefit, of course, is that attitudes can be empirically linked to behaviors in both cross-sectional and longitudinal contexts. Figure 6.2 depicts the relationships between customer-oriented marketing research studies that may be related to CRM.

Note that the relationships depicted in Figure 6.2 can be unidirectional or bidirectional. For example, in some cases the CRM system may supply participants for research studies involving customers. In other cases, research results may be used to update the CRM system itself, such as in the case of customer satisfaction programs. When customers are concentrated geographically, the CRM system may be used to generate focus group participants or respondents for quantitative research involving new product development efforts. This type of effort can produce homogeneous customer samples with respect to past purchases, usage patterns, or other key relationship data. Of course, the CRM system can only generate *customer* samples—if nationally representative research is desired, a different sampling strategy may be in order.

The relationship between CRM and marketing research data is likely to increase in relevance. As Crosby, Johnson, and Quinn (2002) observed, statistical models based on CRM data often lack answers to fundamental questions relating to the psychological underpinnings of behavior. Although descriptive and often quite efficacious, models based exclusively on CRM data often cannot answer questions involving the *reasons* consumers act in

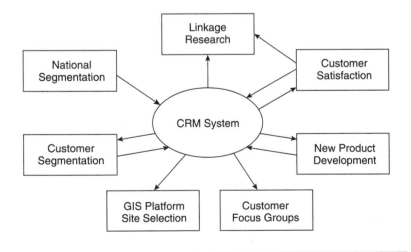

Figure 6.2   Customer-focused marketing research and CRM.

certain ways. They are limited to stimulus-response situations in which, for example, a business variable like price is manipulated and subsequent behaviors are recorded. CRM systems are excellent platforms for this type of experimentation. However, a complete picture requires the integration of psychometric data and transaction-based CRM data.

When customer data include specific geographical information such as latitude-longitude coordinates, the CRM system can feed a variety of geographic information systems (GIS) that overlay census-based demographics and customer information on a computer-based map. Concentrations of customers and a variety of distance metrics can be used to optimize decisions concerning the placement of new branches or stores. Using CRM data in GIS applications can be very powerful visually because a wide variety of high-resolution maps can be employed to illustrate customer distributions. The optimal, fully integrated CRM system should synthesize psychometric, behavioral, demographic, and geographic data as illustrated in Figure 6.3.

Segmentation studies that focus initially on a nationally representative sample can be used to classify customers in a CRM system. Once a set of consumer segments has been developed based on, for example, attitudes toward home ownership, classification algorithms can be developed. Ideally, these equations would employ behavioral or demographic data available in the CRM system. This permits classification of all customers in the CRM system with valid data for the variables in the predictive equations.

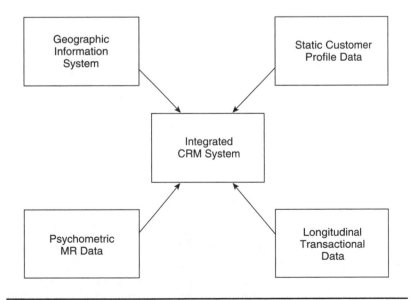

Figure 6.3   Fully integrated CRM system.

This type of project can reveal whether a given national segment is disproportionately represented in the customer database and guide marketing communications based on customer segment affiliation.

Alternatively, CRM systems can be used to facilitate a market segmentation based exclusively on customer data. Because survey data are typically available only for samples of customers, this approach is limited to two types of data. First, static customer profile data based on census block statistics or acquired during the initial sales process may be used in the customer segmentation. These data are combined with transaction-based behavioral data to produce a set of homogeneous customer segments.

Bidirectional relationships involving marketing research projects and CRM should be acutely aware of privacy issues. That is, if primary marketing research data feed a CRM system, the respondent must agree to waive his or her privacy during the interview, regardless of data collection methodology. Telephone, mail, and Internet surveys must contain an item that states the survey data may be shared with the sponsor organization. Respondents must explicitly agree to this waiver before survey data can be uniquely identified to the sponsor.

One of the most appealing bidirectional data linkages to CRM involves customer satisfaction programs. The symbiotic relationship with customer satisfaction measurement is fundamental to the success of CRM programs. After all, the fundamental promise of CRM is enhanced customer satisfaction. The CRM system provides participants for CSM programs and then is updated with this customer feedback data. The CRM–CSM relationship is discussed in greater detail next.

CUSTOMER SATISFACTION DATA AND CRM

The relationship between customer satisfaction surveys and CRM is complex. Increased customer satisfaction is one of CRM's promises. Thus measuring customer satisfaction serves to measure CRM return on investment (ROI). It also provides service and product quality feedback to other functions, of course. As described in Chapter 2, customer satisfaction results may also drive compensation systems, provide competitive intelligence, and serve as a leadership tool tied explicitly to a company mission statement.

A symbiotic relationship exists between CRM and customer satisfaction measurement (CSM) programs. Figure 6.4 illustrates the dual nature of this relationship. That is, the CRM program generates samples for the customer satisfaction program. Customer feedback data are then recorded in the CRM system, assuming, of course, that respondent permission has been procured. A longitudinal analysis of the CSM data can serve as a perform-

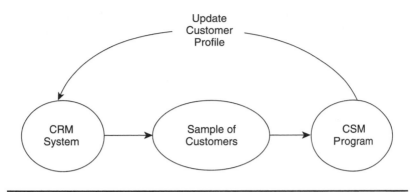

Figure 6.4   Symbiotic relationship between CRM and CSM.

ance evaluation of the CRM program. After all, the organization that fully embraces CRM at both strategic and operational levels should experience increasing levels of customer satisfaction.

As James (2002:15) noted, the integration of customer satisfaction data with CRM is becoming increasingly salient. Many companies are discovering the whole is greater than the sum of the parts. An interaction effect occurs when these two types of data are combined, and it yields a much more valuable platform. The extent of this interaction depends greatly on the depth and breadth of the CRM data, however. Organizations in industries characterized by infrequent customer interactions (e.g., insurance companies) may not experience the rewards yielded by companies with more recurrent, direct customer contact like those in financial services. In the former case, significant customer profile data may be recorded initially, but subsequent interactions usually entail limited communications involving policy status. The exception occurs when the policy owner files a claim, which by definition is not a profitable interaction for the insurance company! Financial services companies—especially retail banking—enjoy frequent customer interactions. These may include high-involvement experiences for the consumer such as home equity loans, mortgages, or the acquisition of various deposit products such as CDs, money market funds, or savings instruments.

One of the key historical differences between customer satisfaction programs and CRM, according to Gupta (2002:19), is that the former has focused on aggregated data, whereas CRM programs are geared toward individual customer-level data. Certainly, customer satisfaction data have been disaggregated based on meaningful business variables such as product ownership, demographics, geography, and especially organizational structure in the form of branch- or store-level performance scores. Nonetheless, a major difference between CRM and customer satisfaction data involves the level of aggregation used. When CRM systems subsume customer satisfaction programs, however, the latter data are more likely to be considered at the individual respondent level in addition to various aggregated levels. The treatment of customer satisfaction data at the individual level has tremendous utility but also may lead to problems.

CRM and psychometric data are typically associated with model development that employs customer satisfaction data on the *predictor* side of the equation with a substantive outcome variable from the CRM data such as a retention or profitability metric. Figure 6.5 illustrates how CSM data may be used on either the predictor or outcome side of regression models to forecast t_2 phenomena using t_1 data. A lag must be accommodated in this framework because a causal relationship is posited and temporal sequencing is presumed. Experimenting with different lags and noting the effect on summary measures like R^2 is advisable. Clearly, the lag that yields the greatest R^2 should be favored.

Companies with extremely large customer databases may never fully populate every customer's CSM data fields because sampling approaches are used to reduce costs and fielding times. If a subset of the overall database has recent customer satisfaction or attitudinal loyalty measures that can be linked to behavioral variables, the approach reflected in the top half of Figure 6.5

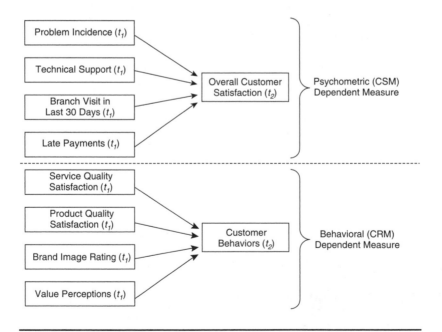

Figure 6.5 CRM and CSM data in predictor and outcome variable roles.

may be appropriate. This involves the development of regression-based models that predict overall satisfaction (or other important attitudinal variables such as loyalty) based on behavioral variables in the CRM database. Assuming reasonable model efficacy (e.g., R^2 greater than 70%), one may *forecast* satisfaction or loyalty levels based on, for example, problem incidence, technical support calls, or other transaction data captured on a continuous basis at the customer level.

This tack involves forecasting based on models that link CRM predictor variables to psychometric outcomes like satisfaction and loyalty. Once a strong model is established based on a sample of customers' psychometric and behavioral CRM data, every customer in the database can be classified into, for example, one of several attitudinal loyalty segments. This approach initially seems somewhat counterintuitive. However, to the extent that loyalty segment affiliation is highly predictive of outcome CRM variables (i.e., it has external validity), it affords a very useful way to relate predictor and outcome CRM data through an intermediate psychometric data link. The importance of psychometric data in explaining relationships between predictor and outcome CRM variables is considerable. In the absence of psychometric data, CRM systems can only record and *describe* behaviors. The addition of customer satisfaction data to the CRM system, therefore, is important if a complete picture of customer behavior is desired.

When behavioral CRM data are highly predictive of customer satisfaction as might be the case with variables involving problem resolution, disputed bills, and various in-person interactions, a continuous cycle of model development, implementation, and feedback such as that depicted in Figure 6.6 can be implemented. The duration of each cycle is limited by three

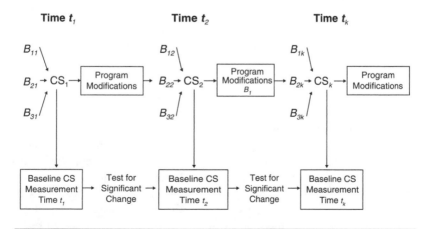

Figure 6.6 Continuous iterative CRM–CSM linkage.

activities: model development, program implementation, and customer feedback data acquisition. This system assumes a continuous effort to improve customer satisfaction by manipulating variables that will affect the service or product quality perceived by customers and will be recorded in the CRM database as, in this case, B_1, B_2, and B_3. These represent customer interactions that are linked to customer satisfaction in the model development phase. Program implementation is based on the behavioral drivers of customer satisfaction and should be aimed at improving the customer's experience with the transaction. Subsequent steps capture customer satisfaction data and develop new models to predict satisfaction based on the most recent behavioral data. Each iteration of this process may take weeks in the case of companies with Internet-based services and customer feedback processes to several months or longer for companies using traditional telephone data collection methodologies and model development strategies.

The continuous process depicted in Figure 6.6 parallels the organization of a typical customer satisfaction tracking program, except that behavioral data are used to model customer satisfaction and these same areas (i.e., B_1, B_2, and B_3) are manipulated in the program modification step. In the traditional customer satisfaction program, self-reported data are used as surrogates for the behavioral data. In either case, psychometric data represent the dependent measures we are trying to optimize because they are, ostensibly, good predictors of consumer behavior, which equates to market share, revenue, profitability, and other critical business outcomes.

As noted earlier, CRM data can be considered in either a predictor or outcome variable context. Indeed, linking transaction-based predictor variables like technical support calls, invoicing problems, and channel activity to dependent CRM data like product purchase, account growth, or relationship termination is possible in the absence of psychometric data. But, as critics have pointed out, this relationship is purely descriptive. The reasons *why* the cause-and-effect relationship exists remain a black box, as shown in Figure 6.7. Psychometric data can reveal why CRM predictor variables affect CRM outcome variables.

One criticism of CRM programs involves the nature of R in CRM. The lack of equity in the relationship is cause for concern; it is decidedly unidirectional, favoring the company. Ostensibly, the customer's main benefit is individualized, seamless interaction with an integrated company. Some feel this represents the basic standard of service: customers, they would argue, deserve this basic level of service. Although they are collecting vast amounts of customer-based transaction and profile data that can be used to the company's advantage, only a modicum of real benefit is apparent to the customer. Certainly, he or she has a more fluid experience dealing with the company, but shouldn't this be expected anyway?

Increasingly, companies appear to recognize the inequity in this situation. Certain luxury hotels, for example, track guests' preferences and tailor

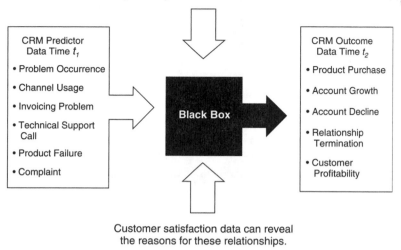

Figure 6.7   Role of customer satisfaction linking predictor and outcome CRM data.

services accordingly. Their CRM programs include tangible customer benefits like upgraded rooms, complimentary wines (based on known preferences), seamless registration, and a team of employees whose goal is to anticipate every guest's needs. This type of program, however, appears to be limited to niche players specializing in very upscale clientele or business-to-business environments in which the value of a customer is substantial. Unfortunately, this may remain the case in the future; companies are unlikely to make the CRM relationship more equitable without direct, immediate benefits, despite the potential increases in customer satisfaction. CRM ROI can be measured in terms of customer satisfaction, and one key approach to increasing the latter involves focusing on the foundation of CRM: the *relationship*.

Clearly, linking customer satisfaction data to CRM systems has certain pitfalls. The data security and privacy issues described earlier must be made very clear throughout the organization. This is compounded in the case of global CRM/CSM systems. If customer satisfaction data are shared within the organization there may be abuses. Despite having waived confidentiality, respondents may not be particularly happy when a sales associate contacts them to follow up on their feedback. The worst case nightmare scenario could involve an employee chastising a respondent for providing undesirable feedback. The end result may be fewer respondents waiving confidentiality and more importantly, a growing lack of candor among a customer base who increasingly suspect their feedback will be uniquely linked to them. The bottom line is that despite confidentiality waivers, uniquely identifying customers based on their feedback can yield undesirable consequences. These proscriptions are especially important in the business-to-consumer environment, but they are also applicable to those working in business-to-business situations.

Global CSM project management is the subject of Chapter 8, but the effects of globalization on the relationship between CRM and CSM merits additional discussion here. Clearly, implementing a global CRM program represents a significant investment in time and resources. The desire to project a consistent, integrated image globally is an admirable objective. As Crosby and Johnson (2002b:10) noted, global CRM programs give rise to questions concerning the standardization of marketing strategy across countries given cultural heterogeneity. Further, they argued, there are few truly global brands like Coca-Cola, Sony, and Microsoft.

The global integration of CRM and CSM programs is exceedingly challenging. On the CRM side, companies face country-level differences in terms of business processes, accounting practices, data formats, database platforms, and data dictionary definitions. Global CSM programs also face numerous hurdles including psychometric issues, data collection methodologies, translations, and timing considerations. A centralized CRM/CSM system may not be practical, in fact. Crosby and Johnson (2002b:11) cited an example involving GE Capital in which foreign privacy regulations restricted the exportation of certain data. This company ultimately conceded that a centralized U.S.-based global CRM system was not viable. Their decision to create a decentralized regional system yielded more flexibility and included basic standardization to facilitate data integration.

THE FUTURE OF THE CRM/CSM RELATIONSHIP

The role of psychometric data—particularly customer feedback data—in the CRM architecture appears quite secure. Indeed, authors like Crosby, Johnson, and Quinn (2002) and Pettit (2002) contend that inclusion of attitudinal data is critical to the long-term survival of CRM. Charges that there is no R in CRM have spawned extensions such as customer experience management (CEM), which in some ways is the mirror image of CRM. Whereas CRM revolves around capturing, sharing, and analyzing transactional data, CEM's focus is the customer experience.

The CEM premise is that every time the customer interacts with the company, the *customer* learns something. Based on this learning, the customer alters his or her behavior. Thus, by managing the customer's *experience,* companies can shape behavior and, ostensibly, customer value. This may involve training front-line employees guided by continuous feedback from customers about the experience.

As Pettit observed (2002:19–20), CEM is highly contextual: "A well-designed CEM initiative begins by precisely defining the types of customer behaviors the company wishes to influence, recognizing how customer needs and expectations change at different points in their lifecycle, and planning experiences that will positively influence customers." A cornerstone of the CEM framework is customer feedback gathered through telephone interviews, e-mail, websites, interactive voice response systems (IVR), and other methodologies. If the future of CRM is CEM, the role of CSM will be very stable.

A comprehensive CEM program also includes key outcome metrics such as profitability, retention rates, purchase behavior, disaggregated sales volumes, and important variables like problem resolution rate. The strength of CEM involves its ability to align business outcomes with experiential data. This continuous interaction facilitates incremental, short-term operational corrections as well as enterprisewide structural or strategic responses.

Partner relationship marketing (PRM) can be used as an adjunct to CRM or CEM. It relates to the channel partnerships a company must maintain in order to relate effectively with its customers. The importance of channel partnerships and the role they play in an overall stakeholder satisfaction system was described in Chapter 2. Including feedback from suppliers, dealers, distributors, franchisees, and other supply chain and distribution system partners provides a more complete picture of a company's (nonfinancial) performance.

7

Linking Customer Satisfaction to Business Outcomes

INTRODUCTION

This chapter reviews the theoretical and empirical foundations underlying linkage research focused on establishing a relationship between customer satisfaction and key business outcomes. Next is a treatment of some important milestones in the quest for an unequivocal demonstration of how customer satisfaction affects business performance. Based on this foundation, a taxonomy of linkage research methods is presented. Hopefully, this will provide you with a firm understanding of your linkage research opportunities and limitations. Efforts to relate service and product quality feedback to business outcomes are often frustrated by data and methodological problems including disparate units of analysis, missing data, insufficient sample sizes, and inconsistent scaling.

Based on the discussion presented in Chapter 1, we know the financial impact of enhanced customer satisfaction may be exerted through one of two mechanisms as depicted in Figure 7.1. The more critical of these involves *customer retention*. When customer acquisition costs are high, averted attrition can yield substantial returns in terms of saved resources. However, the loss of unprofitable customers can actually be beneficial. The second way that enhanced customer satisfaction affects business profitability is more direct. Specifically, customers who are more satisfied tend to purchase more products and services. Many, many intervening variables affect this relationship, of course. Current share of wallet, for example, can affect the extent to which even an extremely satisfied customer can purchase additional products or services.

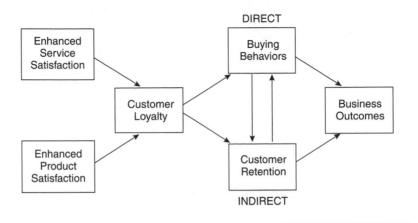

Figure 7.1   Customer satisfaction effects on business outcomes.

LINKAGE RESEARCH TECHNIQUES

Establishing a quantitative relationship between customer satisfaction measures and business outcome variables can be achieved at a variety of levels. These range from an analysis of individual customers to macroeconomic approaches such as that employed by the ACSI study. Thus the *unit of analysis* is of particular concern when embarking on a linkage research project. This represents the individual row in the data set being analyzed. Again, the unit of analysis may range from highly specific such as an individual transaction to macro levels such as entire companies:

- Specific transactions

- Individual customers

- Customer groups

- Organizational subunits

- Organizations

Clearly, the macroeconomic perspective will not have much utility for most organizations other than to demonstrate that companies with higher levels of satisfaction tend to be more profitable. Interorganizational linkage research, therefore, remains largely the realm of academicians. However, intraorganizational research is of great interest to both academics and practitioners. The focus of this discussion concentrates on intraorganizational linkage research.

Once an appropriate dependent measure has been identified, its viability with respect to the unit of analysis must be established. This is perhaps one of the most frustrating aspects of intraorganizational linkage research. To the extent that business outcome data measured at the subunit level are available, aggregation techniques make possible robust linkages. Measures such as retention, share of wallet, market share, revenues, and profitability may not be available at the customer level but often are captured at a higher unit of analysis. These may range from geopolitical boundaries such as states or countries to organizational subunits such as branches or sales districts. In a business-to-business context, customers may be treated in terms of industry segments with known profitability. Thus, even if customer-level profit data are not available, frequently a different unit of analysis may represent a reasonable alternative. Of course, as the unit of analysis is increased beyond the individual customer, sample sizes tend to become smaller and smaller. This reality often forces a longitudinal approach to linkage research, as described next.

Few companies enjoy easily measured customer-level profitability metrics. Financial services organizations appear to have the most advanced business outcome data at the customer level. Even banks must rely on a wide range of assumptions regarding profitability numbers, however. These include estimates of amortized channel access costs (e.g., the cost of visiting a branch to conduct a given transaction), the cost of funds, and a variety of other factors affecting the profitability of a specific customer.

An interesting aspect of linkage research involves the difference between transactional- and relationship-based customer satisfaction data. Linkage research is typically considered to involve relationship satisfaction data and business outcomes. Very little empirical research has focused on the microcosmic link between transaction profitability and transaction satisfaction. Transaction satisfaction data typically focus on a specific process or interaction with known costs and revenues that are measured at the customer level.

Pure transaction satisfaction data such as those gathered by retail fast-food establishments represent an excellent means for establishing a direct relationship between satisfaction and profitability. Indirect outcomes involving attrition are also possible based on transaction data, of course. This may entail a relatively simple approach in which psychometric data (i.e., intention to repurchase) are related to satisfaction. A more sophisticated technique links transaction satisfaction to actual behavior.

Figure 7.2 presents an architecture for understanding and facilitating linkage research. The primary split involves direct and indirect linkages. The latter refers to the effects customer satisfaction has on business outcomes through retention. Direct linkage research, in contrast, involves leveraging covariance between satisfaction and specific business outcome measures such as profitability, revenue, or share of wallet. Within each of these unique branches are two very different approaches to establishing a

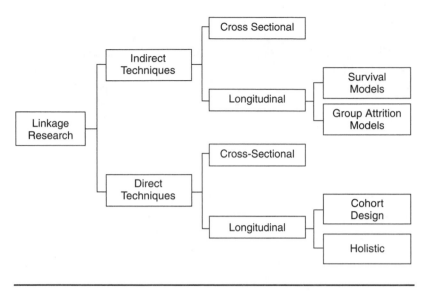

Figure 7.2 Linkage research variants.

relationship between customer satisfaction and profitability. The first relies on cross-sectional data and *implied* causality. That is, covariation is presumed to reflect a causal relationship. Clearly, cross-sectional data do not meet the multiple criteria necessary for establishing causality. The key ingredient—*temporal ordering*—is missing, for example. Nonetheless, a compelling argument can be made by demonstrating that, for example, sales districts with high levels of customer satisfaction also tend to be the most profitable.

The second approach to either direct or indirect linkage research involves longitudinal analysis. This entails relating satisfaction and profitability over time and can take two forms based on the unit of analysis. The first technique is quite simplistic and can be readily accomplished. In effect, this requires that a single profitability or business outcome metric be related to a single satisfaction measure over time. Lagged effects may be tested to determine whether, for example, an increase in satisfaction yields delayed concomitant increases in profitability.

A more sophisticated approach to direct longitudinal linkage research involves multiple *cohort measurements* over time. The key is that the same customers are interviewed at successive periods and changes in satisfaction related to changes in profitability. In this manner we can conclude that customers whose satisfaction increased from time t_1 to time t_2 also were associated with enhanced profitability across the two periods. The application of longitudinal analyses in an indirect linkage context often involves techniques such as survival analysis. In this manner, satisfaction levels (along with other variables) are used to predict attrition at the individual customer level.

Cross-sectional and longitudinal direct linkage analysis are discussed in greater detail throughout the remainder of this chapter. The examples presented focus on both direct and indirect frameworks. Indirect longitudinal research typically involves survival analysis techniques, which are beyond the scope of this chapter. An introduction to the approach is described in Allen and Wilburn (2002:71–85). For more technical treatments of survival analysis techniques, refer to Lee (1992), Allison (1995), or Li (1995).

Prior to a detailed discussion of cross-sectional and longitudinal linkage analyses, a variety of direct linkage dependent measures is reviewed. Most customer satisfaction program managers initially consider financial measures when they attempt empirically to relate customer feedback and business outcomes. Direct linkage with financial dependent measures presents a very compelling case to senior management. Accordingly, the following section reviews a number of financial variables that may be linked to customer satisfaction. The first half of this discussion considers market share as a key dependent measure, and the second reviews specific financial variables and their linkage to customer satisfaction.

DIRECT LINKAGE DEPENDENT MEASURES: MARKET SHARE

Maximizing market share has historically been an unambiguous business objective. Its relationship to profitability is traced to the benefits of substantial market share. The main benefit of superior market share is related to cost, according to Jain (1990:226–27). Market share affects cost in terms of scale and experience. Market leaders are presumed to have lower costs than their competitors as a result of their experience and scale of operations. And, as Jain notes, although maximizing market share is a reasonable goal for businesses, some caveats exist. Of greatest concern are the company's ability to finance the market share objectives and its ability to withstand antitrust actions.

The role of market share in the relationship among service/product quality, customer and employee satisfaction, retention, and financial performance is complex. Barsky (1999:107), for example, maintained that higher market share means *lower* customer satisfaction, which presumably leads to deflated financial performance. His reasoning was that mass producers are less able to satisfy customers in the way that niche players can. This may be true in some cases, but it stands to reason that sophisticated corporations that practice market segmentation and can differentiate their product offerings and marketing communications based on this strategy will be able to satisfy customers despite their dominant market share.

There are a variety of ways to measure market share; they differ considerably with respect to cost. For example, some companies use panel data to estimate market share; others use warehouse withdrawal data. Both are relatively inexpensive. In contrast, larger companies with more resources tend to maintain their own market share estimation programs. This usually involves a telephone survey methodology in which respondents are picked at random from a national sample and asked about their past product purchases and current ownership. In a consumer or retail setting, this might involve random digit dialing from a computer-generated sample of telephone numbers.

When a business-to-business setting is involved, a sample is typically acquired from a supplier like Dun & Bradstreet, and the most appropriate respondent identified through screening questions in the beginning of the survey. In either case, respondents are asked about their past purchase behavior and the brand/model of products they currently own. Occasionally this type of survey also includes items relating to *future* purchases, but unless a follow-up verification survey is conducted, this type of forecast should be considered cautiously. There is some utility in a comparison of current brand ownership and self-reported future behaviors. This can be considered a rough measure of customer retention—respondents who indicate they currently have a given brand and intend to purchase it again in the future may be considered retained customers.

Market share estimates are sometimes calculated at a sales territory level and can entail significant data collection expenditures. For large complex organizations that track key business metrics and customer satisfaction across 100 sales territories, a market share intelligence-gathering program may involve tens of thousands of telephone interviews. For example, in order to achieve a quarterly 95% confidence interval of $\pm 5\%$ for each of 100 sales territories, roughly 400 completed interviews per territory must be completed every three months. On an annual basis, this type of program would entail 160,000 telephone interviews. Assuming an hourly interviewing cost of $25 per hour and a completion rate of 2.0 interviews per hour, the total data collection budget for such a comprehensive program would be $2 million annually.

Market share clearly enjoys a unique role that spans customer retention and profitability. It obviously depends on customer retention. Further, it is a very good indicator of profitability. Its relationship with profitability may very well be curvilinear—as market share increases beyond an optimal point, customer satisfaction may drop. This could be attributed to the need for establishing economies of scale in production to increase share and a consequent drift toward mass production where there is little room for customer-focused marketing activities. Clear evidence suggests that market share does not necessarily equal profitability. Heskett, Sasser, and Schlesinger (1997:20) cite the case of Southwest Airlines, which was never a strong market leader but nevertheless has been consistently rated among its most profitable competitors.

DIRECT LINKAGE DEPENDENT MEASURES: PROFITABILITY

Most companies express their business objectives in terms of profitability, market share, and growth. As an ultimate objective, profitability is a substantive goal. It may be expressed at the corporate level in absolute monetary terms, as a percentage of capital employed, or in terms of total assets, according to Jain (1990:225). The objective may be set for the corporation as a whole or differentiated goals may be set based on customer segment, business line, or specific geographies like sales regions. Optimally, profit goals are set at the same business unit level at which customer satisfaction data are collected.

A number of profitability ratios can be calculated at the strategic business unit level. It is worth briefly describing several of these measures because the manner in which profitability is measured can affect the models we develop. This is particularly important given our interest in linking customer satisfaction—directly or indirectly through retention and market share—to profitability. Profitability can be measured in a number of different ways, so a review of these approaches seems warranted. First, this discussion reviews corporate-level measures of profitability. This is followed by a detailed examination of customer-level profitability.

As noted, profitability can be measured using several different approaches. These include the profit margin on sales, rate of return on assets, and rate of return on common stock equity, according to Kieso and Weygandt (1977: 1026–28). The profit margin on sales is calculated by dividing net income by net sales for a given period. Note that net income may be calculated either of two ways. The capital maintenance approach to net income calculation, according to Keiso and Weygandt (1977:113), "assumes that net income is measured by subtracting beginning net assets from ending net assets and adjusting for any additional investments during the period." In effect, this approach to net income measurement takes the net assets in period t_1 and measures income by the difference in capital values between period t_1 and t_2. Note that using the capital maintenance approach to the net income calculation can be implemented at the strategic business unit level and therefore can be supplied by, for example, sales region, state, or other operating unit.

The preferred method used for calculating net income is the transaction approach. This is an activity-based approach that provides substantially more detail than the capital maintenance technique. The activity-based approach to net income calculation focuses on the activities that have occurred during a given accounting period. Rather than simply providing a net change for a period, the transaction approach discloses the components that comprise the change. This could include items like cost of products sold or interest on long-term debt.

Total average assets is used to determine activity ratios and when multiplied by the profit margin on sales provides better insight into the profitability of a company. Total average assets is calculated as an average value of assets over an accounting period (e.g., fiscal quarter). Banks typically calculate a daily average balance sheet. In particular, the resulting asset turnover ratio tells us how many times the assets turned over during a given period. As Keiso and Weygandt (1977:1026) note, some companies "have a small profit margin on sales and a high turnover (grocery and discount stores), whereas other enterprises have a relatively high profit margin but a low inventory turnover (jewelry and furniture stores)."

Instead of multiplying profit margin by asset turnover, the rate of return on assets can be calculated more simply by dividing net income and total average assets. There has been some debate regarding whether net income before taxes or after taxes should be used, according to Keiso and Weygandt (1977:1029). For management purposes, a pretax measure may be used, because tax expense can fluctuate significantly from year to year due to unrelated tax planning objectives.

Two additional reflections of corporate profitability include the rate of return on common stock equity and earnings per share. The former is the ratio of net income after interest, taxes, and preferred dividends to the average common stockholder's equity. The earnings per share, however, is one of the most familiar metrics used to evaluate a company's performance. A number of caveats are associated with the earnings per share ratio as an objective measure. Keiso and Weygandt (1977:1030), for example, warn that this measure can be increased simply by reducing the number of shares outstanding by purchasing treasury stock. This may happen if a company believes its stock is undervalued in the marketplace. Of more interest is the potential for earnings per share to increase over time. Keiso and Weygandt (1977:1030) suggest that "earnings per share, all other factors being equal, will probably increase year after year if the stockholder reinvests earnings in the business because a larger earnings figure should be generated without a corresponding increase in the denominator, the number of shares outstanding."

The earnings per share and rate of return on common stock equity would be valuable in a meta-analysis that seeks to link customer satisfaction and financial performance across, for example, several hundred companies. Of course, this would assume all of the participating companies used the same customer satisfaction measurements. Interestingly, this is exactly what the American Customer Satisfaction Index (ACSI) program described in Chapter 1 has done successfully.

The preceding discussion has focused on measures of profitability that can be tracked at the corporate or strategic business unit level. When businesses have detailed information concerning their customers' purchasing behaviors, it is possible to calculate profitability at the individual customer level. Financial services providers—banks, in particular—have been very successful over the past 10 years in their efforts to calculate profitability at the customer (household) level. Calculating profitability at the individual customer level requires input from a number of sources. The frequency with which profitability metrics are calculated is another matter. For example, a bank may choose to estimate profitability on a monthly basis, whereas the producer of sophisticated medical imaging devices might be more inclined to estimate net income associated with individual hospitals on an annual basis. Regardless of how frequently profitability is calculated, two inputs are necessary: income from the customer and the cost of doing business with the customer.

First, the income associated with a given customer must be estimated on a yearly basis or more frequently, depending on access to product usage data. Financial services providers face a complex task when assessing the profitability of individual households. Net income must be calculated based on a household's product usage. Deposit and loan balances must be taken into account. Certain costs of capital assumptions must also be made to estimate the net income associated with loan and deposit products.

With respect to the costs associated with a given household, a bank must first estimate the transaction volume and the costs of each transaction type. For example, branch visits are quite expensive—so expensive, in fact, that in the 1990s some banks instituted a fee for branch banking. This was met with incredulity, and those banks that charged for branch banking visits no doubt lost some customers. Nonetheless, when a customer visits a branch it costs the bank in terms of both personnel and the need to have a brick-and-mortar channel for customers to use. If all customers used electronic banking, there would be little need for vast branch networks.

By implementing accounting procedures aimed at quantifying the customer value at the household level, banks are able to differentiate between profitable and unprofitable customers. The former group is of considerable importance because it is not uncommon for the top profit decile to support the remaining customer base. Indeed, members of the lowest profit decile may actually cost the bank money.

Not all organizations have the luxury of estimating profitability at the customer level. In a business-to-business environment, certain manufacturers, however, are able to gauge the value of their customers. When large-scale, low-volume products are considered, the possibility of calculating the net profit associated with each sale is very good. A manufacturer of MRI (magnetic resonance imaging) equipment sold to hospitals is in a good position to calculate profitability at the customer (i.e., hospital) level. The key inputs involve the costs of producing and marketing the equipment and, of course, the revenue its sale yields. Profitability is often enhanced by the revenue stream associated with the continuing technical support and maintenance relationship with the customer.

In many cases the customer relationship is characterized by an initial purchase followed by years of maintenance or technical support. Home and business security systems, for example, start with an initial installation cost followed by continued monitoring costs. Certain computer software and hardware is also characterized by an initial purchase followed by an optional maintenance contract. In retailing, a significant effort has been put forth in an attempt to lure consumers into multiyear maintenance contracts on a wide range of durable goods, such as electronic equipment like printers, stereos, televisions, and DVD players. To retailers the allure of such a proposition is the revenue generated by the maintenance contract and the lengthening of the relationship with the consumer. Of course, the revenue associated with the maintenance contract is offset by any expenses related to repairing or maintaining the equipment. Still, this risk is manageable and has been accommodated in the price of the contract.

Clearly, the profitability of a customer relationship may continue long after the initial sale through maintenance, technical support, and consulting contracts. When this is the case, the profitability of a customer may be calculated by averaging the profitability across the useful life of the product. This helps avoid situations in which customers are highly profitable in the first year and contribute very little to the bottom line in subsequent years. Additionally, averaging the profitability of a customer over the life of the product facilitates comparisons of customers at any point in the product life cycle. That is, without averaging profitability (or any other financial performance variable) across the product's life, customers who made the initial purchase will be very profitable and those in the maintenance phase may be less profitable. This type of comparison fails to take into consideration the *lifetime value* of a customer.

Heskett et al. (1997:60–65) describe the lifetime value of a customer as a much more encompassing measure that accommodates future purchase behavior. This measure further subsumes the value of word-of-mouth advertising: referrals. The authors cited the instance of Domino's Pizza, which calculated the lifetime value of a loyal pizza buyer to be $4,000 in revenue. A more dramatic example involved a Texas Cadillac dealership that estimated the lifetime value of a loyal customer to be $332,000 in new vehicles and service. Clearly, the lifetime value of a customer is simply the sum of the value (either in terms of revenue or profit) of the relationship across its lifetime.

A variety of approaches to modeling the relationship among customer satisfaction, employee satisfaction, and profitability are possible. Companies without access to profitability measures at the customer level must strive to develop a longitudinal database that measures both customer satisfaction and profitability simultaneously monthly or quarterly. With a sufficient number of observations, they may attempt to relate the measures statistically using time series analysis. Other companies that may not have profitability data available at the customer level may be able to conduct cross-sectional analyses by measuring customer and employee satisfaction at the organization subunit (e.g., strategic business unit) level. Assuming a sufficient number of subunits, satisfaction—both internal and external—can be linked with financial performance variables. Finally, some organizations enjoy the ability to calculate measures of performance at the individual customer level. For these companies typically a wealth of information can be mined. For banks, this includes a variety of demographic and product ownership variables. Using one of these approaches, virtually any organization can attempt to link internal and external satisfaction with financial performance data.

CROSS-SECTIONAL LINKAGE TECHNIQUES

As illustrated in Figure 7.2, cross-sectional linkage analysis may involve direct or indirect relationships. Our discussion is limited to direct linkage analysis because this is an area of great interest to customer satisfaction program managers. Direct linkage analysis provides compelling evidence with respect to the effects of customer satisfaction on business outcome measures. Of course, it is important to concede at the outset that the cross-sectional analyses presented in this section do not provide unequivocal evidence of causality. With cross-sectional data, there is no temporal ordering—a fundamental requirement for demonstrating that one construct causes another.

The general dependence model framework for establishing cross-sectional linkage analysis typically involves a series of independent variables that reflect service and product quality issues. The dependent measure may be any appropriate business outcome variable, depending on the unit of analysis. Thus, within the retail financial services industry, in which the unit of analysis could be an individual (or household), the dependent measure is likely to be profitability. Again, the unit of analysis and industry dictate the nature of the outcome variable. As noted earlier, appropriate dependent financial metrics include revenue, profitability, share of wallet, and market share.

Dependence models such as multiple regression analysis and structural equation modeling *imply* causality. The causal relationship is typically intuitive, but not proven. Keep in mind that these types of models leverage cross-sectional covariance and, in the absence of temporal ordering, can only confirm the data are consistent with the hypothesized cause-and-effect relationship(s). Of the two types of dependence models referenced earlier, structural equation modeling (SEM) provides a platform for the most interesting cross-sectional linkage analysis. Most of the major statistical packages have modules for conducting this type of analysis. The most important aspect of SEM is that it is a *confirmatory* approach to data analysis. Unlike exploratory data analysis, confirmatory analytic techniques require the researcher to specify a priori the hypothesized causal links. The model is then tested and based on a variety of fit statistics; the model is either accepted as consistent with the relationships in the data or discarded. This involves an explicit hypothesis test regarding the consistency between the hypothesized model and the data. For a more substantive, mathematical treatment of the subject, see Bollen (1989). A less technically demanding discussion may be found in Schumacker and Lomax (1996).

In the typical SEM model there are multiple dependent measures. This is quite different from multiple regression models in which a single outcome measure (y) is presumed to depend on a series of predictor variables. With multiple dependent measures, a causal chain may be developed and tested mathematically. As a result, it is possible to hypothesize that service quality satisfaction (x_1) and product quality satisfaction (x_2) affect overall customer satisfaction (y_1), which in turn affects profitability (y_2). Mathematically, this relationship involves two regression equations, one for each dependent measure.

Figure 7.3 illustrates the type of causal modeling that can be conducted using the SEM modules in any of the advanced statistical analysis packages available today. The conceptual relationship depicted in the figure suggests that technical support satisfaction (x_1), product quality satisfaction (x_2), and sales service satisfaction (x_3) jointly affect overall satisfaction (y_1), which, in turn, affects the second dependent measure (y_2), profitability.

Causality is assumed to flow from the left of the figure to the right. Thus an arrow links each of the three predictors to the first dependent measure. Further, there are paths from product quality satisfaction to profitability and from overall satisfaction to profitability. The former path involves direct effect on the second dependent measure and is one of the most desirable aspects of path analytic modeling. That is, the predictor variables are not constrained to affect the second dependent measure indirectly or through overall satisfaction. Any of the predictor variables may affect the final dependent measure either indirectly (through overall satisfaction) or directly, as illustrated by the path from product quality to profitability.

Because the causal model shown in Figure 7.3 contains two dependent variables, two linear equations summarize the relationships. These are summarized in Equations 7.1 and 7.2:

$$y_1 = 0.31x_1 + 0.42x_2 + 0.50x_3 \qquad (7.1)$$

$$y_2 = 0.14y_1 + 0.26x_2 \qquad (7.2)$$

To researchers with no exposure to causal modeling, the most disconcerting aspect of these equations is the role of y_1 as both dependent (Equation 7.1) and predictor (Equation 7.2) variable. Indeed, overall satisfaction depends on technical support satisfaction, product quality satisfaction, and sales service satisfaction. Overall satisfaction is a predictor of profitability, however. As a result, it is present as the dependent measure in the first equation and a predictor variable in the second equation.

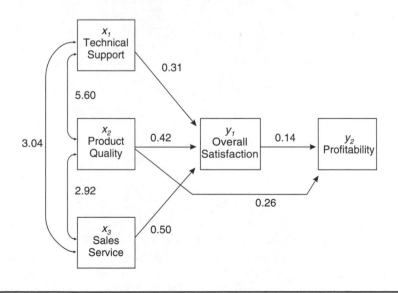

Figure 7.3   Path analysis model with two dependent measures.

Interestingly, each equation is associated with a separate R^2 statistic. Generally, researchers encounter very high R^2 statistics associated with the former equation, which relates psychometric predictors to a psychometric outcome variable (overall satisfaction). Significantly less efficacious models are typically encountered in the second equation. That is, it is difficult to account for a substantive proportion of the variance in a financial dependent measure using psychometric predictors. It is uncommon to encounter R^2 values much greater than 0.20 when financial variables depend on customer feedback data. The most problematic aspect of modeling financial outcome variables is that many extraneous, uncontrollable factors influence variation. These range from economic trends such as changes in the prime rate to more idiosyncratic and difficult-to-control issues such as accounting procedures.

Despite yielding R^2 statistics that would ordinarily be considered abysmal with psychometric data, the ability to affect even 20% of the variation in profitability by manipulating service and product quality issues is noteworthy. Models similar to Figure 7.3 can be very beneficial in directing management attention to the causal sequence that yields the greatest profitability. In particular, service or product issues that have both indirect (i.e., exerted through an intermediate variable like overall customer satisfaction) and direct effects on business outcomes should be of great interest.

LONGITUDINAL LINKAGE TECHNIQUES

Linkage analysis aimed at establishing a more defensible direct relationship between customer satisfaction and profitability often leverages a longitudinal design. The temporal ordering often encountered in longitudinal linkage analyses makes arguments that satisfaction *causes* desirable business outcomes more compelling. For example, consider a group of customers whose satisfaction drops from time t_1 to time t_2 and another group whose satisfaction increases over this same period. If the profitability of the former group is lower at time t_2 and the second group is associated with an increase in this outcome measure, a quite convincing case can be made for the financial effects of satisfaction.

Table 7.1 summarizes a relatively simple approach to longitudinal analysis. In this case, two time periods (t_1 and t_2) are involved. A relationship satisfaction survey was administered at each time period roughly six months apart. The rows of the table relate to changes in satisfaction among consumers who have been categorized based on their satisfaction level. For example, the first row in Table 7.1 represents the group of respondents who were characterized by low levels of satisfaction at time t_1 and low levels of satisfaction at time t_2. In other words, over the course of the six months between the two measurements, the satisfaction levels of these customers did not change. In fact, this is true for the first three rows of the table. In each case, the t_1 satisfaction level is equivalent to the t_2 satisfaction level.

The second block of rows in Table 7.1 represents those customers who experienced increases in satisfaction over the two measurement periods. Finally, the last three rows of the table relate to customers whose satisfaction in time t_1 was higher than in time t_2. These customers experienced decreases in satisfaction over the study period. Collectively, the table depicts three broad categories of customers: those whose satisfaction did not change, those for whom satisfaction increased, and customers who experienced declines in satisfaction over the six-month period. Three distinct cases within each of these categories yield nine specific conditions (e.g., low -> low).

The nine unique conditions reflected in Table 7.1 are depicted as a matrix form in Figure 7.4. The top-left cell, for example, represents the group for whom satisfaction was low in both measurements. Conversely, the bottom-right cell reflects customers whose satisfaction was high in both measurements. The diagonal cells, therefore, indicate no change in satisfaction from time t_1 to time t_2. The off-diagonal elements of the matrix presented in Figure 7.4 indicate changes in satisfaction over the two study periods. The three upper off-diagonal cells depict increases in satisfaction, whereas the three lower off-diagonal cells reference the customers whose satisfaction dropped.

The arrows included in each cell represent the average change in profitability among the customers in each cell. Customers in the upper-left cell (low -> low) were characterized by decreased profitability over the two periods. The bottom left cell (high -> low) indicates that for this group of customers who experienced a very large drop in satisfaction there was a substantial dip in average profitability. The converse situation is reflected

Table 7.1 Longitudinal differences in satisfaction.

Time t_1	Time t_2	Difference
Low	Low	No change in satisfaction
Medium	Medium	
High	High	
Low	Medium	Increase in satisfaction
Low	High	
Medium	High	
Medium	Low	Decrease in satisfaction
High	Medium	
High	Low	

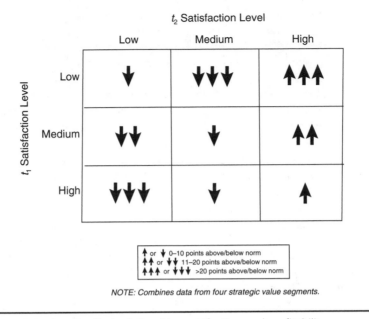

Figure 7.4 Longitudinal relationship: satisfaction and profitability.

in the upper-right cell (low -> high). In this case, customers whose satisfaction greatly increased were also associated with significant increases in profitability.

The study results illustrated in Figure 7.4 provide compelling evidence that a relationship between *changes* in satisfaction and *changes* in profitability may exist. This type of relationship is more robust and defensible than a purely cross-sectional analysis. The reason for this is that in a cross-sectional design we are limited to inferences related to covariance. For example, dissatisfied customers also are less profitable possibly because of some third, extraneous variable. We cannot reasonably conclude they are less profitable *because* they are dissatisfied. The longitudinal example presented in Figure 7.4 does not unequivocally establish causality, of course. Although temporal ordering has been introduced to the design, we did not control for many other confounding variables that could be responsible for the differences in profitability. Nonetheless, the results presented in Figure 7.4 are quite strong and should be convincing to most managers.

SUMMARY

Linkage analysis is one of the final frontiers of customer satisfaction and loyalty research. Relating psychometric data to financial outcome data in a causal framework is problematic from a variety of perspectives. Numerous sources of error attenuate the relationship and measurement—particularly with respect to financial variables—is often subject to uncontrollable forces such as macroeconomic conditions.

The growing applied and academic body of experience in linkage analysis strongly confirms a significant link between customer satisfaction and business outcomes. The ultimate linkage analysis effort would span three core data types: engineering performance, customer feedback, and business outcomes. If objective product performance data can be linked to customer feedback, which, in turn, is used to predict business outcomes, a complete sequence may be established. Thus changes in product performance variance can be related through satisfaction to business outcomes. In this manner, the financial outcomes of product enhancements can be gauged. This approach is discussed at length in Chapter 9.

8

Managing Global
CSM Projects

INTRODUCTION

This chapter focuses on management and analysis associated with global customer satisfaction research programs. Program management, reporting, survey translations, cultural biases, data collection, and a variety of other considerations make global customer satisfaction studies very challenging. One of the most troublesome issues involves comparing psychometric data—particularly customer satisfaction data—across countries.

Advances in information technology and international distribution systems, universally accepted quality standards, political shifts in Asia and Europe, and a host of other factors such as the Internet have contributed to an increasingly global economy. The emergence of a few truly global brands like Coca-Cola, Nike, or McDonald's is noteworthy. Not withstanding numerous cultural gaffes and translation difficulties over the years, the ability to market products internationally has never been stronger.

Failure to accommodate language and cultural differences has resulted in humorous misunderstandings such as that encountered by the Milk Processor Board's "Got Milk?" campaign (Mahajan and Wind, 2002:40). The campaign's well-known rhetorical question was translated for Spanish audiences and became "Are You Lactating?" The list of examples depicting how U.S. companies failed to accommodate cultural and language differences seems endless.

Global marketing efforts often require research that crosses national and cultural boundaries. Global marketing research results must often be reported at a country level. In the case of particularly large or strategically important countries, results may be further driven down to the regional level. Pricing models, segmentation studies, product optimization, market potential studies, customer satisfaction and loyalty programs, brand image assessments, usage and awareness studies, and other marketing research efforts often must produce psychometric data that will facilitate strategic implementation at the country and, ultimately, global level.

Global customer satisfaction programs are of special concern for a variety of reasons. In particular, they involve inferences concerning service or product quality performance levels based on psychometric data. The collection and measurement of customer feedback data are sources of potential bias and error that may affect inferences concerning performance. As a result, special attention to these areas is warranted.

Because psychometric data are subject to numerous measurement and collection biases, it may be prudent to supplement customer feedback with objective data involving, for example, technical support calls, complaints, or problems. In this regard, actual business performance must be considered in conjunction with customer feedback data in a global satisfaction study. If satisfaction levels in a particular country are lower than the regional norm but sales and profitability are quickly escalating, the program manager should initially consider the validity of the psychometric data. If no substantive cultural or data collection biases appear to be affecting the service or product quality feedback data, this situation could foretell customer retention problems. The bottom line is that in large-scale global customer satisfaction programs, it is prudent to compare quality feedback data with objective performance measures such as sales, profit, and market share. The combined data will yield better insight into the idiosyncratic needs of each country in the program.

GLOBAL PROGRAM MANAGEMENT

One of the first questions a company must address following the decision to conduct a global customer satisfaction study is whether to engage a consultant or use in-house resources. In either case, project management should be considered in terms of the five main project stages depicted in Figure 8.1. These involve the initial project definition phase, followed by continuous cycling through data collection, analysis, reporting, and implementation.

The duration of each iteration shown in Figure 8.1 is one of the key project parameters established in the project definition stage. Cycle length may be determined by a number of factors including costs and implementation. Monthly reporting, for example, is considerably more expensive than a quarterly program. Further, few organizations can react to customer feedback data this quickly. Most companies simply cannot evaluate monthly feedback data and implement organizational changes on a monthly basis. Exceptions may involve systems that can be modified centrally with ease, such as call center scripts and websites.

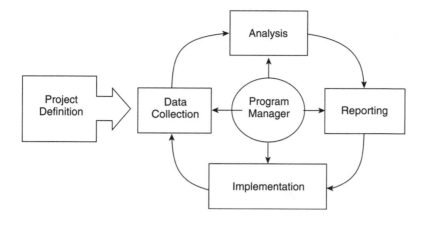

Figure 8.1 Primary phases of global customer satisfaction projects.

Vavra (1997:444–46) reviews the administration of global projects in terms of three architectures: centralized, coordinated, and decentralized. The author concludes that although centralized management provides the most control over a variety of issues (including instrument development, fielding, and reporting), it may also introduce certain ethnocentric biases and may potentially alienate local operating units. These concerns were also expressed by Naumann and Giel (1995:343). Coordinated management, in contrast, involves cooperation between a central corporate department and an objective third-party consulting organization. This is preferable to the centralized approach, Vavra argues, because the consulting organization introduces elements of objectivity and expertise. Nonetheless, this approach may further exacerbate relationships with local operating units, who perceive the consulting organization as an unwanted outsider. The ideal structure, according to Vavra, is decentralized. In this approach, the corporate client establishes the objectives and reporting requirements while a consulting organization manages a decentralized fielding program that solicits significant input from local operating units. This approach creates a sense of ownership among operating unit managers and (hopefully) integrates corporate and consultant design and content ideas. Despite these advantages, Naumann and Giel (1995:344) warned that this is a more expensive tack than a centralized architecture.

Table 8.1 presents a checklist for global customer satisfaction studies. Although relatively exhaustive, keep in mind that this list is restricted to relatively high-level tasks. There are myriad considerations within each of the items in the list—far too many to describe and discuss adequately in a

I. Project definition
  1. Scope and parameters
    • Region/country rollup structure
    • Subregion definition
    • Desired confidence level/country
    • Key tracking metrics: satisfaction vs. loyalty
    • Relationship or transaction focus
    • Customer sample: availability and format consistency
  2. Instrument development
    • Qualitative review
    • Item generation
    • Scale selection
    • Logic structure
    • Cultural bias assessment
    • Translations (bidirectional)
    • Field reviews
  3. Data collection methodology
    • Frequency and duration
    • Quotas and subquotas
    • Mail program
      —Format: scanner technology
      —Frequency and duration
      —Printing: regional vs. central
      —Address data file format
      —Outbound facility
      —Inbound facility
      —Prenotification postcard
      —Cover letter with signature
      —Respondent incentive
    • Telephone program
      —CATI program(s)
      —Phone number format
      —Language character sets
      —Midprogram language change
      —Respondent incentive

    • Internet program
      —Programming platform
      —Database link
      —Customer e-mail list
      —E-mail solicitation
      —Security and access issues
  4. Data processing
    • Data dictionary
    • Unique survey ID numbering system
    • Encryption/security/data exchange
    • Backups and archiving system
    • Record suppression
    • Data cleaning
  5. Reporting definition
    • Aggregation structure
    • Key reporting metrics
    • Weighting
    • Key-driver status indicator
    • Comparisons to norms
    • Significance testing/level
    • Graphics and color
    • Web-based reporting
    • Report generation programming
      —Application development language
      —Report format/layout
      —Testing/QA procedures
      —Subroutine library
  6. Implementation issues
    • Performance norms
    • Statistical testing
    • Bonus system payout
    • Best practices database
II. Data collection
  1. Sample data processing
    • Suppression rules
    • Randomization procedure
    • Replicate generation and size

continued

Figure 8.2 Global customer satisfaction project management checklist.

continued

2. CATI parameters
   - Suppression rules
   - Number attempts
   - Callback procedures
   - Customer problem resolution
   - Legitimacy contact phone number

3. Mail parameters
   - Prenotification postcard
   - Country coding on survey
   - Monetary incentive
   - Suppression rules
   - Fielding close date—late arrival disposition
   - Scanning procedures—OMR and OCR
   - Comment transcription/coding
   - Customer problem resolution

4. Internet parameters
   - E-mail solicitations
   - Unique password linked to org. unit
   - Respondent incentive system

II. Analysis and programming
   1. Data preparation
      - Minimum observations/unit
      - Data cleaning
      - Open-ended question codes
      - Weighting
   2. Univariate and bivariate analysis
      - Confidence level
      - Finite population correction
      - Significance testing
      - Item analysis: univariate EDA profile
   3. Multivariate analysis
      - Missing value imputation
      - Key driver derivation
      - Collinearity warnings
      - ANOVA: Key metrics/country
      - Cultural bias assessment

4. Report generation programs
   - Missing value imputation
   - QA comparison with statistical package
   - Rollup structure

IV. Reporting
   1. Quality assurance
      - Univariate check
      - Bivariate check
      - Key driver check
      - Pre- and postimputation match
   2. Rollup structure
      - Branch/store label changes
      - New/deleted units
      - Region/country changes
      - Rollup implications of unit changes
   3. Report distribution
      - Random QA checks
      - Web-based results
        - Security: multilevel report access
        - Password-user database
        - Access
      - Hardcopy results
        - Print quality check
        - Printing anomaly check
        - Backup copies
        - Provision for reprints
        - Shipping

V. Results implementation
   1. Incentive/Bonus pool system
      - Statistical testing confidence level
      - Bonus pool eligibility calculation
      - Communication and distribution
      - Recognize top performers

continued

2. Best practices database
   - Top performance deciles on key measures
   - Facilitate communication: top/bottom deciles
   - Six Sigma team
3. Process change implementation
   - Link to Six Sigma efforts
   - Corporate process experts identified
   - Country-specific process experts
   - Focus groups with customers
   - Key-driver patterns and customer verbatims
   - Customer advisory panel
   - Link customer and employee feedback data
   - Employee communication and training
4. Linkage research
   - Focus on behavioral linkage
   - Link customer, employee, and channel feedback
   - Relate feedback to business outcomes
   - Develop simulation or forecast models

single chapter. Different aspects of the checklist are considered throughout this book. For example, performance-reward programs and implementation issues comprise entire chapters.

DATA COLLECTION CONSIDERATIONS

One very appealing aspect of customer satisfaction research from a data collection perspective is that a relationship with the respondent already exists. As a result, response rates are generally high, telephone and address data are typically very accurate, and with the proper controls nonresponse bias can be minimized. These factors make the transition from domestic to international data collection somewhat less problematic. Still, international customer satisfaction programs face considerable hurdles when it comes to gathering feedback across multiple countries.

Just as in any domestic customer satisfaction program, international data collection can take several forms. The most common methodologies include mail, telephone, personal interviews, panels, and the Internet. The strengths and weaknesses of each are summarized in Table 8.2. One of the key issues driving data collection methodology involves the extent to which the relationship has been documented, thereby yielding unique contact information for each customer. Clearly, for some low-involvement products, it is difficult to gather detailed customer profile information. Even when warranty cards are used to collect customer information, low return rates yield a somewhat skewed perspective of the customer base.

Table 8.1 International data collection methodologies.

Methodology	Strengths	Weaknesses
Telephone survey	Flexible, allows clarification, fast turnaround, multiple attempts/callbacks, real-time statistics, global availability. Item rotation within battery.	Expensive, difficult to provide respondent incentive, low penetration in some countries, not appropriate in some cultures.
Mail survey	Inexpensive, can include incentive, cover letter possible, respondent can complete at any time.	Slow, inflexible, no clarification possible, unknown respondent, items in battery cannot be randomized without significant cost.
Personal interview	Control of interview situation, extensive clarification, probing, and explanation possible.	Expensive, slow, and time consuming.
Internet survey	Very inexpensive, fast, real-time statistics, sample and survey control, incentive systems can include Web-based prize fulfillment systems. Items rotation within battery possible.	Unknown respondent, lower control, response rate issues, Internet access/penetration may skew results.
Interactive voice response (IVR)	Very inexpensive, fast and efficient, multiple languages, digital comment recording, respondent incentives.	Limited length, no probing or clarification, unknown respondents, low penetration in some countries, rotary phones precluded.
Panel-based survey	Very effective when customers are unknown and purchase incidence is low.	Panel bias, limited respondent access.

TELEPHONE SURVEYS

Clearly, a successful international customer satisfaction program that employs a telephone data collection methodology must rely on an accurate database of customer phone numbers. Even though services exist that can provide telephone numbers based on address information in Europe and the United States, this process rarely exceeds a 60% accuracy rate, thereby introducing a source of systematic nonresponse bias. In Europe, it is necessary to engage a separate address-matching service for each country. This further complicates the process from a program and data management standpoint.

Although generally not an issue in North America or Western Europe, the penetration of telephones in consumer households should be considered for international projects that include data collection in Eastern Europe, Asia, South America, and Africa. Less affluent households in these areas may not have telephones in their homes or telephone service may be erratic.

In either case, these conditions may lead to situations in which certain customers are systematically excluded from the sample. Of course, this rarely is a consideration in business-to-business studies. However, in some Asian countries, executive interviews must be conducted in person.

Assuming telephone data collection is appropriate, it may be necessary to manage multiple data collection facilities. In a perfect world, all telephone interviewing would be conducted from a single location. Unfortunately, the reality is that for a large-scale program spanning three or more continents, data collection must often be managed from key cities with a rich source of multilingual interviewers. Toronto is a reasonable choice for North America because Spanish, French, and Asian language interviewers are widely available. Similarly, London is a logical data collection hub for Europe. In South America, a Brazilian operation will cover a large proportion of the population, but subcontractors may still be necessary to address pockets in Central America. Separate call centers should be used for Chinese, Japanese, and Korean data collection to ensure against language problems.

The concession that one must use multiple data collection centers for large-scale global customer satisfaction programs further exacerbates data management issues. When different computer-aided telephone interviewing (CATI) programs are used, a data processing step is required to ensure consistency. A *global* data dictionary is a necessity! However, just because a data dictionary exists does not mean it will be adhered to. The need for consistent data structures and definitions is discussed in greater detail later. This is a crucial issue; ignoring it can yield erroneous reporting results and jeopardize the entire program.

Telephone data collection, although expensive, clearly enjoys significant advantages over alternatives. It is flexible, permitting changes to survey structure during the fielding process. This methodology also lets researchers attempt to reach respondents over numerous calls, thereby reducing nonresponse bias. In the case of very affluent consumers or difficult-to-reach business respondents, it is sometimes helpful to call from outside the respondent's continent. For example, certain respondents in the United States and Canada are more likely to participate in a survey when the call is from London. The novelty factor and implied importance of an overseas call lead to lower refusal rates. Enhanced call productivity offsets the marginal cost of the international (versus domestic) telephone call. The net result is less nonresponse bias. As international calling costs continue to drop, this tactic is being considered more frequently.

MAIL SURVEYS

Mail surveys are attractive from a cost standpoint. The mail packet can include a monetary incentive intended to increase response rates. Mail programs in the

United States are quite predictable in terms of delivery and return times, but international studies are more vexing. The mail systems in some countries are not very efficient, and the result can be delivery delays that may exceed several weeks. Clearly, this is not a desirable outcome for a tracking study involving a scheduled mail-out every quarter.

As in the case of telephone data collection, a regional approach may be appropriate. That is, centralized mailing facilities in Hong Kong, Toronto, London, and São Paulo could effectively cover a large portion of an international customer satisfaction study's data collection needs. Business reply envelopes in which respondents send their completed surveys may go to a centralized collection point, or a separate postal box can be set up in each country. Although the latter may appear less costly initially because of domestic versus international postal rates, the cost and time required to set up return sites in each country is one downside. More importantly, perhaps, is the requirement to print separate business reply envelopes for each country. Some researchers have suggested that international mail programs that involve industrial customers will be more successful due to fewer postal problems (Vavra, 1997:435). Vavra suggested that mail delivery to business addresses may be more reliable than to residences.

For international tracking programs that rely on a quarterly reporting cycle, mail surveys may be problematic. Long delays in the data collection cycle can result in situations in which too few surveys are returned for a particular country or a lag effect in which surveys from one quarter are used in the next quarter's reporting. If managed properly, however, a mail-based, international tracking study can be a very cost-effective approach to global customer satisfaction measurement and reporting.

PERSONAL INTERVIEWS

In some cultures, personal interviews are requisite. This may be due to a lack of reliable telecommunication infrastructure or cultural norms. In Asia, for example, interviews in a business-to-business context must be conducted face to face. In some countries, the relatively low incidence of home telephones, attractive labor rates, and high population density makes personal interviews a logical choice. Its primary advantage is that the interviewer can probe, clarify, assist, and facilitate during the survey process. A high level of rapport develops between the interviewer and respondent, and, as a result, it may be possible to gather more insightful or otherwise inaccessible attitudinal data.

When personal interviews are used, it is not necessary to completely concede national (or other) projections. If random sampling techniques are employed in which, for example, every nth household is interviewed, the types of systematic bias associated with available samples can be largely avoided. When interviewers are permitted to choose respondents in a "mall intercept" fashion, a wide variety of error sources are introduced. Respondents who appear more approachable, educated, or affluent will likely be targeted at a disproportionate rate by interviewers who are not guided by a randomized sampling plan.

Computer-aided personal interviewing (CAPI) combines the benefits of CATI telephone interviewing and the personal interviewing channel. In this scenario, the interviewer is provided with a small laptop computer containing the programmed survey. Data are entered directly into the computer as the survey proceeds. The most sophisticated CAPI systems make real-time database updates possible so researchers may access and review the data as the fielding progresses. This allows programming errors to be identified and corrected at any time during the interviewing process.

THE INTERNET

The Internet has emerged as a major player in terms of customer satisfaction data collection. It is cost effective and permits a wide variety of interesting survey variations including photographs or even short movies. The typical Internet customer satisfaction survey begins with an e-mail solicitation in which customers are asked to visit a particular website using a unique key and password combination. Ilieva, Baron, and Healey (2002) provide an interesting review of online surveys in marketing research.

International customer satisfaction studies—particularly those involving business-to-business applications—may enjoy substantial savings over telephone administration. For example, one international study involving 20 countries and over 5000 business-to-business telephone interviews had fielding costs nearing $1 million. A migration to a Web survey platform yielded a slightly reduced response rate (47%) and a fielding budget reduction of nearly $800,000! Clearly, Web surveys in an international business-to-business context provide an extremely attractive alternative to traditional telephone data collection methodologies.

The downside of Internet surveys is that the customer's e-mail address must be known. In some product categories and particularly in business-to-business applications, this is not an issue. However, in cases where the most basic customer information is not present, the e-mail solicitation is obviously precluded. In such cases it may be possible to direct website visitors to a survey. Although this may yield completed surveys, the extent to which the sample is representative of the overall customer population is questionable.

Even companies that have recorded customer e-mail addresses are often surprised at the extent to which these data are inaccurate. It is not uncommon to have more than 30% of the e-mail solicitations bounce back due to bad addresses. Finally, the preceding points assume a very large proportion of the customer base has e-mail access. If this is not the case, a substantive source of bias may be introduced. If less than 60% of your customers have Internet access, this methodology may not be appropriate unless you can demonstrate empirically that Internet access is statistically unrelated to satisfaction levels. In consumer studies this is especially important because Internet access is related to socioeconomic status. As Internet household penetration across the globe increases, this will become less of a concern. Of course, in business-to-business applications, this is really a moot issue now.

When customer e-mail addresses are available and a high proportion of customers have e-mail access, an international Internet-based study is quite attractive from both cost and logistics perspectives. The flexibility of Internet surveys, fast turnaround time, ability to present graphics, and low cost are all compelling reasons to consider this methodology. Perhaps even more enticing is the ability to manage the international data collection effort from a central point, virtually anywhere in the world.

There are a variety of ways to ensure the successful execution of an Internet customer satisfaction study. For example, requiring the respondent to enter a long string of digits and characters as an identification number will reduce participation rates. E-mail solicitations containing an active link to the survey website should also include the respondent's unique identification number. Technically, this involves passing a parameter with your URL so a hot link can be established enabling automatic log-ins. This permits your program to link the identification number dynamically to the customer database and provide an individualized welcome screen containing the respondent's name or company information. In certain situations, of course, confidentiality and anonymity concerns outweigh this convenience.

The initial e-mail solicitation to participate in the online satisfaction survey must be recognized by the customer as originating from a legitimate source—either a consultant or the client organization. Because an estimated 30% or more of all e-mail in 2002 was *spam* (unsolicited advertising messages), the legitimate e-mail survey invitation must be recognized as such. One way to ensure that customers will identify the e-mail invitation is to announce to all customers that a survey is planned. This information can be communicated through a website, an insert in mailed invoices, or other vehicles already in place. Once the primary invitation has been sent, it is advantageous to check completed surveys and purge responders from the original e-mail list before sending a reminder e-mail. This process can be repeated three or four times until the fielding deadline approaches. Because the reminders are sent via e-mail, the cost of this process is minimal and the effects in terms of enhanced response rates can be substantial.

INTERACTIVE VOICE RESPONSE (IVR)

One of the newest approaches to global customer satisfaction data collection involves interactive voice response (IVR) technology. This system requires respondents to dial a toll-free telephone number and participate in a survey guided by a recorded or computerized voice. To indicate their levels of satisfaction and respond to other categorical questions, the telephone keypad is used to provide numeric feedback.

The primary advantages of IVR technology in global customer satisfaction programs are fiscal efficiency and simplicity. IVR interviews tend to be very inexpensive. They must, however, be short and not exceed five minutes or so. Even with this constraint, IVR surveys cost a small fraction of a telephone survey of similar length.

One area where IVR survey systems excel involves respondent incentive fulfillment. The typical IVR system is based on a sales register tape, programmed to make the survey offer to every *n*th customer. The receipt is printed with an invitation for the customer to call a toll-free number and participate in the survey and a coupon for a free gift. They are told that if they complete the survey they will be provided with a confirmation number to write in under the coupon, which they may then redeem at any participating branch. Fast-food organizations typically give respondents a free sandwich. Pizza franchises often provide a free pizza. Unlike other data collection methodologies (e.g., mail surveys), IVR technology is more efficient in that incentives are provided only to consumers who participate in the survey.

Of course, the IVR data collection platform is not without certain disadvantages. Among these are a lack of telephone access in some countries, the limited survey length, and inability to screen respondents for validity. Of course, rotary telephones are precluded because a keypad must be used to generate the appropriate signal. In some less well-developed countries, the need for touch-tone phones may systematically bias the results. The extent to which this affects global programs depends on the affluence of the respondent universe and the countries that will be included in the study. Further, it is presently not realistic to have a single, global toll-free number for all countries to call. The current global telecommunications picture requires establishing a separate toll-free number for each country in the study. Finally, 10-point scales may be somewhat problematic because there is no 10 on most phone keypads. Instead, either a range of 0 to 9 must be used, or alternatively, the 0 may be used in place of the 10.

PANELS

In situations characterized by customer anonymity and a low purchase incidence, panels may offer the most cost-effective way to gather feedback data. Many companies do not have the opportunity to gather customer information at the point of sale or through warranty card registration programs, and in these cases panel data can prove invaluable.

Both Internet and conventional mail panels are available in the United States and Europe. Consumer and business panels are available on both continents. Panel availability in other parts of the world is spotty and available on an individual country basis in many cases. There are specialized business panels focusing on, for example, executives in Asia, but it is not clear how representative or well-maintained these are. Other companies are feverishly working on the development of consumer panels in countries like China and Russia.

Because no single source for a worldwide panel exists, multiple sources must typically be used. Understandably, the companies that offer panels are quite protective of their respondent pools. In most cases, the panel company retains control of the data collection process, thereby protecting their valuable assets. This concession may be problematic for program managers who want more access to respondents. Actual data collection may rely on mail, telephone, or Internet methodologies.

Methodological concerns involving participant recruitment, panel maintenance, and attrition rates are largely overshadowed by the benefits afforded in situations characterized by low incidence and customer anonymity. Nevertheless, it would be judicious to understand the panel's design, maintenance, and recruitment methodologies thoroughly in order to anticipate possible biases.

In certain cases, multiple methodologies must be used for data collection in international customer satisfaction programs. As noted earlier, in some business-to-business situations it is necessary to conduct in-person interviews. Clearly, limiting the number of data collection methodologies used in a single study would be prudent. The measurement effect of multiple methodologies is of concern when comparing customer satisfaction scores across countries or regions. If, for example, personal interviews are used in Japan and telephone interviews are used in other countries, one could reasonably argue that differences in scores are a likely artifact of using disparate data collection methodologies. This further compounds a related issue involving the effects of cultural bias on survey data. The only way to sidestep this issue is to make comparisons within countries to a best-in-class normative score or to only compare countries with similar data collection methodologies within the same world region. These issues are discussed in greater detail later in this chapter when the psychometric effects of cultural bias are considered.

INSTRUMENT DESIGN

Sources of variation in customer satisfaction scores in international studies include data collection methodology, cultural bias, and, of course, actual service or product quality differences. Instrument design and content should not represent additional sources of variation. Indeed, every effort should be made to ensure the same *core content* is present in all countries and basic structural and measurement characteristics are consistent globally.

The most important instrument design considerations for international customer satisfaction studies involve scaling, core content, nesting structure, and the placement of critical dependent measures. These issues are not unique to international studies, of course, and should be considered when embarking on domestic projects that span multiple organizational strata as well.

One objective of global customer satisfaction programs is to compare service and product quality feedback at a regional or country level. Based on this performance data, a number of management systems may be affected. For example, country or regional managers may participate in incentive or bonus systems. The data may also help shape service or product quality strategies. When units within an organization will be compared based on service or product quality feedback, the criteria they are contrasted across must be completely parallel. In short, a set of common attributes should be administered to respondents in all countries. Although there may be a need to accommodate a set of unique questions to address the idiosyncratic market dynamics of each country, there must be a set of core attributes administered to all respondents worldwide.

At the risk of stating the obvious, the same scaling must be used throughout the program. Permitting individual country managers to dictate the type of scale used in their survey is a recipe for disaster if comparisons between countries or regions will be of interest. Clearly, if a seven-point anchored scale is selected, it should be used in every country without exception. Comparing performance levels across disparate scales is highly problematic and should be avoided at all costs.

Every effort should be made to ensure that endpoint anchor translations are equivalent. Because endpoint labels tend to be extremes such as Very Satisfied and Very Dissatisfied or Poor and Superior, translations generally do not pose a serious problem. However, fully anchored scales in which each point value has a label may be more troublesome. Fully anchored scales usually involve four or five points, with a neutral midpoint in the case of the latter. Thus ensuring the labels are consistent across multiple languages can be more challenging. There are good reasons to avoid fully anchored scales, of course. With fewer points, these scales tend to yield less variance and, as a result, less efficacious key-driver models. Further, no compelling evidence suggests that in customer satisfaction research fully anchored four- or five-point scales produce more desirable (i.e., normal) distributions.

One issue that emerges in European surveys involves the direction of the satisfaction scale. In many European countries good grades are associated with low numbers. In North America, the opposite is true. A 4.0 is a perfect grade point average in the United States, for example. In many European customer satisfaction studies, lower scale numbers are associated with high levels of satisfaction and the highest point on the scale reflects the lowest level of satisfaction. Some European companies require that this direction change be maintained in North American customer satisfaction studies. This is not a particularly troublesome scaling issue, but program managers should be aware that changing scale direction across countries or continents is a potential problem from both logistic and statistical standpoints. The bottom line is that every effort should be made to use the same scale in the same fashion in every country whenever possible.

Assuming parallel core content and scaling, a further consideration in global customer satisfaction instruments involves the placement of dependent measures. In short, should the overall satisfaction question be placed at the beginning or end of the survey? There are differing opinions concerning this issue. Some argue that placing the dependent measures at the beginning of survey yields a more realistic top of mind response. Others maintain that overall satisfaction should be placed at the end of the survey because this permits the respondent to consider a variety of specific service and product quality issues before providing a summary evaluation. The former approach likely is more appropriate for low-involvement goods. Placement of the dependent measure at the end of the survey should be reserved for higher involvement products and services. Of course, it is imperative that the same dependent variable placement—whether in the front or end of the survey—be used globally.

In many consumer satisfaction surveys, a limited amount of demographic and profile information is collected at the end of the interview. Measures of socioeconomic status are often used as a means to disaggregate the data. In global studies, capturing data relating to household income, home value, and other measures of affluence can be more problematic. Respondents in some cultures are averse to providing this type of information. In Russia, for example, respondent affluence is inferred based on a series of questions relating to product ownership and shopping habits. When reporting data based on these types of demographics, remember that definitions of affluence differ tremendously around the world. A $800 monthly household income in the United States is near the poverty level, but it is considered a reflection of prosperity in many countries.

Another issue affecting instrument content involves the *scope creep phenomenon,* which occurs when the customer satisfaction instrument grows to include other agendas such as brand awareness, segmentation, product positioning, and pricing. In many cases, program managers must decide to do a thorough job on one front or a mediocre job on many fronts. Keep the survey focused on service or product quality feedback. Although it is tempting to address unrelated topics because the marginal cost of adding questions is low, the result may be an unfocused and excessively long survey. Respondent fatigue emerges after approximately 15 minutes and eventually yields less introspective answers.

An overriding concern in the instrument development process should be to minimize the number of biases that can affect customer feedback measurement. Particularly when your end goal is a comparison of satisfaction levels across regions, countries, or continents, strive to control as many sources of measurement error and bias as possible. Survey instrument design and content represents a *potential* source of error that is highly manageable.

THE DATA DICTIONARY

The importance of a data dictionary in global customer satisfaction projects cannot be overstated. A data dictionary represents a formal specification of data standards including the format and content of all variables considered in a given study. The data dictionary is critically important when multiple data collection points are used.

Table 8.3 presents a sample data dictionary for a global research project spanning Asia, Europe, and North America. The key components of this type of documentation involve the columns representing the variable names, values, missing response instructions, variable types, and additional comments with respect to discrepancies or exceptions. Without this type of documentation, a global research project may at worst be doomed to failure and at best plagued by inconsistencies, errors, and other seemingly intractable data problems.

The integral role played by the data dictionary makes it a critical aspect of any global (or domestic) customer satisfaction research program. Data from all areas should be forced to conform to the data standards documented in the data dictionary. If multiple file formats are being created in different countries, it may be beneficial to require an ASCII format that can be read and converted to a database (or other) format centrally.

Table 8.2 Sample data dictionary for global research project.

Question number on survey	Variable name	Question text	Values	Missing	Type	Discrepancies
101	Q101	What would you describe as the best characteristic of your new automated dispensing machine?	1. Its ability to dispense without coordinating phase interrupts. 2. The price-sensitivity ratio and digital torsion bars. 3. The ability to reduce phase shift error. 4. None **(Do not read)** 5. Not sure **(Do not read)**		Integer	Asked only on questionnaire for Japan.
102	Q102	Do you think that changes in the automated dispensing machine will affect your business?	1. Yes 2. No 3. Not sure **(Do not read)**	6	Integer	Asked only on questionnaire for Japan.
103	Q103	The United Nations is considering providing automated dispensing machines to countries in Asia. Do you feel this is equitable?	1. Yes 2. No 3. Not sure **(Do not read)**	3	Integer	Asked only on questionnaire for France.

continued

continued

Table 8.2 Sample data dictionary for global research project.

Question number on survey	Variable name	Question text	Values	Missing	Type	Discrepancies
104	Q104	If you were to recommend an automated dispensing machine to a colleague in another country, what one reason would you give him or her?	1. The machines work regardless of current type. 2. Dispensing works even in extreme temperatures. 3. Ability to phase shift according to GMT. 4. Multiple digital torsion bars. 5. Other **(please specify___)** 6. Not sure **(Do not read)** 7. Not sure **(Do not read)**		Integer	Asked only on questionnaire for France.
	Q104o_1 Q104o_2	Other Specify			2 variables, each String 72	Asked only on questionnaire for France.
105	Q105_1 Q105_2 Q105_3 Q105_4 Q105_5 Q105_6 Q105_7 Q105_8 Q105_9 Q105_10	If multiple phase shifting were possible in your current automated dispensing system, would you adopt it if the cost were less than the cost associated with leasing a Sigma-3 centroidal device? *(multiple variables specified here to capture all of the answers)*			10 variables, each String 72	Asked only on questionnaire for Germany.

continued

Table 8.2   Sample data dictionary for global research project.

Question number on survey	Variable name	Question text	Values	Missing	Type	Discrepancies
106	Q106	Some automated dispensing machine producers have considered developing a system of rigid, digital torsion exchange bars with heat dissipators. Do you agree with this approach to phase shift problems?	1. Yes 2. No **(skip to Q98)** 3. Not sure **(Do not read)**	5	Integer	Asked only on questionnaire for Germany.
107	Q107	Do you think that phase shifting will continue to be problematic in Arctic regions?	1. Yes 2. No 3. Not sure **(Do not read)**	4	Integer	Asked only on questionnaire for Germany.
45	Q45	Will the availability of digital spectroscopic ICR devices change how you purchase automated dispensing machines?	1. Yes 2. No **(Skip to 47)** 3. Not sure **(Do not read; skip to 47)**	3	Integer	
46	Q46	As you know, digital spectroscopic ICR devices permit automated dispensing machines to operate under −200° Celsius. Under what applications would you use the capability?	1. Axial radiant temperatures 2. Thermographic imaging 3. Subnuclear amalgamation 4. Hemophasic testing 5. Particle acceleration 6. Jet propulsion 7. Other 8. Not sure **(Do not read)**	8	Integer	

continued

Table 8.2 Sample data dictionary for global research project.

Question number on survey	Variable name	Question text	Values	Missing	Type	Discrepancies
47	Q47	Compared to your colleagues, are you living in better economic conditions now?	1. Yes 2. No 3. Not sure (**Do not read**)	3	Integer	
48	Q48	Do you expect your children to live in better economic conditions than you?	1. Yes 2. No 3. Not sure (**Do not read**)	3	Integer	
901	Q901	What is your age?	Valid range 1–110	111	Integer	
903	Q903	Which of the following best describes your highest level of education?	1. Less than high school graduate 2. High school graduate 3. Some college 4. College graduate 0. Refuse (**Do not read**)	0	Integer	
913	Q913	Which of the following best describes your occupation?	1. Managerial/Administrative 2. Medical 3. Professional/Technical 4. Sales 5. Research 6. Executive 7. Manufacturing/Production 8. Other (**please specify** _____) 9. Not sure (**Do not read**) 0. Refuse (**Do not read**)	0, 13	Integer	

continued

Table 8.2 Sample data dictionary for global research project.

Question number on survey	Variable name	Question text	Values	Missing	Type	Discrepancies
914	Q914	Which of the following best describes your marital status?	1. Married 2. Single, never married 3. Divorced/widowed/ separated 4. Not married/living together 5. Not sure/Refuse **(Do not read)**		Integer	
922	Q922	Gender	1. Male 2. Female		Integer	

PSYCHOMETRIC ISSUES: CULTURAL BIAS

In the typical customer satisfaction program conducted in North America, we assume there are no substantive cultural differences across strategic business units that affect our measurements. Increasingly, multinational corporations are requiring customer satisfaction programs to be conducted at a global level. In this case the strategic business unit is assumed to be a country or, in some cases, regions within countries.

It is likely that subtle cultural differences within countries affect customer satisfaction scoring. For example, we have encountered significant differences between rural and urban customers with respect to their overall satisfaction levels. That regionally based cultural differences may also exist is a distinct possibility despite the general assumption that the United States is a melting pot and culturally homogeneous.

Although it is questionable whether cultural differences within the United States affect customer or employee satisfaction results, a great deal of evidence suggests there are differences across countries. For multinationals interested in comparing performance levels across a global network of operations, cultural differences may make measuring and comparing customer satisfaction across countries somewhat problematic.

When a multinational corporation is interested in comparing how different country operations perform with respect to customer satisfaction, some interesting questions arise. In particular, it is unclear if differences in performance across countries are attributable to cultural variations or real differences regarding the extent to which managers in each country have satisfied their customers.

Note that cultural differences may affect customer satisfaction statistics in a variety of ways. In the simplest case, the summary reporting metric may be affected. For example, respondents from certain cultures may be more inclined to give positive satisfaction scores because it is less acceptable to express dissatisfaction. Of course, not only mean or percentage scores can be affected by cultural differences. The distribution of scores may also be affected. In cultures that tend to provide positive scores because of the social desirability of doing so, distributions may be even more skewed than normal. As a result there may also be a concomitant decrease in variance around the mean score.

It is also possible for cultural differences to affect key-driver analyses. This would require us to consider the possibility that covariance structures may be affected by cultural differences across respondent groups. Focusing exclusively on the predictor side of the equation, we must consider the possibility that the correlation matrices of customer satisfaction items differ substantively across two or more countries. For example, the null hypothesis would be that the correlation matrix in one country is equivalent to all of the others. Covariance structure analysis provides a platform for conducting this type of test.

Most research related to how cultural differences affect customer and employee satisfaction measurement programs has focused on how to modify simple reporting metrics like the mean or top-two box score to reflect these differences. Interesting theoretical perspectives are offered by Van de Vijver and Poortinga (1982), England and Harpaz (1983), McCauley and Colberg (1983), and Bhalla and Lin (1987). Several approaches to developing cultural bias adjustments are possible. Two relatively unsophisticated approaches involve regional comparisons and normative indexing.

The regional comparison approach to the cultural differences problem involves simply constraining reporting to a given geographic region. Thus Denmark might be compared only with other Scandinavian countries and Brazil compared only to other countries in Latin America. The most important potential problem with this approach is that there may still be cultural differences among the countries in a given region.

A more refined approach to adjusting for bias attributable to cultural differences involves normative indexing. This approach can take two forms. First, a corporate norm can be established for a given country. Performance scores can then be expressed as values relative to the country or regional norm. This technique helps managers compare their performance levels to the country standard, but it does little to facilitate intercountry comparisons. Another approach to the normative indexing technique is to assess performance relative to another multinational brand or corporation's performance. For example, Coca-Cola could gauge its performance in terms of distribution, access, price, and other variables against Pepsi, its main competitor. Similarly, an auto manufacturer in Europe might choose to use the performance of Mercedes as a benchmark.

A more sophisticated approach to assessing cultural bias was developed by Crosby (1992). Crosby's approach presumed there was a fixed cultural bias error term for every country. This could be used to adjust scores for each country in the following manner:

$$PQ_o = f(PP - EXP) + RB_j + e$$

where

$$PQ_o = \text{Observed rating}$$
$$PP - EXP = \text{Perceived performance minus expected performance}$$
$$RB_j = \text{Response bias common to a specific country}$$
$$e = \text{Random error}$$

Although this seems straightforward enough, the method used to determine RB_j is more complicated. The adjustment factor is developed using a standard set of questions that represent different levels of performance in a variety of settings. These range from a theater performance to airline travel delays:

> "There is one awkward pause in a professional theater performance as an actor tries to recall his lines."

> "An astronomer in your country discovers a star."

> "Your arrival by air on a one-hour flight is delayed by 15 minutes."

> "A supplier averages 10 minutes late for most meetings."

Responses to a set of 30 day-to-day occurrence items like these are used to develop a unique adjustment factor for every country in a study. The adjustment factors are calculated using the grand mean across all 30 questions for each country. A global mean is then calculated using the responses for all the countries combined. Next, one country is chosen as a benchmark against which all other countries will be compared. For a U.S. multinational, the United States would typically be selected as the benchmark. Following the selection of a benchmark, each country's mean is then subtracted from the global mean to calculate the individual country adjustment factors. These are then applied to the actual performance scores.

Crosby's approach to developing cultural bias adjustment factors is based on certain fundamental assumptions. Among these are that respondents in a country are more likely to use multipoint scales the same way as people in different countries. Perhaps more important is the assumption that the 30 items in the day-to-day occurrence battery are answered in a manner that is transportable to the specific case where product or service quality is being evaluated.

As globalization escalates there will be an increasingly compelling call for customer and employee satisfaction programs that include comparisons across countries. The development of techniques such as those introduced here will be important cornerstones for multinational service and product quality programs. The possibility that covariance structures are also affected by cultural bias is worth additional focus.

9

Linking Customer Feedback to Business Processes

INTRODUCTION

This chapter focuses on an often ignored area of customer satisfaction research. Indeed, organizational change aimed at enhancing customer feedback metrics is even often neglected by consultants, theoreticians, and academicians. The topics addressed here draw heavily on the derived importance discussion presented in Chapter 5. Thus an understanding of the fundamental implications of derived importance is critical to a good grasp of the managerial responses to these data.

Most marketing research consulting firms specialize in the measurement and analysis aspects of customer satisfaction data. The implicit assumption is that implementation issues are the domain of the department responsible for the customer satisfaction project: the market research department, service quality area, marketing department, or branch operations group. Consulting firms may also avoid implementation issues because they have little organizational clout or insight into many idiosyncratic political realities. Finally, the typical marketing research consultant's interest lies in measurement, analysis, and interpretation rather than management operations per se.

Figure 9.1 summarizes the service and product quality feedback program from a systems perspective. As shown, the system's core involves an iterative cycle of measurement, analysis, and implementation. Measurement and analysis issues have been the subjects of innumerable books, articles, conferences, and papers. Implementation topics, however, have not received as much attention. And yet ostensibly the implementation step is directly responsible for any increases in service or quality evaluations in subsequent iterations of the process. Without management action in response to the analysis and reporting phase, there is not a compelling reason to continue the process. In the absence of a managerial response to the customer feedback data, we should expect service or quality evaluations to

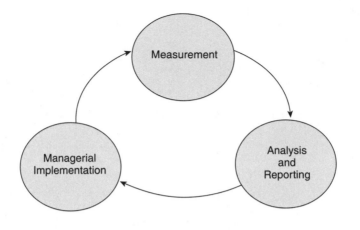

Figure 9.1 Iterative customer satisfaction system components.

remain unchanged or subject to other influences such as random quality variations.

Do not lose sight of the fact that the customer feedback system's superordinate objective is a sustained, long-term increase in a critical dependent measure such as overall satisfaction or loyalty. This chapter focuses on the customer feedback system's implementation phase, which is critically important to the overall system's fundamental objective. It involves linking customer feedback to business processes. These linkages typically rely on marginal resource allocation models, which are based on one of the multivariate dependence techniques described earlier. In short, derived importance results direct management decisions toward enhancing the business processes that will yield the biggest improvements in overall customer satisfaction. This in turn is presumed to affect profitability primarily through improved customer retention. The empirical linkage between customer satisfaction and business outcomes was discussed in Chapter 7.

The strength of derived importance models to management decision making aimed at improving customer satisfaction is virtually unmatched. Derived importance models reveal to managers the service or product quality issues that if improved will yield the biggest increase in overall satisfaction or any other critical dependent measure such as customer loyalty. By focusing on key-driver business processes, managers can maximize their impact on the dependent measure they are trying to maximize: overall customer satisfaction.

Keep in mind that derived importance models facilitate decisions concerning *marginal* resources. It would be a mistake, for example, to reallocate resources based on derived importance results because doing so would likely increase the perceived or actual quality variance. For example, consider a situation in which parking availability emerged as characterized by high levels of satisfaction and very low derived importance. Conversely, assume the company's invoicing system was determined to be a strong driver of overall satisfaction with relatively poor performance levels. In this extreme example, the manager might be tempted to rent half of the company's parking spaces to a neighboring business and use the proceeds to purchase a state-of-the-art computerized invoicing system. The results of this action would likely be recognized after the next data collection and analysis iteration. In short, satisfaction with accessibility would plummet while its derived importance would skyrocket, reflecting customers' frustration with the intense competition for a place to park their cars. Invoicing satisfaction might be very high and its derived importance considerably diminished following this action, but the manager is now faced with a completely new problem.

Thus management action based on derived importance modeling must recognize that *marginal resources* are the key to successful strategy deployment. Shuffling existing resources based on derived importance and performance levels yields undesirable results, as illustrated in our parking example. This rule is not unequivocal, however. Possibly the astute manager will recognize situations not nearly as egregious as the parking example. That is, there may be situations where reallocation may be successfully achieved without disturbing low-importance issues. Only managers with considerable operational familiarity will be able to assess accurately the extent to which a small portion of resources may be shifted from low-importance to high-importance quality issues. Each situation will be unique, of course, and reallocation should be approached very cautiously with the knowledge that excessive resource shifting may yield dysfunctional results.

KEY DRIVERS AND IMPROVEMENT COSTS

Figure 9.2 presents a typical performance-importance quadrant map and summarizes the strategic implications of positioning a service or product quality issue in each sector. Those appearing in the top half of the quadrant clearly are drivers that when addressed appropriately will yield the greatest improvements in a dependent measure like overall satisfaction or loyalty. The primary difference across items in the top half of the quadrant involves current performance level. The typical strategic quadrant map focuses management attention on low-performance drivers because these offer the greatest upside potential for increases in the dependent measure. This discussion focuses on an important aspect of *x*-axis position and the cost of moving a

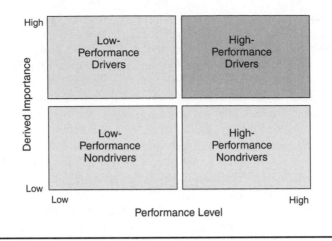

Figure 9.2 Performance-importance quadrant chart.

given service or product quality issue to the right—that is, increasing its performance level.

In an ideal world, improving various service and product quality issues would be inexpensive and it would cost the same to improve the scores of dissatisfied customers as moderately satisfied customers. Unfortunately, this is not realistic. The decision tree presented in Figure 9.3 summarizes the process most managers go through when considering results presented in a quadrant chart (performance-importance) format. First, driver status is identified in terms of vertical position. Next, current performance levels are considered in terms of *x*-axis position. Those with low levels of current performance are identified. Finally, the third step involves assessing the cost of improving performance levels for a given service or product quality issue. If it is excessive, the manager returns to the second step and identifies the issue with the next highest level of performance and subsequently assesses the cost of improving it.

When implementing key-driver strategies, two unique relationships should be considered. The first issue is explicitly included in Figure 9.3 (Step 3) and involves the *absolute cost* of improving current performance levels. The second area of concern involves the relationship between improvement cost and customer satisfaction. The linearity of the cost–performance relationship is of special concern here. The remainder of this section first addresses absolute cost issues and then turns toward a more advanced topic: nonlinear cost–performance functions.

Managers who have struggled with the realities of linking customer feedback analysis to business processes will appreciate the difficulties asso-

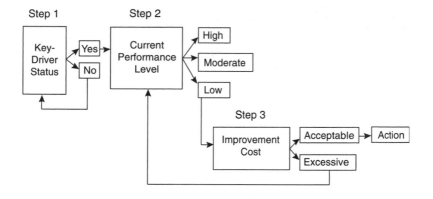

Figure 9.3   Key-driver implementation decision tree.

ciated with assessing the costs of improving performance levels. When addressing performance levels among key-driver issues, *consumer perceptions are reality*. In short, if an organization can enhance the extent to which it is *perceived* as delivering high levels of quality for a given service or product issue, this will be as effective as actually making physical or otherwise tangible process or product changes. The key is that driver status—technically covariance with the dependent variable—is based on the existence of variation in satisfaction for a given item. Without variance, there can be no covariance. Variance is attributable to actual or perceived variation in quality.

Consider the implications of the data presented in Table 9.1, which includes three predictor variables and two outcome measures (overall satisfaction and repurchase likelihood). These data are artificial and were constructed to demonstrate the effect of minimal variance on key-driver status. As shown, two of the three predictors have little response variation on the 10-point satisfaction scale. Of the 15 responses on the product delivery variable, only one entry is not an 8 on the 10-point scale. The second column reflects the entries for the next predictor variable—service quality. There is considerable variation in the responses for this variable and somewhat less for the technical support measure. Such is also the case for the third predictor variable and the primary dependent measure (overall satisfaction). The second dependent variable (likelihood to repurchase), however, is characterized by low variance. This could reflect a captive audience phenomenon in which even dissatisfied customers expect to repurchase.

The means and variances of the five variables are presented at the bottom of Table 9.1. The first predictor variable is characterized by very low variance; the second distribution is much less abnormal. The third predictor is interesting because the mean is very low and the variance is moderate. Of

Table 9.1 Implications of variance on driver status: raw sample data.

	Product delivery	Service quality	Technical support	Overall satisfaction	Repurchase likelihood
	8	4	3	6	9
	8	8	2	10	9
	9	5	3	7	9
	8	9	2	9	10
	8	10	3	10	9
	8	2	5	4	9
	8	4	3	5	10
	8	5	4	6	9
	8	9	3	8	9
	8	10	2	9	9
	8	8	6	7	9
	8	7	4	8	10
	8	7	3	8	9
	8	8	7	9	9
	8	2	3	4	9
Mean:	8.06	6.53	3.53	7.33	9.20
Variance:	0.07	7.24	2.10	3.92	0.17

Note: Responses based on a 10-point scale where 1=Poor and 10=Excellent.

the two dependent measures, the first (overall satisfaction) enjoys substantial variance around the mean, and the second dependent measure reflects a more unusual situation with very little variation.

Although the presence of variance in a measure does not *ensure* covariance with a dependent measure in a multiple regression context, its absence *in general* does tend to preclude meaningful covariance. This is evidenced by the correlations presented in Table 9.2. The lack of variance in the first predictor measure (product delivery) is associated with a very low correlation ($r = -0.04$) with overall satisfaction.

The point here is that *generally speaking,* variance must exist in perceived quality measures for key-driver status to occur. This variance can occur at the high end of the scale or the low end, and it may or may not be associated with *covariance* with a dependent measure such as overall satisfaction or loyalty. Given a moderate level of covariance between a predictor and dependent measure, a reduction in the former variable's variance will typically yield a concomitant drop in its key-driver status. Clearly, it is possible to have a survey item characterized by extremely limited variance covary strongly with another equally constrained variable. In this case, it would benefit the manager to know that the strong covariance is actually attributable to a very small proportion of the respondents. Two variables that have highly

Table 9.2   Implications of variance on driver status: correlations.

	Product delivery	Service quality	Technical support	Overall satisfaction	Repurchase likelihood
Product delivery	1.00				
Service quality	−0.16	1.00			
Technical support	−0.10	−0.13	1.00		
Overall satisfaction	−0.04	0.92	−0.19	1.00	
Repurchase likelihood	−0.13	0.02	−0.19	0.00	1.00

Note: $r_{ij} > 0.90$ is significant at 95%.

limited variance and yet still covary strongly should be scrutinized. Possibly a small group of individuals is responsible for this relationship.

Addressing various key drivers from a managerial perspective involves assessing the costs associated with changing customer quality *perceptions,* as just discussed. Satisfaction with certain service or product quality issues will be relatively inexpensive to increase; other issues may be cost prohibitive. The primary components of an exhaustive customer satisfaction survey instrument may include a diverse array of issues such as service quality, technical support, product quality, brand reputation, problem resolution, sales process, and others, depending on the product or service category.

Experience across a wide variety of high-involvement product categories such as financial services, telecommunications, and luxury consumer packaged goods suggests that *brand image* issues consistently emerge as strong drivers of satisfaction and loyalty. Brand perceptions involving social responsibility, environmental concern, prestige, and trustworthiness are not particularly dynamic, nor are they highly elastic with respect to communications efforts. In short, it could require tens of millions of dollars to elicit a significant change in brand image through traditional advertising communications.

Satisfaction with other service or product quality issues may be enhanced in a more cost-effective fashion. The absolute cost of affecting positive change in satisfaction across service and product quality issues varies by industry and organization, of course. The most flexibility is afforded organizations that collect customer feedback data at the lowest reporting unit level. For a large restaurant chain, this would involve customer satisfaction surveys administered at each restaurant. Banks typically collect customer satisfaction data at the branch level. When sufficient data is collected to permit development of key drivers at the unit level, management tactics can be tailored to the unique driver profile of each branch, restaurant, or outlet. This optimizes deployment tactics for each unit and may ensure the greatest return on investment, depending on the magnitude of resources necessary to collect and analyze data at the unit level.

Certain quality issues clearly should be addressed at the organizational subunit level, and others will be the domain of corporate interests. Brand image, for example, is typically an area ostensibly controlled by corporate advertising, public relations, and marketing communications. Similarly, pricing issues are usually manipulated centrally with little room for autonomous decisions by branches. In the case of consumer durables, product quality is often considered static across branch or unit networks. If product quality varies, it is most often attributable to the production facility. If there are multiple production facilities, an effort may be made to link product quality feedback metrics to specific production units. Often a simple F-test will suffice in determining if such a relationship exists. Only in cases where the product is *produced* at the subunit level should product quality feedback be linked to the subunit.

Service quality, accessibility, and other support issues involve subunit management. The implications of linking these issues to reward systems were discussed in greater detail in Chapter 4. Quality issues that can be directly addressed by branch or subunit managers have the greatest flexibility within measurement and reporting frameworks that involve collecting and reporting data at the subunit level. Although more costly, this type of customer satisfaction program facilitates driver-based implementation decisions at the unique subunit level and the corporate level. Thus corporate strategists can address issues such as pricing, product quality, and brand image while subunit managers focus on the drivers that emerge from analysis of data provided by their own customers. As a result, the types of analyses presented in the following discussion may be conducted at two distinct levels.

At this stage a third variable clearly has been introduced to the performance-importance quadrant framework that is the foundation of management implementation decisions. This third variable is cost, which can be measured at a ratio level such as dollars or in a relative fashion using interval measures. Less ideal is the use of ordinal (rank) metrics that simply order costs from lowest to highest. Figure 9.4 summarizes the four levels at which improvement cost may be measured. These same measurement levels are used to describe psychometric data obtained using survey instruments. Typically, for example, quality feedback data are collected at the interval level using 7-point or 10-point scales anchored with endpoints such as Poor to Excellent.

Data related to the cost of improving various service and product quality issues may be measured at any of the levels summarized in Figure 9.4. It is considerably more advantageous to consider costs in ratio-level terms. This means that for a given service or product quality issue, the cost of improving average satisfaction must be estimated in terms of *actual money*. Regardless of the measurement level, assigning costs to improvement efforts requires management insights and justification. Based on the earlier

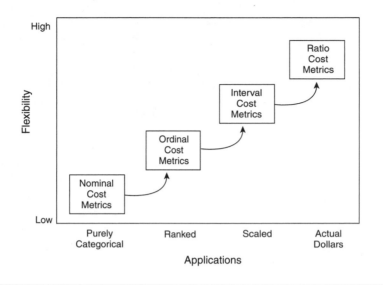

Figure 9.4 Improvement cost measurement levels.

discussion of corporate versus unit-level implementation issues, it should be evident that assigning costs to quality issues must consider these realities. That is, unit managers will have more insight into implementation costs associated with improving quality issues that they directly control. Conversely, corporate strategists will be more adept at gauging the cost implications of enhancing issues such as pricing or brand image.

Meaningfully assigning costs to service or product quality satisfaction is at best problematic and will almost always entail some form of estimate. This estimate may be based on actual experience or empirical grounds. In the former case, managers may rely on case studies, their own judgment, or colleagues to establish the costs associated with enhancing satisfaction. This approach may be more amenable to lower ordinal or interval level measurements. Often managers are hesitant to provide actual monetary costs associated with increasing customer satisfaction. Estimates in terms of rank orders or an interval-level scale, ranging, for example, from Very Inexpensive to Very Expensive may be perceived more favorably because these metrics are more easily defended.

A more desirable tack that is quite feasible in distributed organizations with many branches or subunits involves empirically based cost estimates. Consider a bank with 1000 individual branches, for example. Assume for the purposes of illustration that we are considering only one variable controllable by managers at the branch level: teller line waiting time. If customer satisfaction is measured at each branch on a semicontinuous basis, corporate-level researchers may provide branch managers with a simple statistical model relating teller expenditures and satisfaction with waiting time. The predictor variable (expenditures on teller salaries) must be scaled to the average daily number of customers visiting a branch. By scaling the teller expenditure variable in this manner, the effects of branch size are removed from the equation. That is, larger branches typically have larger teller salary expenditures than small branches. Our interest is in the relationship between the amount of money spent on tellers to satisfaction with waiting time. Clearly, it stands to reason that branches with higher teller-to-customer ratios will have shorter waiting times, all else being equal.

Based on the regression analysis implied, a quantitative relationship between teller expenditures and waiting time satisfaction can be established. The proportion of variance shared by the two variables (R^2) will provide insights into the strength of the relationship. If the results suggest that branches with higher staff-to-customer ratios have higher satisfaction levels, it is a simple matter to determine the cost of adding additional tellers. In short, the empirically based approach to establishing improvement costs may be the most valuable tool for managers. Unfortunately, branch managers typically must rely on corporate research departments to provide these types of insights. Nonetheless, armed with actual cost functions, managers can make meaningful judgments regarding the most cost-effective approaches to maximizing overall customer satisfaction or loyalty.

Based on an exercise that spans a variety of key-driver issues that may be controlled at the branch level, managers may evaluate their situation using three key variables: performance, importance, and improvement cost. Figure 9.5 integrates the importance-performance chart with a presumed

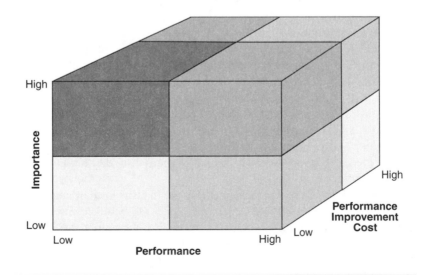

Figure 9.5 Strategic management cube.

improvement cost z-axis. This enhanced "strategic management cube" incorporates three characteristics of every service or product quality issue: performance, importance, and improvement cost. With respect to Figure 9.5, managers should focus their attentions on issues characterized by low importance, high performance, and low improvement costs. Note that the cube axes essentially subsume the second and third steps in the decision tree presented earlier in Figure 9.3.

IMPROVEMENT COST FUNCTIONS

One issue that deserves further elaboration involves the nature of the satisfaction-cost function. The most simplistic approach assumes that the cost of enhancing satisfaction scores is constant across the entire range of experiences. This implies it is equally costly to improve service or product regardless of current performance level. This simplifying assumption is typically used because the alternative to the constant cost function is more difficult to communicate to managers.

When establishing implementation priorities, consider the three variables that define the strategic management cube presented in Figure 9.5: performance, importance, and performance improvement cost. The latter typically is defined as a constant with respect to performance. That is, cost is assumed to be uniform across performance levels. Common sense suggests this may rarely be the case, however. As performance level increases, it stands to reason that enhancements will be more and more costly. Moving an individual respondent from a 9 on a 10-point scale to a 10 may be four times as expensive as moving from a 5 to a 6 on the same scale. Unfortunately, little empirical evidence confirms this supposition.

Figure 9.6 presents a series of cost functions including constant, linear, and nonlinear forms. Improvement costs are depicted for five hypothetical services. The first (Service A) is associated with a constant performance improvement cost function. The cost of improving satisfaction for this service is the same regardless of current performance level. In the case of Service A, the cost of improvement is the same no matter how satisfied customers are. Of course, this same straight line could also be depicted anywhere along the y-axis. The function related to this line can be expressed as shown in Equation 9.1 where the cost (y_a) associated with improving Service A is 60 units regardless of satisfaction level.

$$y_a = 60 \tag{9.1}$$

Service B in Figure 9.6 is associated with improvement costs that increase in direct proportion to current performance level. Improving this

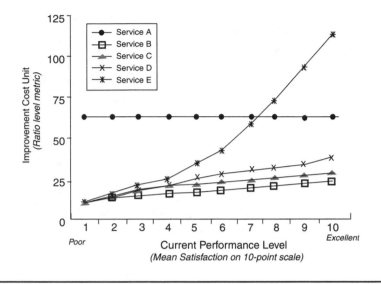

Figure 9.6   Constant, linear, and nonlinear cost functions.

service when performance is low costs considerably less than when performance levels are high. The cost function for this service is reflected in Equation 9.2, which suggests that as x (performance level) increases, y (enhancement cost) increases proportionately. Note there is a fixed cost of 10 units, which is reflected in the y-intercept in the figure. That is, enhancements to Service B will minimally cost 10 units regardless of the performance level or enhancement magnitude.

$$y_b = 10 + 2x \qquad (9.2)$$

The third function relates to Service C and suggests that improvement cost increases in a linear fashion but at half the rate associated with Service B. The fixed component of 10 units is depicted in Figure 9.6 as the y-intercept. Equation 9.3 summarizes the cost function for enhancing satisfaction with Service B. As shown, there is a fixed cost component of 10 units. Thereafter, the variable cost of increasing satisfaction is directly related to the current performance level.

$$y_c = 10 + 1x \qquad (9.3)$$

Two quadratic cost functions are presented in Figure 9.6. In the cases of Service D and Service E, the cost of enhancing performance level increases in a nonlinear fashion. Functions of this nature are particularly conservative because they acknowledge that performance enhancements become much more costly at higher levels. The level of nonlinearity is controlled by the power to which the variable cost component is raised. This involves raising the performance level by a factor greater than one. Squaring or even cubing the performance level yields variable cost components that increase dramatically and focus managerial attention away from drivers associated with even moderately high satisfaction levels.

The first nonlinear cost function is presented for Service D in Equation 9.4. In this case, enhancement costs increase rapidly once an intermediate level of satisfaction has been achieved. Note that a fixed improvement cost of 10 units is assumed for this service.

$$Y_d = 10 + x^{1.5} \qquad (9.4)$$

An even more aggressive cost function is depicted for Service E in Equation 9.5. Here, the variable cost component is equal to the square of current performance. Note that the fixed cost of 10 units has been retained in this function as well. The result, as shown in Figure 9.6, is rapidly escalating enhancement costs as current performance increases. This is the most conservative performance improvement cost function shown in Figure 9.6. More dramatic nonlinearity may be achieved by raising the variable cost component to even higher powers.

$$Y_e = 10 + x^2 \qquad (9.5)$$

The most conservative, nonlinear cost functions may be employed when there is a great deal of uncertainty concerning improvement costs or when it is clear a tremendous effort would be required to boost performance. In the absence of stable empirical data relating to improvement costs, managers may opt to choose two cost functions—one relatively conservative and another more optimistic—and assume the actual cost may be somewhere in between the two extremes.

MANAGERIAL STRATEGIES: PRODUCT QUALITY

Much of the discussion to this point has focused on enhancements to service and intangible quality issues. For many manufacturing organizations, product quality is the primary focus. Manufacturers with highly evolved customer satisfaction programs can demonstrate linkages empirically from engineering data to psychometric data and subsequently to business outcome measures such as profitability. Of course, product quality will only be relevant to organizations for which product issues are substantive drivers of key dependent measures like overall satisfaction or loyalty.

Figure 9.7 presents a causal chain that begins with engineering data. These are linked to psychometric data involving customer satisfaction. In turn, customer satisfaction data are used to predict business outcomes such as profitability, revenue, or market share. Establishing this type of chain is very demanding and requires that engineering data be provided for specific product units, which are subsequently tracked in terms of customer feedback. This is a particularly effective means for linking specific engineering metrics to customer feedback data in the form of customer satisfaction.

Typically, the linkage between engineering data and customer feedback data must be established at the product unit level. One approach is to take a random sample of, for example, 400 product units and subject each to a series of objective quality tests. In some cases it is possible that product quality is so well controlled, no variance may be associated with these measurements. If this were true, we would expect that product quality could not emerge as a key driver because variance is necessary to establish covariance. Of course, even with no actual physical quality variations, *consumer expectations* may vary, which could potentially be the source of the covariance underlying key-driver status.

Assuming a set of objective quality metrics can be obtained for the test units, each must be uniquely identified and placed in a test consumer environment. Ideally, the placement will be blind so that end users are not aware of the interest in linking physical product characteristics to customer satisfaction. Assuming the product quality variance is within acceptable limits, there should be no reason not to sell the units in the general market. It will be imperative to record the purchaser of each unit, of course. If a more controlled situation is desired, the units may be placed in businesses or households for long-term usage. This approach will typically require some form

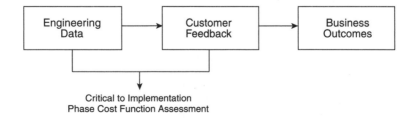

Figure 9.7 Product quality implementation chain.

of monetary or other compensation that may include final ownership of the test unit depending on its cost. When product placement involves end users who are provided incentives to participate in the study, considerably more flexibility is possible in terms of collecting psychometric data. Multiple measurements over the course of a year or more are possible when end users are compensated for participating in the research.

The key to establishing the linkage between physical product characteristics or performance levels and customer evaluations involves an analysis in which both the engineering data and psychometric data can be related in a dependence model framework. At a macro level, the researcher may initially use canonical correlation analysis to link a set of exogenous engineering variables to a set of endogenous psychometrics. Subsequently, more refined explorations should involve a single psychometric dependent measure such as overall satisfaction and a series of physical predictor variables.

Once an organization has established a relationship between specific engineering metrics and psychometric data such as satisfaction or repurchase likelihood, estimating costs for increasing various aspects of product quality are relatively straightforward. Engineering staff will be able to estimate the costs associated with addressing the various product performance variables. This exercise will enable marketing and engineering to determine the most effective course of action. Interestingly, organizations that have also established an empirical linkage between satisfaction and profitability may be in a position to determine the actual return on investment associated with various product quality enhancement strategies.

Organizations that have established linkages between physical product characteristics and satisfaction and, in turn, between satisfaction and profitability are in a unique—and enviable—position. Consider the illustrative set of regression models presented in Equation 9.6 and 9.7 linking product characteristics to overall product satisfaction (Y_{ps}) and various satisfaction measures to overall profitability (Y_{π}).

$$Y_{ps} = 3.2 + (0.34x_1) + (0.21x_2) + (0.06x_3) \qquad (9.6)$$

$$Y_{\pi} = 8.7 + (8.2x_1) + (3.1x_2) + (1.2x_3) + (1.7x_4) \qquad (9.7)$$

Typically, we would expect the former regression model to be considerably more efficacious than the latter. Profitability is notoriously difficult to model because it is subject to innumerable economic vagaries, accounting preferences, and competitive forces. Thus an R^2 of 0.70 or greater could be expected for the equation predicting overall satisfaction (Y_{ps}), whereas a level of 0.20 would be extremely gratifying for the profitability model. Assume that x_1 through x_4 are the following psychometric variables: x_1 = service satisfaction, x_2 = product satisfaction, x_3 = technical support satisfaction, x_4 = reputation/image satisfaction. Thus the dependent measure in Equation 9.6 is actually a predictor variable (x_2) in Equation 9.7.

Given the preceding two equations, a researcher could establish the effect of increasing each predictor variable by 10% in terms of the forecasted change in the dependent measure (Y_{ps}). Note that depending on the sample size and variance associated with each predictor variable, a 95% confidence interval around Y_{ps} can be established. This will yield upper and lower bounds for our estimate of the new value of the dependent variable. The dependent measure in Equation 9.6 is a predictor variable (x_2) in Equation 9.7, and as a result we can use the upper- and lower-bound values of Y_{ps} to forecast changes in the profitability measure (Y_{π}). Table 9.3 presents a hypothetical example of this type of exercise.

The illustrative data presented in Table 9.3 demonstrate how enhancements to product features can be linked to forecasted changes in overall product satisfaction. Note that this example uses the 95% upper- and lower-confidence limits of both dependent measures (Y_{ps} and Y_{π}) to provide ranges for the estimated profit results. Specifically, for each of the three predictor variables, a current performance level is enhanced by 10% and linked to an improvement cost. The cost for decreasing the noise level from 65.2db to 58.7db is $700,000, for example. The impact of this product enhancement on overall product satisfaction (Y_{ps}) is associated with a lower confidence limit (LCL) estimate of 7.8 and an upper confidence limit (UCL) of 8.1. These bounds are entered into the second regression equation and used to produce profitability forecasts. The worst case is based on the LCL value of product satisfaction (Y_{ps}), and the best case is based on the UCL value. Note that these two scenarios also have UCL and LCL values around the forecast of profitability (Y_{π}). This gives us ranges around the optimistic and pessimistic return on investment predictions.

Based on Table 9.3 we can conclude that decreasing the noise level of the product by 10% will generate a return on investment ranging anywhere from $100,000 to $600,000 based on a $700,000 improvement cost, a worst case LCL of $800,000, and best case UCL of $1,300,000. Of course, this is a somewhat simplified example; its purpose is simply to illustrate the types of analytical tacks that may be embraced. When a manufacturing organization has empirically linked engineering, psychometric, and business outcome data, the type of analysis presented in Table 9.3 can provide a compelling framework for understanding the implications of product enhancements.

Referencing the cost functions introduced in Figure 9.6, it is now possible to include these in our discussion. Until now, the focus has been on

Table 9.3 Linking engineering data to profitability through satisfaction.

Engineering variables	Current level	Enhanced level	Cost to improve	Forecast (Y_{ps}) Product Satisfaction				Forecast (Y_π) Profitability			
				Worst Case				Best Case			
				LCL	UCL	LCL	UCL	UCL	LCL	LCL	UCL
x_1 Noise level (db)	65.2	58.7	$0.7	7.8	8.1	$0.8	$1.1	$1.1	$1.0	$1.0	$1.3
x_2 Finish depth (microns)	15.4	16.9	$0.5	7.6	7.9	$0.4	$0.7	$0.7	$0.6	$0.6	$0.9
x_3 Weight (grams)	35.6	39.2	$0.6	7.4	8.0	$0.1	$0.3	$0.3	$0.2	$0.2	$0.4

Note: Financial entries presented in millions of dollars.

linking specific engineering design enhancements to customer satisfaction, resulting in the cost-benefit analysis presented in Table 9.3. Clearly, the costs associated with a 10% enhancement for each of the design features will increase as more aggressive improvements are required. That is, it is highly probable that a 20% improvement in noise level will cost more than twice the amount necessary to improve by 10%. Indeed, in some cases the optimal enhancement may not be physically possible regardless of the resources available to engineering. A completely quiet dishwasher with a sound level lower than 20db may not be possible with today's electric motor technology. Still, clearly the constant, linear, and nonlinear cost functions described earlier play an integral role in determining costs for various product improvement initiatives.

MANAGERIAL STRATEGIES: SERVICE QUALITY

Much to the chagrin of managers in service organizations, the exact state of the myriad variables that affect a customer interaction defies precise measurement. Unlike in the case of a specific product, which can be physically measured across a variety of features, the service interaction is subject to a tremendous amount of random error and fluctuation that is extremely difficult to gauge numerically. Consider this seemingly innocuous situation at a suburban bank branch:

> It is a hot summer day in Dallas when a customer pulls in and, with some difficulty, manages to find a parking spot next to a 25-year-old behemoth vehicle. With this in mind, our customer enters the branch building and encounters a rather long line. Despite the branch manager's best efforts, the building's HVAC system is still unreliable, and the air conditioning on this particular day is not working especially well—the temperature is a balmy 78°F in the building. After a 12-minute wait in line, the customer approaches one of several teller windows and is courteously greeted by a veteran bank employee who is recovering from the flu. Having overslept on this morning, the teller is a bit hurried and despite having past transactions with this particular customer, fails to engage in small talk and simply processes the deposit. The customer notes the lack of air conditioning, and the teller empathizes briefly and concludes the transaction with a receipt, thanks the customer, and dryly calls for the next in line. The customer leaves the branch building, finds a minor door ding, and drives off.

Clearly, an enormous number of highly variable factors affect the customer's service experience. Many of these simply are beyond the control of branch or unit managers. Perhaps the most vexing of these factors are those that directly affect the human interaction portion of the customer's experience. Idiosyncratic reactions to physical, emotional, environmental, and social factors frustrate attempts to model mathematically these effects on service quality feedback measures. Although this was relatively straightforward in the product quality example presented earlier, it is highly problematic in a service quality framework.

Service and product quality issues controlled at the branch or organizational subunit level may be amenable to the less conservative cost functions depicted in Figure 9.6. Many corporate-level issues, however, are probably best considered with nonlinear enhancement cost functions. For example, consider two drivers of overall satisfaction and customer loyalty at a large retail bank: *teller friendliness* and a critical aspect of brand image, *financial stability*. The service quality issue is best addressed at the branch level, whereas the brand image issue must be the domain of corporate marketing or advertising departments.

For the branch manager interested in enhancing feedback ratings associated with teller friendliness, costs will be associated with training and role-playing sessions for staff. A concerted effort to make this issue salient among the front-line employees through training combined with some form of incentive system may have relatively modest costs that do not accelerate dramatically as performance level increases.

In contrast to branch-level staffing and training solutions, corporate strategies involving mass communications and the manipulation of *perceptions* may demand more conservative enhancement cost functions. Advertising communications leveraging broadcast media are a relatively inefficient means of affecting customer perceptions, depending, of course, on market share. Targeted mailings when customer address information is known will permit more focused communications. Regardless of the media or message format, however, issues involving intangibles such as brand image may be more difficult to enhance. The depth and breadth of communications aimed at enhancing corporate image issues may have to increase geometrically in order to gain even modest improvements in satisfaction levels. Clearly, the more conservative improvement cost functions will be appropriate when changes to relatively static issues involving brand image are sought.

SUMMARY

Managerial actions based on customer satisfaction results often receive too little attention from research consultants whose interest typically revolves around the psychometric and analytic aspects of a project. And, to a certain extent, implementation issues are often considered the client's domain in a consulting relationship. Because of this, less progress has been made establishing empirical relationships between improvement efforts and concomitant increases in customer satisfaction.

Managerial actions aimed at product or service quality enhancements represent a critical link in the continuous improvement process. This underscores the importance of establishing empirical relationships between these activities and subsequent changes in customer satisfaction. The need to present this relationship as causal suggests that every effort should be made to meet the requirements for demonstrating a cause-and-effect link. Thus, if possible, an experimental design with test and control sites is advisable.

10

Creating and Managing Loyalty Segments

INTRODUCTION

In Chapter 2 and elsewhere, we noted a shift from tracking overall satisfaction. It appears that a focus on satisfaction exclusively may be somewhat myopic. To the extent that alternative constructs like loyalty are *better predictors of consumer behavior,* they should certainly be examined. This chapter introduces a simple operational definition of loyalty and a highly effective means for developing robust, optimized key-driver models. The use of multinomial logistic (MNL) regression has several very compelling advantages. Of key interest is the explicit recognition that what drives loyalty among the least loyal segment may be different from the driver model for customers at the other end of the distribution. As a result, differential service and product quality improvement strategies may be developed to address the idiosyncratic driver profiles of each loyalty segment.

The primary impetus for the search for alternatives to satisfaction is the recognition that satisfied customers still defect. Measures of loyalty—even the relatively simplistic one presented in this chapter—appear quite promising in terms of greater predictive efficacy in the consumer behaviors that drive market share and profitability. Of course, each organization must evaluate the extent to which customer satisfaction has performed with respect to its relationship to business outcomes. It has become increasingly clear that simple loyalty indexes are performing quite well in this regard, particularly when they fully subsume a measure of overall satisfaction.

LOYALTY: OPERATIONAL DEFINITIONS

Chapter 2 introduced the use of a composite loyalty index and its subsequent decomposition into four customer segments. The three-item loyalty index ranges from 3 to 30 and is the sum of overall satisfaction, willingness to recommend, and likelihood to repurchase. A scoring mechanism that illustrates the intersection of the three items graphically is presented in Figure 10.1. The number presented in the center of the three intersecting circles is the proportion of respondents associated with a top-box score on all three measures. This composite is a useful way to track the three individual components of the index and the ultimate measure simultaneously.

Avoid creating an index with too many components; it is preferable to have no more than three items. The danger associated with too many items involves the difficulty with demonstrating performance improvements. A large number of items, each with its own variance and error, is likely to produce an index that is very difficult to move from a performance improvement standpoint. It will be highly *insensitive* to management action and, as a result, yields a frustrating program that may ultimately be abandoned. A benefit of this lower degree of sensitivity is a reduction in volatility. The three-item loyalty index described here is generally associated with less longitudinal variance than the single measures that comprise it.

Not only are multi-item indexes more difficult to move, they also tend to yield regression equations with lower predictive power. This tends to be directly related to the average scale item intercorrelation. Cronbach's alpha—a reliability coefficient—is an effective way to summarize the inter-

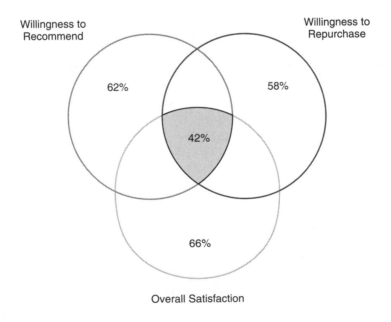

Willingness to Recommend

Willingness to Repurchase

62%

58%

42%

66%

Overall Satisfaction

Figure 10.1   Loyalty index of three key items.

nal consistency of a multi-item index. Of course, perfect correlations among the variables (i.e., Cronbach's alpha = 1.0) in the scale would suggest that any of the individual items would suffice. It is reasonable to expect reliability coefficients greater than 0.70 for loyalty indexes composed of three items.

The data summarized in Figure 10.1 are decomposed into four segments. Figure 10.2 illustrates how the four groups are defined based on the range of their scores on the cumulative frequency distribution. It is typically preferable to work with between three and five segments. Performance scales with more points will enable up to five or six segments, although this will require a substantial number of respondents and no fewer than 200 per group. A 10-point scale and 2000 observations could support up to six loyalty segments, for example, assuming the data are not excessively skewed.

LOYALTY SEGMENT DRIVERS

Ordinarily, a single regression model is used to develop the key-driver profile for a group of customers. This could involve an entire customer base or separate model development for each of many organization subunits such as branches or geographically defined areas. The dependent measure is typically overall satisfaction, and on the predictor side of the equation is a set of service and product quality satisfaction items. The resultant model is then applied to the entire distribution. That is, it is presumed the effect of enhancing a given predictor variable is equal across the entire distribution. Highly dissatisfied customers are assumed to be affected by this service or product quality enhancement at the same rate their more satisfied counterparts are. This may be a gross simplification. It is likely, for example, that what drives

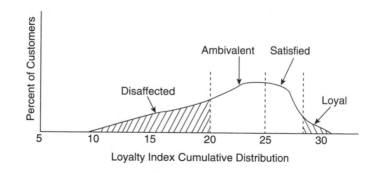

Figure 10.2 Cumulative loyalty index frequency distribution and segment formation.

satisfaction at the low end of the distribution (i.e., dissatisfied customers) is not effective among highly satisfied customers.

ASSESSING DRIVER HOMOGENEITY

The likelihood that various service and product quality issues exert differential effects across the distribution of overall satisfaction or a loyalty index can be checked quite easily. An examination of the residuals obtained from multiple regression analysis will reveal a lot about the model's ability to predict accurately at the extremes of the dependent measure.

In regression analysis, residuals are simply the difference between the predicted value and the actual value of the dependent variable. Minimizing the total squared error (Equation 10.1) is the basis for the objective function in ordinary least squares (OLS) regression.

$$\sum_{i=1}^{n}(y_i - \hat{y}_i)^2 \qquad (10.1)$$

Heteroscedasticity and *homoscedasticity* are used to describe the distribution of the residuals in regression analysis. The latter term refers to the desirable instance in which the residuals are uniformly distributed over the range of $\hat{y}$ as depicted in Figure 10.3. In contrast, heteroscedasticity is a condition characterized by unequal residual variance over the dependent measure. Figure 10.4 presents three residual plots that reveal heteroscedasticity.

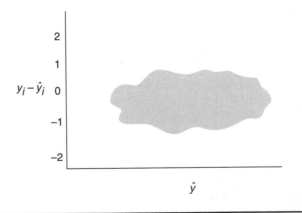

Figure 10.3 Homoscedasticity of regression residuals.

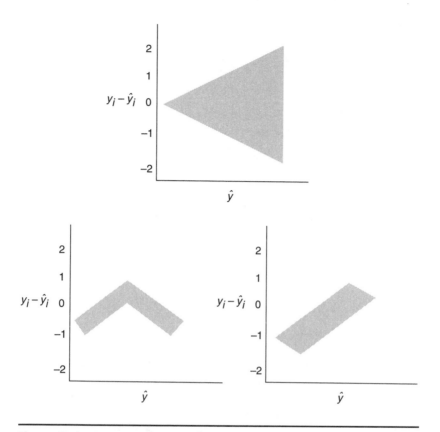

Figure 10.4 Heteroscedasticity of regression residuals.

A variety of factors may be responsible for the types of heteroscedasticity illustrated in Figure 10.4. In some cases, the distribution of the dependent measure may be problematic and require transformation. When the residual distribution appears nonlinear, it is likely a quadratic term or cross-product term may be required in the model.

Although it is seldom conducted in applied research, an intensive review of residuals is often fruitful and will reveal influential observations that could be unduly influencing the model. Numerous test statistics are available for assessing the effects of observations associated with excessively large residuals. Among these are DFBETA, DFFIT, and studentized residuals. These are described in great detail by Belsley, Kuh, and Welsch (1980:6–84).

When developing driver analyses that use a loyalty index (or simply overall satisfaction) as the dependent measure, a check for homoscedasticity will reveal whether the drivers are uniform over the entire distribution. If heteroscedasticity is present, the technique described in the remainder of this chapter may be appropriate. The ensuing discussion and case study present a means for developing simultaneous driver equations unique to each loyalty segment as described earlier.

INTRODUCTION TO BINARY LOGISTIC REGRESSION

Establishing marginal resource allocation models for the segments would typically be conducted across the entire dependent measure distribution. That is, a multiple regression model would be developed using a series of service and product quality satisfaction measures as predictors and the loyalty index as a dependent measure. The same model would then be used to understand how to move members of one segment into the next most loyal group. The implicit assumption is that the same driver profile will be applicable to each segment. For example, a 10% increase in satisfaction with technical support would yield an equal effect on each group.

This section presents an alternative key-driver model that has proven to provide tremendous insights into how loyalty segments differ. The technique described is also quite robust in conditions characterized by substantial collinearity. Indeed, unlike a number of other approaches, the results did not reflect typical manifestations of ill conditioning. In particular, the statistically significant, reversed sign beta coefficient problem was circumvented using the approach described here.

The classic regression analysis framework is generally used in the following manner. A series of one or more independent variables (e.g., satisfaction with service, billing, and product quality) are used to predict one *numeric* dependent variable (e.g., overall satisfaction). The outcome side of this equation must be numeric and is assumed to be normally distributed. The predictor variables, however, may be interval- or ratio-level metrics. Categorical variables can be accommodated with a series of dummy variables.

Occasionally, the dependent variable is categorical and has two or more values. This might be the case when we want to differentiate between two groups such as high and low loyalty. Similarly, we might want to understand the differences between customers who are very satisfied and those who are very dissatisfied or those who purchased a product and those who did not. These are examples of dichotomous dependent measures. Other categorical measures may be associated with more than two levels such as region: West, South, East, and Midwest. It is also possible to accommodate ordinal dependent measures, which have a rank order.

When a regression analysis employs a series of numeric independent variables to predict a single binary dependent variable, the classic ordinary least squares model tends to be inadequate (Hosmer and Lemeshow, 1989:5–7) based on two important criteria. First, the conditional mean of y is constrained to take only two values—for example, zero and one. More technically, the conditional mean of the outcome variable $E(y|x)$ is limited and as it approaches its extremes (zero or one) becomes increasingly curvilinear or S shaped. The second difference between binary and interval- or ratio-level dependent variables cited by Hosmer and Lemeshow involves the distribution of the error term ϵ. In short, the distribution of ϵ under the conditions of a binary outcome variable violate the assumptions associated with ordinary least squares. Based on these violations, researchers rely on logistic regression analysis, which is summarized in Equations 10.2, 10.3, and 10.4.

The logit link is nonlinear and has several advantages for classification purposes. In the binary dependent variable case, the logit $g(x)$ is:

$$g(x) = \ln \frac{\pi(x)}{1 - \pi(x)} \tag{10.2}$$

and

$$\pi(x) = \frac{e^{g(x)}}{1 + e^{g(x)}} \tag{10.3}$$

where $\pi_{(x)}$ is equal to the *probability* of being a member of the highly (dis)satisfied group. The logit $g_{(x)}$ is calculated as one would if classical regression analysis was used:

$$g_{(x)} = \beta_0 + \beta_1 x_1 + \beta_2 x_2 + \cdots + \beta_k x_k + e \tag{10.4}$$

An example will facilitate an understanding of how the technique is applied. Consider the product quality example presented in Figure 10.5. There are five numeric predictor variables and a single binary dependent measure. Each predictor variable score reflects the respondents' satisfaction and was measured using a 10-point scale.

Recall that respondents were asked how satisfied they were with each of these aspects of their product. In the present case, these five questions are followed by a single outcome item that elicits a binary response: "Will you purchase additional Stilletto products . . .?" Only two responses are possible: yes and no.

Based on the preceding, our model takes the familiar form, as shown in Equation 10.5:

$$g_{(x)} = \beta_0 + \beta_1 x_1 + \beta_2 x_2 + \cdots + \beta_k x_k + e \tag{10.5}$$

Welcome to the family of Stilletto product owners. We make every effort to ensure your feedback is considered and utilized in our product development and enhancement programs. Your input is integral to our success.

We're interested in your experience with your new **Stilletto Jumar device**. Please take a moment to fill out the questionnaire below and return it in the postage-paid mailer.

	Very Dissatisfied									**Very Satisfied**
Overall finish	1☐	2☐	3☐	4☐	5☐	6☐	7☐	8☐	9☐	10☐
Spring quality	1☐	2☐	3☐	4☐	5☐	6☐	7☐	8☐	9☐	10☐
Camming action	1☐	2☐	3☐	4☐	5☐	6☐	7☐	8☐	9☐	10☐
Grip comfort	1☐	2☐	3☐	4☐	5☐	6☐	7☐	8☐	9☐	10☐
Overall design	1☐	2☐	3☐	4☐	5☐	6☐	7☐	8☐	9☐	10☐

Considering all these issues, will you purchase additional Stilletto products for future expeditions?

1☐ Yes   2☐ No

Figure 10.5   Illustration of survey structure for binary logistic regression.

Note that $g_{(x)}$ is the outcome variable—technically, the logit x. Calculation of $g_{(x)}$ employs maximum likelihood analysis. An explanation of this technique is well beyond the scope of this book. You may wish to refer to Hosmer and Lemeshow's (1989) exhaustive treatment of the logistic regression analysis technique.

For the purposes of this illustration we focus on the five predictor variables and the binary dependent variable. When we examine the average satisfaction scores between the two groups, it becomes clear that those who indicated they would purchase again were, in general, more satisfied with the five product quality variables. This is depicted in Figure 10.6.

When multiple logistic regression is used, the dependent variable can take on two values. In the present case they were coded N and Y, indicating that the respondent would not or would purchase Stilletto products again. Table 10.1 suggests that the overall finish (x_1) has the greatest impact on intended repeat purchase. The implication of the negative sign preceding the parameter estimates β_k is discussed later. The logistic regression analysis confirms the second best predictor of the dependent variable is overall design (x_5). These conclusions are based on the probability of the β^2 statis-

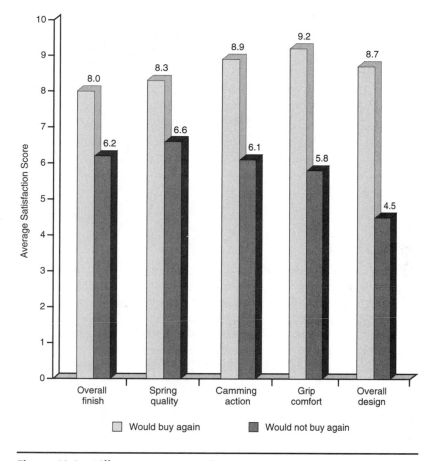

Figure 10.6 Differences across predictor variables.

tic associated with the parameter estimate. Note the column in Table 10.1 labeled Odds ratio. Deviations from 1.0 indicate *higher* or *lower* probability of membership in the group who indicated they would *not* purchase from this company in the future. The reason for this is discussed later.

Equation 10.6 represents the first step in calculating the probability of group membership. The logit (g_x) is calculated in a manner reminiscent of ordinary regression analysis. Thus a respondent who rated each of the five areas as a 9 would have $g_{(x)}$ value of –2.77, which by itself has little meaning. Interpreting $g_{(x)}$ requires us to return to the logit link shown in Equation 10.7.

$$g_{(x)} = 3.26 - .47_{(X_1)} - .08_{(X_2)} - .02_{(x3)} + .03_{(x4)} - .13_{(x5)} \qquad (10.6)$$

Table 10.1 Logistic regression analysis results.

Variable	Parameter estimate	Standard error	Pr > chi square	Standard estimate	Odds ratio
Intercept	3.26	0.47	0.00		
x_1. Overall finish	–0.47	0.05	0.00	–0.58	0.66
x_2. Spring quality	–0.08	0.08	0.56	–0.05	0.94
x_3. Camming action	–0.02	0.04	0.98	–0.00	1.00
x_4. Grip comfort	0.03	0.04	0.81	0.00	1.00
x_5. Overall design	–0.13	0.07	0.02	–0.16	0.87

$$\pi(x) = \frac{e^{g(x)}}{1 + e^{g(x)}} \tag{10.7}$$

If we now insert the value of –2.77, the value of $\pi_{(x)}$ becomes 0.06 over 1.06. Thus the value of $\pi_{(x)}$ is approximately 0.06, or 6%. This means the customer who gives all 9's on the survey has a 94% chance of purchasing additional products from this supplier based on the self-reported intention data. Remember that in this case the dependent measure is attitudinal and does not necessarily translate directly into behavior.

Different statistical packages approach the interpretation of $\pi_{(x)}$ in one of two ways. Most notably, SAS considers this the probability of being in the *lower valued* binary code, which, in this case, is indicative of the N response that is treated as 0 mathematically. In contrast, SPSS produces the opposite output; the value of $\pi_{(x)}$ is considered the probability of membership in the *higher valued* binary code, 1.

Logistic regression can accommodate other scenarios as well. In particular, multinomial logistic (MNL) regression is intended for dependent variables that take more than two values. Consider the case of a dependent variable with three possible values (0, 1, and 2). A conditional probability for each value must be considered, as shown in Equations 10.8 through 10.10.

$$P\left(Y = 0 \middle| x\right) = \frac{1}{1 + e^{g_1(x)} = e^{g_2(x)}} \tag{10.8}$$

$$P\left(Y = 1 \middle| x\right) = \frac{e^{g_1(x)}}{1 + e^{g_1(x)} + e^{g_2(x)}} \tag{10.9}$$

$$P\left(Y = 2 \middle| x\right) = \frac{e^{g_2(x)}}{1 + e^{g_1(x)} + e^{g_2(x)}} \tag{10.10}$$

This approach addresses the multinomial logistic regression model for a nominal dependent variable that takes three values. Other models that accommodate ordinal-level multinomial dependent variables are also available. A thorough review of these and other variants is discussed in McCullagh and Nelder (1983). Hosmer and Lemeshow (1989:216–45) also provide guidance concerning multinomial model building strategies. Multinomial logistic regression models for ordinal response variables include three approaches: adjacent category logits, continuation-ratio logits, and cumulative logits. All three leverage the ordering in the ordinal dependent measure. Agresti (1990:319–46) provides an excellent discussion of these techniques.

The role of MNL regression to accommodate the ordinal loyalty segment variable presented in Figure 10.2 is significant. When applied to the loyalty segments, MNL regression will yield a separate driver equation for moving customers from a lower segment to a higher segment. The major benefit of this approach is that a single driver equation is not imposed on all customers. Instead, there is an explicit recognition that the factors affecting loyalty at one point in the distribution may not be relevant in another part. The previous discussion on heteroscedasticity was presented to facilitate the identification of situations in which OLS regression fails at the extremes of the dependent measure.

CASE STUDY: MNL REGRESSION AND LOYALTY SEGMENTS

This case study involves the customer satisfaction and loyalty data for a global telecommunications company. In total, 16 predictor variables and nearly 2000 observations were used to model a dependent composite index parallel to that described earlier and in Chapter 2. Specifically, the index was developed by summing three key questionnaire items: willingness to recommend, repurchase likelihood, and overall satisfaction. A 10-point scale was used, and, as a result, the dependent index ranged from 3 to 30. A 10-point scale is generally preferred in customer satisfaction and loyalty research because it yields more refined distributions and permits the development of more segments. Of course, 10-point scales are also superior in terms of multivariate model development ranging from multiple regression to dimension reduction techniques like principal components analysis.

Based on judgment and a desire to produce baseline segments that meet a minimum size level of 250, the cumulative frequency distribution was used to produce four segments, as shown in Table 10.2. Their sizes reflect the general shape of the overall distribution. The large sample size permitted four segments to be developed. Fewer observations might dictate only three segments. Conceivably, five segments could be developed with the nearly 2000 observations used here. Too many segments, however, become unmanageable and should be avoided.

The initial decision concerning the scoring cutoffs for segment classifications is obviously quite important. The initial size of the Loyal group, in particular, will have significant political and analytical implications. Setting the bar too high may frustrate managers who perceive the goal as unrealistic. Conversely, creating a very large Loyal group from the outset may produce a false sense of security and reduce interest in further increasing the size of this segment. Of course, the same is true on the opposite end of the loyalty continuum. Creating an initial segment distribution that reflects a disproportionately large group of Disaffected customers may result in overwhelmed managers. They may perceive the segment size(s) as either erroneous or indicative of impending organizational failure.

From a purely univariate perspective, Table 10.2 reveals that 14% of the company's customers are in the Disaffected segment. This is somewhat disconcerting because it is very likely the largest proportion of annual customer attrition is attributable to members of this group. Thus, to the extent these customers are profitable, increasing their loyalty levels (and decreasing attrition risk) may yield substantive indirect and direct returns. The indirect benefits associated with increasing loyalty among these customers are enjoyed in the form of lower replacement costs. In short, customers who do not leave do not have to be replaced. Direct benefits include increased purchase volume or frequency. In some situations the return on improving the loyalty of Disaffected customers may greatly exceed that of similar enhancements among other more satisfied segments. This is particularly true when the fixed costs of customer acquisition are high and the variable costs associated with retention are low.

One way to validate the segment formation technique just described is to contrast the mean or top-two box scores of key variables presumed to affect the dependent measures used to create the groups. In this case, a total of 18 service and product quality variables are presented across the four loyalty segments (Table 10.3). As expected, the satisfaction scores drop consistently across the segments for each variable. Indeed, in no case is there a reversal of scores; the less loyal groups virtually always have means lower

Table 10.2 Loyalty segment composition and size.

Segment	Scoring range	Number	Proportion
Loyal	>28	414	21%
Satisfied	>24<29	799	40%
Ambivalent	>19<25	496	25%
Disaffected	<20	281	14%

Table 10.3 Mean scores on predictor variables across loyalty groups.

Quality measure	Loyal	Satisfied	Ambivalent	Disaffected
x_1 Tech support	8.7	7.9	7.2	7.1
x_2 Knowledge	8.2	7.5	7.2	6.6
x_3 Invoice	8.8	8.1	8.0	7.1
x_4 Sales	9.4	8.7	8.5	8.0
x_5 Delivery	8.7	7.9	7.4	6.9
x_6 Sound quality	8.2	7.5	6.5	6.5
x_7 Price/Value	8.2	7.4	6.7	6.2
x_8 Warranty	8.6	7.7	6.9	6.3
x_9 Instructions	8.9	8.1	7.7	6.9
x_{10} Access	8.0	7.6	7.3	7.2
x_{11} Upgrades	8.7	7.9	7.6	6.9
x_{12} Accessories	8.7	7.8	7.9	6.6
x_{13} Design	8.8	8.1	7.3	7.4
x_{14} Software	7.9	7.1	6.8	6.3
x_{15} Hardware	8.3	7.5	7.1	6.2
x_{16} Mobility	8.5	7.9	7.1	6.8
x_{17} Brand	8.8	8.1	8.1	7.4
x_{18} Weight	8.9	8.2	7.9	7.4

than the adjacent, more loyal group. There is one exception to this involving the Sound quality (x_6) variable. In this case, the Ambivalent and Disaffected segments emerged with the *same* mean score. Nonetheless, contrasting the segments across the 18 exogenous variables unequivocally lends credence to the segment formation technique used in this approach.

TRADITIONAL MODEL DEVELOPMENT

The predictor side of the equation—a series of 18 service and product satisfaction items—was introduced in Table 10.3. The MNL model of interest involves an ordinal dependent measure and 18 interval-level predictor variables. The rationale underlying the decision to pursue this form of model is the likely heterogeneous driver profile across the distribution. In short, issues that drive loyalty among highly dissatisfied customers may not be relevant at the other end of the distribution.

It should come as no surprise that the 18 variables are highly interrelated. This is not at all unusual in a customer satisfaction and loyalty measurement context. Collinearity has plagued the development of robust dependence models from the earliest applications of derived importance analysis. In this case, the condition index exceeded 37, which, according to authors like Belsley et al. (1980:105), is a reflection of "strong relations" among the independent variables. Accordingly, manifestations of harmful collinearity may be expected when regression-based procedures are used.

Table 10.4 presents an interesting review of various approaches to deriving the importance of the 18 variables using the interval-level loyalty scale, which ranges from 3 to 30. Five different approaches to derived importance metric development were utilized: OLS regression, Pearson correlations, partial correlations, Kruskal's technique, and a neural network approach. Pearson correlations are the only bivariate technique among the five and are included to provide a clear picture of the pairwise behavior of each predictor variable with the loyalty index. Note that the Pearson correlations range from a low of $r = 0.46$ to a high of $r = 0.76$ and that all are positive.

The effects of the strong bivariate—and possibly multivariate—correlations among the 18 predictor variables is apparent in the OLS results presented in Table 10.4. That the first variable (x_1) is associated with a statistically significant negative beta coefficient (–0.12) suggests a pathological condition and model instability. Clearly, the suggestion that increasing customers' satisfaction with technical support (x_1) will *decrease* loyalty would be met with skepticism among managers.

The partial correlation results closely parallel those of the OLS regression. In particular, the partial correlation of x_1 with the dependent index is negative and statistically significant. This measure reflects the covariance of a single variable (x_1) when the effects of the remaining variables (x_2-x_{18}) are removed mathematically. The statistically significant negative partial correlation is in stark contrast to the Pearson's correlation of 0.57.

The results for Kruksal's relative importance algorithm (Kruskal, 1987) are also presented in Table 10.4. Recall that Kruskal's technique is computationally intensive and involves averaging the squared partial correlation for each predictor variable with the dependent measure over all permutations of the former variable set. In this case, there are 18 predictor variables and, therefore, *millions* of unique sets. Because the Kruskal's metric is a *squared* partial correlation, negative coefficents are precluded.

The Kruskal's results are consistent with OLS, the bivariate correlations, and partial correlations with respect to identifying the variable (x_9) with the strongest relationship to the dependent measure. These four approaches are not in perfect agreement, however. The partial correlation results, for example, suggest that x_2 and x_9 are equally strong predictors of the loyalty index, whereas OLS and Kruskal's clearly favor x_9.

Finally, the use of an artificial neural network yielded a driver profile that was parallel to those associated with OLS and Kruskal's. Nonetheless, x_1 emerged with a negative coefficient, which is in agreement with the par-

Table 10.4 Comparison of dependence model approaches.

Service/Product quality variable	OLS Beta	p-value	Pearson	Partial r	p-value	Kruskals	Neural
x_1 Tech support	−0.12	0.02	0.57	−0.05	0.02	0.03	−0.90
x_2 Knowledge	0.46	0.00	0.57	0.23	0.00	0.09	3.30
x_3 Invoice	0.19	0.00	0.70	0.06	0.00	0.09	1.30
x_4 Sales	0.11	0.10	0.65	0.04	0.10	0.06	1.10
x_5 Delivery	0.09	0.15	0.66	0.03	0.15	0.06	0.90
x_6 Sound quality	0.08	0.16	0.59	0.03	1.60	0.04	0.70
x_7 Price/Value	0.08	0.15	0.63	0.03	0.15	0.05	0.60
x_8 Warranty	0.32	0.00	0.74	0.12	0.00	0.09	2.40
x_9 Instructions	0.72	0.00	0.76	0.23	0.00	0.15	5.40
x_{10} Access	−0.09	0.17	0.46	−0.03	0.17	0.02	−0.20
x_{11} Upgrades	0.01	0.81	0.65	0.00	0.81	0.05	0.20
x_{12} Accessories	0.29	0.00	0.72	0.11	0.00	0.10	2.40
x_{13} Design	0.02	0.73	0.60	0.00	0.73	0.04	0.30
x_{14} Software	0.15	0.00	0.50	0.09	0.00	0.05	1.10
x_{15} Hardware	0.15	0.00	0.67	0.06	0.00	0.07	0.90
x_{16} Mobility	0.23	0.00	0.65	0.09	0.00	0.05	1.80
x_{17} Brand	0.24	0.00	0.65	0.09	0.00	0.04	1.80
x_{18} Weight	0.32	0.00	0.65	0.11	0.00	0.06	2.30

Notes: (1) Condition index is 37. (2) All Pearson correlations are statistically significant at < 0.05. (3) OLS $R^2 = 0.74$.

tial correlation and OLS. The benefits of artificial neural networks relative to other techniques include the ability to accommodate nonlinear relationships and automatic interaction estimation. For an explanation of the differences between neural networks and regression-based techniques in customer satisfaction research, refer to Gronholdt and Martensen (2002:2).

MNL MODEL DEVELOPMENT

We turn now to the collapsed loyalty index as described earlier and summarized in Table 10.2. By collapsing the loyalty index into four discrete segments, the nature of the dependent measure changes substantially. It is now an ordinal-level variable. Further, the MNL model development process will yield not one but *three* regression equations. In MNL regression with k variables, n observations, and j dependent measure levels (i.e., segments) there will be $j - 1$ equations. This actually reflects a constraint in the data. That is, we can model the movement of customers from the Disaffected group to the Ambivalent group ($j = 1$ versus $j = 2$). Similarly, we can model what drives Ambivalent customers into the Satisfied segment ($j = 2$ versus $j = 3$). Finally, a separate equation will reflect the drivers of movement from the Satisfied group to the Loyal segment ($j = 3$ versus $j = 4$). However, we are constrained with respect to moving members of the Loyal group ($j = 4$) further up the distribution because they represent its pinnacle.

A parenthetical issue that should be addressed at this point involves the benefits of MNL regression versus a series of binary logistic regressions. That is, we could definitely approach the problem just described in terms of three separate binary logistic regression models, one for each pairing of adjacent dependent measure levels ($j = 1/2$, $j = 2/3$, and $j = 3/4$). The simultaneous versus separate model fitting question was addressed by Agresti (1990:310–12). Like other authors, he concluded that simultaneous model development using MNL is preferable due to greater efficiency and smaller standard errors.

Table 10.5 presents the results for the three-equation MNL analysis of the loyalty segments. The results are somewhat parallel to those presented earlier (Table 10.4) in that x_2 and x_9 are consistently the strongest drivers of loyalty. Interestingly, x_1, which was associated with a statistically significant negative coefficient in the OLS regression analysis, is not problematic in the MNL analysis.

Based on the results presented in Table 10.5, it is clear there are disparate driver profiles across the loyalty segments. The first of these involve x_4 and x_8, which are significant only for the Disaffected group. The next instance of different driver patterns involves x_{15}, which is not a factor for the Disaffected group but is significant for the two more satisfied segments.

Table 10.5 Summary of MNL driver status.

Service/Product quality variable	Disaffected	p-value	Ambivalent	p-value	Satisfied	p-value
x_1 Tech support	−0.04	0.64	−0.11	0.09	−0.11	0.06
x_2 Knowledge	0.66	0.00	0.40	0.00	0.23	0.00
x_3 Invoice	0.09	0.40	0.04	0.55	0.06	0.36
x_4 Sales	0.27	0.01	−0.05	0.53	−0.00	0.92
x_5 Delivery	0.09	0.33	0.00	0.96	0.00	0.97
x_6 Sound quality	0.09	0.29	0.06	0.38	−0.04	0.48
x_7 Price/Value	0.10	0.18	0.04	0.56	0.03	0.63
x_8 Warranty	0.26	0.00	0.14	0.06	0.01	0.84
x_9 Instructions	0.58	0.00	0.41	0.00	0.39	0.00
x_{10} Access	−0.01	0.89	−0.00	0.94	−0.03	0.67
x_{11} Upgrades	−0.00	0.96	0.00	0.94	−0.02	0.72
x_{12} Accessories	0.39	0.00	0.20	0.00	0.24	0.00
x_{13} Design	0.17	0.07	0.03	0.61	−0.09	0.15
x_{14} Software	0.26	0.00	0.14	0.00	0.10	0.04
x_{15} Hardware	0.12	0.13	0.16	0.01	0.13	0.03
x_{16} Mobility	0.22	0.01	0.26	0.00	0.15	0.01
x_{17} Brand	0.25	0.00	0.13	0.02	0.12	0.02
x_{18} Weight	0.40	0.00	0.18	0.02	0.05	0.44

Notes: (1) Drivers significant at 95% have been highlighted. (2) Loyal group is not modeled as a data constraint.

Finally, note that x_{18} is significant for both the Disaffected and Ambivalent segments but not their more satisfied peers.

These results point toward very different profiles across the cumulative loyalty frequency distribution. From a managerial standpoint, these results suggest that the Disaffected segment will respond to the sales process (x_4) and warranty (x_8) enhancements. Further, this group appears to be considerably more sensitive to the drivers that transcend the three groups: Knowledge (x_2) and Instructions (x_9). The unique driver profiles of each segment can be exploited to produce product and service enhancement strategies customized for each group. This approach will yield returns that exceed a single equation strategy based on a one-size-fits-all model, as described next.

SEGMENT DYNAMICS FORECASTING

It is possible to use the MNL models introduced in Table 10.5 to assess the effects of enhancements to any combination of the 18 service and product quality items on the predictor side of the equation. In order to do this effectively, the best course of action is to generate a new frequency distribution across the segments using the equations presented in Table 10.5. This is because even a very good MNL model will not be able to reproduce exactly the original distribution based on the input data set. Once a baseline distribution has been established using the model, it is possible to enhance systematically one or more of the predictor variables. This is achieved by multiplying each score by a constant such as 1.20, which would imply a 20% increase in satisfaction at the individual respondent. In effect, each respondent's score is multiplied by the enhancement constant. The MNL equations are then used to generate a new segment distribution. A comparison of the enhanced distribution to the baseline distribution permits inferences concerning the impact of a change in terms of segment dynamics.

It can be readily demonstrated that a 20% enhancement to x_2, for example, will yield very different effects across the segments. Figure 10.7 reveals how each segment's size will change as x_9 is enhanced by 10% and 20%, respectively. With respect to the Disaffected segment, for example, we see that a 10% enhancement to x_2 yields a reduction of 2.1 percentage points in this group's size. A 20% enhancement to the same predictor variable results in a 3.9 percentage point drop in size. We can naturally assume that these customers are moved up the distribution—most probably into the Ambivalent segment.

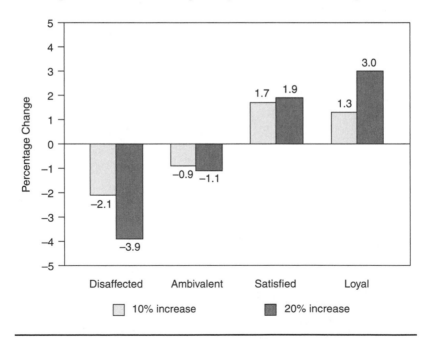

Figure 10.7 Differential effects of 10% and 20% enhancement to x_9.

Figure 10.7 also indicates that the 10% and 20% enhancements to x_2 would result in less substantive reductions in the size of the Ambivalent segment. Of course, we must consider this as the net effect because this segment has new members and has also lost members. That is, we have established that a significant number of the Disaffected moved up the distribution based on the 20% simulated enhancement. These customers presumably will move into the Ambivalent segment. And, based on the same increase, many of the Ambivalent customers have moved into the Satisfied segment. Thus the net effect for the Ambivalent segment is a reduction of either 0.9 percentage points or 1.1 points in the case of enhancements to x_2 of 10% and 20%, respectively.

As implied in the discussion of the Ambivalent segment dynamics, the Satisfied segment appears to grow substantially based on the enhancements to x_2. Note that a 10% increase to x_2 yields a 1.7 percentage point increase in the Satisfied segment size; a 20% increase results in only a slight marginal impact. Again, we must assume this is the net effect on the Satisfied segment because many of these customers will have moved into the top, most loyal group. Indeed, the Loyal segment grows by either 1.3 or 3.0 percentage points with the 10% and 20% increases to x_2. Because there is nowhere for Loyal segment members to move, this group can only increase in size under the current scenario. Of course, had we simulated a *reduction* in satisfaction, the reverse would be true. That is, a 20% reduction in x_2 would result in a drop in the size of the Loyal and Satisfied segments and proportional increases in the remaining two segments.

Any number of complex simulation scenarios could be tested using the procedures described here. Multiple variables may be changed simultaneously; some may be associated with increases and others may reflect reductions in satisfaction. The net effect, however, can be modeled in terms of segment-size dynamics. The most powerful and efficient means of facilitating a deeper understanding of these dynamics is to program the MNL equations in a simple user interface that permits testing numerous what-if? scenarios. This is readily accomplished using any of the programming languages currently available including C++, Visual Basic, or others.

IMPLEMENTATION ISSUES

The downside of a single driver equation for the entire loyalty distribution is that it is a one-size-fits-all solution that assumes dissatisfied customers will respond to the same service or product quality enhancements as their highly satisfied peers. The presence of heteroscedasticity in the regression residuals is a good indication that this phenomenon is present. In effect, this type of model frequently is highly efficacious in the middle two-thirds of the distribution but is less accurate at the tails.

Clearly, the MNL regression approach in which a unique driver equation is developed for each loyalty segment has an advantage in terms of sensitivity to the idiosyncratic needs of each group. However, a significant hurdle remains when this type of analysis is conducted based on *sampling* from a customer population. Specifically, although the MNL approach may confirm that different segments have varying driver profiles, it provides little insight into how we can reach members of each segment should we desire to implement unique programs aimed at each group. If every customer is associated with a segment affiliation, it is possible to direct targeted marketing and direct mail programs to members of each group.

In Chapter 6 we explored the linkage between customer satisfaction programs and CRM. As part of this discussion the notion that satisfaction could be predicted from CRM behavioral and demographic profile data was introduced (Figure 6.5). This technique is applicable in the present context as well. In short, if it is necessary to append a loyalty segment code to each customer record based on the decomposition of a cumulative frequency distribution obtained from a *sample*, then we need some means of predicting segment affiliation for the population.

Customer satisfaction, or, more generally, customer loyalty, is presumed to be an outcome of a longitudinal series of service and product quality encounters interleaved with media-based brand imagery. In many organizations characterized by substantive customer relationships, it is possible to leverage demographic and behavioral profile data to predict satisfaction accurately. In this instance, our interest focuses on predicting customer loyalty segment. Variables such as tenure, past purchases, problem resolution (or lack thereof), geodemographics, and others can be used in a model development strategy aimed at predicting loyalty segment. The use of MNL regression is appropriate at this stage as well. The discussion in Chapter 6 provides more detail concerning the use of CRM data to predict satisfaction level.

IMPLICATIONS FOR INCENTIVE SYSTEMS

As implied in Chapter 4, the loyalty segment approach to customer satisfaction program management has significant implications for management incentive systems. The most typical customer feedback linkages to management incentives involve a simple proportion. Quite simply, the modal system varies manager bonuses based on the proportion of their customers that fall into the most desirable (i.e., highly satisfied or loyal) categories. Often this calculation involves the percentage of top-two box scores at the branch level. Managers whose scores significantly exceed a baseline corporate norm or reflect an improvement over time are rewarded.

But this typical top-box-oriented reward system tends to be myopic because it focuses managerial attention on the most satisfied group of customers. Most such systems do not even include a metric that reflects the total number of dissatisfied customers in a given manager's customer base. Substantive anecdotal evidence suggests that highly dissatisfied customers are more likely to relate their *negative* experiences to friends than highly satisfied customers are apt to discuss their *positive* experiences. It certainly makes sense that the least satisfied customers are also those at highest risk of attrition. Accordingly, a management incentive system that rewards employees for increasing the overall satisfaction or loyalty level of any customer should have a greater impact on the entire customer base.

A strategically more desirable approach to customer feedback management incentive systems rewards employees for increasing loyalty levels anywhere in the overall distribution. The focus on a single key metric like proportion of highly loyal customers may be retained as a useful yardstick for progress. It should be considered, however, only in light of the remainder of the distribution. A very high proportion of extremely loyal customers can be easily offset by a large number of highly dissatisfied customers. The ideal incentive system rewards managers for their total net positive customer shift across all segments. This system gives the same weight to reducing the size of the least satisfied segment as it does to increasing the size of the most satisfied segment.

One caveat, however, is that this approach requires larger sample sizes than those normally associated with branch-level customer satisfaction programs. As a result, it may be necessary to (1) gather more data each reporting iteration, (2) run the loyalty segmentation step annually at the branch level, (3) reduce the number of segments to three, or (4) combine branches based on proximity or organization structure. The last option, which involves combining branches, is probably the least desirable from a managerial standpoint. It fails to differentiate performance levels within a branch grouping and may not recognize strong performers because of their peers' failures.

FUTURE DIRECTIONS

The decomposition of cumulative frequency distributions in an effort to develop unique loyalty segments has tremendous possibilities. Of greatest interest is the ability to generate unique driver profiles for each segment. This makes possible an optimized solution in which a unique implementation plan is developed for each group. The likelihood that less satisfied segments have greater upside potential in terms of profitability and relationship depth or breadth is very real. Certainly, members of the least satisfied loyalty segments will be at greatest attrition risk. To the extent that the fixed costs associated with acquiring new customers is high and the variable costs of retaining them is low, a focus on retaining profitable members of the Disaffected and Ambivalent segments seems mandatory.

There is a clear recognition in the customer satisfaction measurement and reporting arena that a certain amount of myopia has been present. Attrition among ostensibly satisfied customers tended to defy traditional models. The shift toward more sophisticated metrics aimed at gauging customer loyalty represents a positive step forward for the industry. A parsimonious operationalization of the loyalty construct will likely be one of the greatest challenges in applied customer psychometrics. Future measures of loyalty must strive to become more predictive of desirable customer behaviors. This is the critical test of any outcome measure whether it is termed satisfaction, loyalty, or commitment. The key is that the ultimate dependent psychometric measure will be clearly linked to outcome behaviors and, in turn, be predicated on actionable service and product quality issues. The strength of these relationships will most certainly shape the future of customer feedback research.

Appendix A

Customer Satisfaction Data Analysis Tips

INTRODUCTION

This appendix presents a series of useful strategies and heuristics for analyzing customer satisfaction data using any of the well-known statistical packages. Most large-scale tracking studies involve static, programmed reports, but ad hoc requests and other analytical issues likely will involve the use of statistical analysis software. The bulk of the tips presented in this section involve documenting, organizing, and testing. Following these guidelines or insisting that your analytical staff or consultants adhere to these suggestions may save many hours of frustration. Surprisingly, many experienced senior-level analytical consultants fail to maintain documentation, save critical code, or test various data transformations adequately. The suggestions in this appendix are presented in three broad categories: documentation, validation, and data management. The guidelines are applicable to a wide variety of statistical data analysis projects, not just customer satisfaction research.

DOCUMENTATION

1. Use comment syntax. It is not at all unusual to return to code after months or even years and find it difficult to understand. Generous use of comment syntax to document what your code is doing will facilitate its reuse or reorient the original author should the project be revisited. It is very helpful to use a standardized heading on all statistical analysis program code to document the original author, date written, project, and what exactly the code is intended to do.

2. Organize directories. Clearly, the use of directories and subdirectories can ensure an organized statistical analysis. Separate subdirectories for raw data, cleaned data, and data with imputed missing values may be warranted in some cases. The thoughtful and judicious use of directories and subdirectories will virtually ensure a good level of organization and help minimize the possibility of errors.

3. Structure program naming. It is very desirable to use a standardized program-naming convention to associate various parts of a larger project. Although directories certainly go a long way in this regard, the programs within a given directory can be self-documenting to a certain extent if their names coincide with their intended use. The newest operating systems do not restrict users to eight character file names, so there is no longer any excuse for file names that do not reflect an overall organization and specific purpose.

4. Save code. One would think this would be so self-evident it need not even be addressed here. Quite astonishingly, many senior-level statistical analysts simply submit interactive code and save the hard copy results. Their assumption is that they can conveniently replicate this and the costs of documenting and saving their code are too high for ad hoc or other occasional jobs. Unfortunately, this approach can—and often does—prove very disappointing. There is absolutely no excuse for not saving code, documenting it, and guaranteeing that the results can be reproduced exactly. If you work with an analyst who does not save code and simply hands you hard copy statistical output, be prepared for a disaster.

5. Take and save notes. It is very helpful during the course of a large-scale research project to maintain a daily diary in which various tasks, findings, outcomes, and decisions are documented. This will facilitate examinations of problems and help determine how to approach similar projects in the future. A diary containing notes will also help document the entire project because in most cases substantive decisions are made based on unforeseen analytic outcomes. Copious daily notes regarding outcomes, conversations, and unforeseen circumstances can prove invaluable should the need to justify a decision become necessary.

6. Use variable value labels. Most researchers who are intimately familiar with the data they are working with do not necessarily benefit from value labels. But end users, managers, and those with little exposure to the survey content will find the absence of value labels most disconcerting. Creating value labels for key ordinal and nominal variables is critically important. It requires very little initial effort and will save a tremendous amount of confusion later when results are shared. Failure to provide this fundamental level of documentation to users reflects a real problem. If your analytical staff—whether in house or consulting—consistently fails to provide value labels for categorical and rank variables, you will eventually encounter significant problems.

7. Use variable titles. When providing tables or other output from the standard statistical analysis packages, all variables should have titles. When programming with standard statistical packages it is highly advantageous to use variable names that are sequential and reflect the instrument structure. Unfortunately, this heuristic is not especially user friendly. Referring to variables Q15_a–Q15_c in a statistical analysis programming package is much more efficient than a list of disparate although presumably meaningful variable names like CONFIRM, CONFIDE, and TOTLLRS. When combined with value labels, variable titles completely document the data regardless of the statistical procedures being used.

DATA MANAGEMENT

8. Save log files. In addition to saving the code used to generate statistical output, it is also wise to retain the log files associated with the executed source code. Log files produced by the main statistical analysis packages contain confirmations that various procedures executed successfully, the number of observations that were included or excluded from procedures, and any relevant warnings concerning issues like convergence, variable names, or file sizes. When connected to the original source code and output, log files completely document and substantiate the analytical work. They serve as a validation that the output is authentic and was run successfully with a specific set of data, in a presumably error-free manner.

9. Separate analysis and data management. When possible, separate data manipulation and data analysis. The use of highly structured directory architectures as described earlier will facilitate this, of course. Manipulate data in one step that yields a production data set that serves as the input to multiple, subsequent analytical steps. This approach minimizes the possibility of error and reduces computing cycle time. With respect to the latter, even though CPU speeds seem to double every few years, data manipulation often is still time consuming. The time requirements, however, should be a minimal concern. The biggest potential problem associated with not separating the manipulation and analysis stages is that should an error be identified or a change required, it is highly advantageous to address a single program. In short, if every analysis program contains the same data manipulation code, a relatively innocuous change may become highly problematic.

10. Back up judiciously. Long-term and volatile storage media are now so inexpensive it would be extremely negligent to fail to back up critical data and program files adequately. This can be taken to the extreme, however. Too many backups combined with a lack of organization and documentation can lead to a very undesirable situation. It is very difficult to differentiate among a series of undocumented data files with varying numbers of observations and variables.

VALIDATION

11. Exploratory data analysis. Univariate profiling should precede more sophisticated multivariate analysis whenever possible. The univariate stage will clearly reveal the most egregious failures in the validation stage. Indeed, the univariate analysis step may, for many, represent the validation phase. An examination of each critical numeric variable in terms of range, missing values, and distribution will quickly and concisely expose potential problems that, if unchecked, could subtly (or overtly) affect more sophisticated multivariate analyses.

12. Missing values. The treatment of missing values in a psychometric research setting is a vast subject that has been the topic of numerous books. This single paragraph, therefore, can by no means provide an exhaustive discussion of missing values. Anyone with even modest experience in this area, however, will recognize the importance of the topic to multivariate analysis. From a data validation standpoint, the imputation of missing values is a process through which a number of troubling errors can emerge. Intensive data validation should follow the imputation process to ensure, minimally, the face validity of the imputed data. Of course, a more rigorous level of testing should follow and involve pre- and postimputation comparisons of summary statistics. A demonstration that the mean and variance are not substantively affected by a missing value imputation step will go a long way in engendering comfort among knowledgeable end users.

13. Mathematical transformations. Transformations intended to change distribution forms or to yield new variables should be scrutinized with great care, particularly when others will rely on the transformed data in subsequent analytic steps. The use of exploratory data analysis techniques to examine the distribution of derived variables is highly recommended. The distributions of derived variables should be of significant interest prior to full-scale deployment. The major statistical packages provide excellent univariate analysis procedures that will help identify potential problems based on a review of output associated with these. A simple normal-probability plot, for example, will reveal a lot in terms of the success of an effort to correct excessive kurtosis, skewness, or other problems. Derived variables should always be considered as suspect before they are unleashed to other users who may be less aware of potential problems. Finally, when deriving complex variables, break up long equations and provide comment syntax to describe what is being done at each stage. The use of inter-mediate variables will help other users isolate problems later and facilitate an understanding of how the derived variable is being calculated.

14. Frequency distributions. Simple frequencies can be very helpful in the data validation step. Two-way classification tables, for example, can instantly identify problematic cases involving instrument structure and rout-ing. When a particular response must precede a battery of items, it is very helpful to generate tables that confirm the presumed sequencing or logic structure. In many cases, this approach can identify logic errors in com-puter-aided telephone interviewing (CATI) or Web survey programs or data entry and validation systems for paper-and-pencil surveys. It is often pru-dent to perform this type of check immediately after data collection has begun.

Appendix B

Useful Statistical Tests for Customer Satisfaction Research

ROLE OF INFERENTIAL STATISTICS

In most customer satisfaction programs, samples are drawn from a population of customers and these data are used to generate performance metrics. The foundation of inferential statistics involves the extent to which our samples are representative of the overall population. Scientific survey sampling offers tremendous cost savings over a census approach in which an attempt is made to contact every customer. The exception typically involves situations characterized by a relatively small number of high-value customers.

Unlike descriptive statistics, which simply describe the obtained data, inferential statistics use the obtained data in drawing conclusions or making inferences about a population based on sample data. The majority of inferential statistics are performed through the use of samples from infinite populations, and random samples as small as $n > 30$ have been used successfully in representing normally distributed populations.

The two main purposes of inferential statistics are hypothesis testing and parameter estimation. In hypothesis testing, the alternative hypothesis asserts that the difference in the results of two or more conditions is due to one or more independent variables. The null hypothesis asserts that the difference in results between the conditions is not due to the independent variable. The independent variable in any experiment is the variable systematically manipulated by the researcher. The dependent variable is the variable used to measure the effect of the independent variable. The underlying assumption is that all other characteristics of or influences on the various conditions are held constant and any resulting difference between the conditions can be attributed to the effects of the independent variable.

Rejecting the Null Hypothesis

Although data can be collected and used in the absence of any hypothesis, the application of statistical tests used in the scientific methodology provides objective verification by disproving the null hypothesis. Because it is impossible to calculate the probability of the alternative hypothesis, we calculate the probability of getting the results due to chance alone—the null hypothesis. If that probability is equal to or less than a preset critical probability level named alpha level (α), we can reasonably reject the null hypothesis and accept the alternative hypothesis as the only other logical explanation for the obtained results. The most common alpha levels used are $p < .05$, and $p < .01$, where p is the probability of having obtained the results due to chance alone.

Interval Estimation

Interval estimates usually are more informative than hypothesis testing procedures, which only allow for the rejection or acceptance of any given hypothesis. The confidence interval is the range of scores or values, which is most likely to contain the population mean. The confidence limits are the critical values that border the confidence interval. The most commonly used confidence intervals are 95% and 99%, where the probability that the interval contains the mean difference is .95 or .99. This value is expressed as $1 - \alpha$ (alpha). Critical values such as the t-value and z-value represent the distance from the mean known to contain 95% or 99% of the normal curve, as shown in Figure B.1.

Confidence Interval Selection

Because researchers are looking to find statistical significance based on sample data, the chance of making an error in their estimate needs to be kept minimal. Thus it has been determined that the smallest acceptable possibility of the occurrence of an estimation error is 5%, which is represented by a 95% confidence interval. Any larger percentage possibility of error in inferential statistics cannot constitute statistical significance. The ability to make accurate predictions and use inferential statistics is based in part on the central limit theorem, which states that the sampling distribution of the mean will be normally distributed as the sample size (n) increases, even if the population distribution is not normally distributed. Once n, the sample size, is larger than about 1000, the distribution of population scores becomes irrelevant. For all purposes the mean of the sampling distribution will differ so insignificantly from the mean of the population distribution that researchers

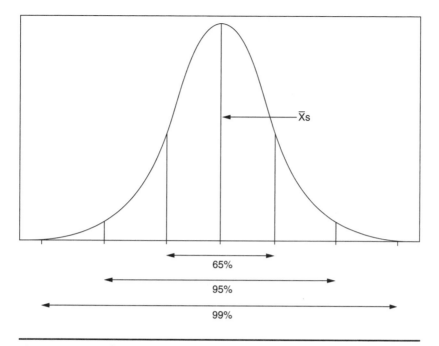

Figure B.1   Confidence intervals and the normal curve.

can make highly accurate predictions and their conclusions can be regarded with great confidence. In order to allow for predictions and conclusions to be formed in the absence of finite measurable populations, and to allow for the detection of relationships and variable effects, the criterion for determining statistical significance often cannot be set too stringently. A 99% confidence interval ($\alpha = .01$) often results in what is called a Type II error, which disallows for conclusions to be drawn and hypotheses to be accepted, even if the data at the slightly more generous .05 alpha level would have been significant. The 95% confidence interval is the most often applied confidence interval in inferential statistics. This interval keeps the estimation error so small that inferences can be drawn with a very high level of accuracy, without making it impossible to detect important effects and relationships embedded in the data.

Standard Deviation and the Normal Curve

Many inference tests analyzing experiments and survey data require normally distributed sampling distributions. With increasing sample size, sampling distributions become normally distributed, which is the basic tenet of

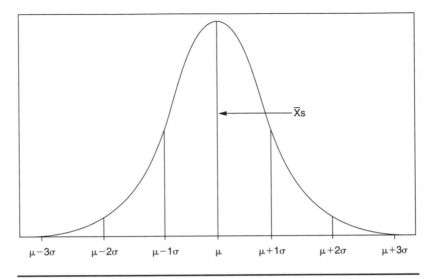

Figure B.2 Standard deviations and the normal curve.

the central limit theorem. This in turn allows for the application of the normal curve, which is mathematically generated and a theoretical distribution of the population scores. The standard deviation is a measure of dispersion of the scores relative to the mean of such distribution. In a normal distribution, approximately 65% of all scores will fall within the first standard deviation (one standard deviation from the mean in both directions), approximately 95% of all scores will fall within the second standard deviation, and approximately 99% of all scores within the third standard deviation, as shown in Figure B.2. Through score transformation a raw score can be changed into a z-score, which expresses how many standard deviation units a raw score is above or below the mean. This transformation allows for comparisons of scores whose measurement units might otherwise be incomparable, based on their respective positions within the population of scores.

One-Tailed versus Two-Tailed Hypotheses

When a hypothesis is nondirectional, the evaluation of the resulting data will be two tailed. When the hypothesis is directional and any resulting data turns out to be in the opposite direction but will be of no practical importance, the evaluation of the results will be one tailed. Accordingly, the critical values used to evaluate nondirectional hypotheses are different from those used for directional hypotheses. Figures B.3 and B.4 illustrate this concept.

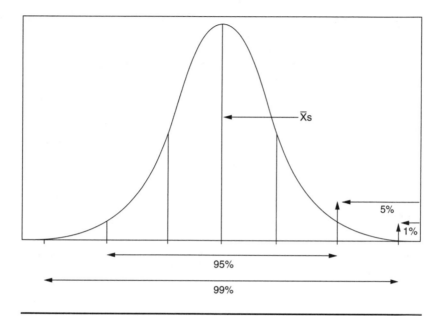

Figure B.3 One-tailed hypothesis and the normal curve.

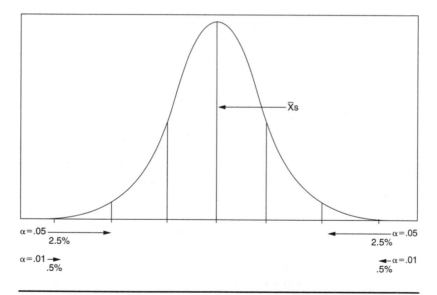

Figure B.4 Two-tailed hypothesis and the normal curve.

Type I and II Errors

The decision of how stringent to set the alpha level is based on the type of error a researcher is willing to make when analyzing the data. The Type I error occurs when the null hypothesis has been rejected even though the null hypothesis is true. The probability of making a Type I error is greater when a less stringent alpha level is used. The Type II error occurs when the null hypothesis is retained even though the null hypothesis is false. The more stringent the alpha level, the greater the probability of making a Type II error. However, the probability of making a Type II error decreases with the number of independent replications of the experiment.

Power and Statistical Tests

Depending on the data and the hypothesis, the researcher must choose the statistical test that is most powerful and best fits the raw data. In statistics, power, also known as beta (β), reflects the ability to detect the effect of the independent variable if in fact there is one and thus being able to reject the null hypothesis. Beta (β) is also described as the probability of making a Type II error. Increasing the sample size (n) increases the power of an experiment. Power decreases the more stringent alpha levels are set, because it becomes significantly more difficult to detect relationships or variable effects. It is therefore imperative to use the most powerful test that fits the data under analysis.

Data Types

In statistical terms, there are only four kinds of measurement scales. *Nominal scales* are used when the data is qualitative rather than quantitative. *Ordinal scales* are used with data that is rank ordered, yet the size of the difference between the individual ranks is not known or is arbitrary and inconsistent. *Interval scales* are used when adjacent units of data are separated by equal intervals but do not have an absolute zero point. *Ratio scales* are used for data whose individual adjacent units are separated by equal intervals and the data has an absolute zero point. Ratio scale data is the only one of the data types that can be manipulated and calculated using all mathematical principles.

Correlation and Regression

Correlation and regression involve the relationship between two or more variables. Where correlation establishes a relationship and expresses the magnitude and direction of such relationships, regression uses the data in order to make predictions. Both employ paired sets of scores obtained from the same or matched subjects. Perfect linear relationships result in perfect predictions. When the relationship is not perfect there will be prediction errors, which can be computed by calculating the standard error of estimate. If this error is determined to be minimal, predictions may be made with relatively reliable accuracy.

Univariate, Bivariate, and Multivariate Methods

Univariate designs measure multiple dependent variables separately with separate statistical analyses. Multivariate designs combine three or more variables in a single statistical analysis. When correlational designs combine multiple variables, researchers often evaluate relationships among variables by using bivariate (pairwise) correlation analyses, even though it is often more advantageous to use a multivariate design and analyze all variables in just one statistical test. In experimental research, multivariate tests prove to be more powerful because the correlations between the dependent variables are taken into account and complex relationships can be detected with a significantly smaller possibility of making a Type I error.

FINITE POPULATION CORRECTION FACTOR

In most consumer-oriented customer satisfaction programs, the customer populations are quite large. Typically, the customer population size is many, many times larger than the sample used to generate service or product quality performance metrics. For example, a sample (n) of 400 from a customer population (N) of 10,000 (or more) is not uncommon. In this case, the ratio of n/N is very small (.04). Clearly, the sample is a small fraction of the population.

Occasionally, the ratio of the customer population to the research sample is much higher. This is often the case in business-to-business customer satisfaction programs. When the sample represents more than about 5% of the population, it is desirable to apply the finite population correction (FPC) factor. As demonstrated next, incorporating this factor in customer satisfaction programs can be economically advantageous from a data collection standpoint.

In effect, the FPC factor reduces variance estimates (technically, the standard error) as a function of the ratio n/N. Conceptually, this is attractive because the notion we can reduce our estimate of variance as our sample size (n) approaches the universe size (N) is intuitively palatable. Once $n = N$, of course, $s^2 = \sigma^2$ and we have conducted a census. The FPC factor is something to consider when sample sizes are at least 5% of the population. At this low end of the spectrum, applying the FPC factor yields only very modest reductions in sample size requirements. However, as the ratio n/N increases past about 0.15, there can be tremendous savings.

Equation B.1 presents the FPC factor as described by Everitt (1998:126). An equivalent, slightly less conservative form described by Crow et al. (1960:39) is presented in Equation B.2. The latter form is typically applied directly to the standard error of the mean or proportion and is used predominantly throughout this section. The square root of Equation B.1 produces the equivalent of Equation B.2.

$$(1 - n / N) \tag{B.1}$$

$$(N - n) / (N - 1) \tag{B.2}$$

Table B.1 illustrates the impact of the FPC factor across a range of n/N from 5% to 40%. Because the FPC factor effectively reduces variance estimates, a value of 1.00 will leave s^2 unscathed. As shown, when the sample size represents 5% of the population, the FPC effect is only very slight. As the sample becomes increasingly large relative to the universe size, however, the impact of the FPC factor on variance estimates becomes more substantial.

Sample Size Requirements

The most typical FPC factor application involves sample size estimation. It is here that the use of this tool can yield significant data collection cost savings. Frequently, we encounter situations in which an organization strives for a ±4-points top-two box accuracy level at 95% confidence across a multibranch distribution system. That is, the performance metrics must be accurate within 4 points, with 95% confidence for each branch in the net-

Table B.1   Illustration of FPC factor effects.

(*n*) Sample Size	(*N*) Population	(*n/N*) Ratio	FPC[1]
50	1000	5%	.97
100	1000	10%	.95
150	1000	15%	.92
200	1000	20%	.89
250	1000	25%	.87
300	1000	30%	.84
350	1000	35%	.81
400	1000	40%	.77

[1] See Equation B.2.

work. In this situation, if the population of customers at the branch level is relatively small versus the sample size, application of the FPC factor can substantially reduce the number of interviews required. This may translate into direct monetary savings for customer satisfaction program managers depending, of course, on the branch-level ratio n/N.

Equations B.3 and B.4 are frequently used to determine sample size requirements based on a desired level of error (E), estimated standard deviation (S), and confidence level (Z_c) for means and proportions, respectively.

$$n = (S^2 Z^2) / E^2 \qquad\qquad (B.3)$$

$$n = (S^2 Z^2) / E^2 \qquad\qquad (B.4)$$

With respect to the first equation relating to means, a typical check involves the sample size required at 95% confidence when the standard deviation is 1.0 and the desired level of error is 0.1. Given this, the required sample size is 384 as shown here:

$$((1.0^2)(1.96^2)) / 0.1^2 = 384$$

Similarly, to check Equation B.4 relating to proportions we can assume the most conservative case of a 50% metric with an error of ±5 points at 95% confidence. Based on these parameters, the sample size requirement is calculated in the following manner:

$$((1.96^2)(.5 * .5)) / .05^2 = 384$$

Based on the preceding two calculations, the importance of the number 384 as a heuristic to guide estimates of sample size requirement based on the standard parameters introduced earlier should be clear. When calculating sample size requirements for proportions, the most conservative (50%) case was assumed. In customer satisfaction research, data are typically skewed and, as a result, we may refine our sample size estimates accordingly. Departures from the most conservative case should only be undertaken based on empirical evidence or substantive experience in similar industries using parallel methodologies and survey instruments.

Given the calculations just presented that both resulted in sample size requirements of 384 interviews, it is of great interest now to introduce the effects of the FPC factor assuming the same general parameters. Equations

B.5 and B.6 introduce the FPC (Equation B.1) to the calculation of sample sizes for means and proportions, respectively.

$$n = \text{FPC} * ((S^2 Z^2) / E^2) \qquad\qquad (\text{B.5})$$

$$n = \text{FPC} * \frac{(Z^2(p_1(1 - p_1)))}{E^2} \qquad\qquad (\text{B.6})$$

Applying the FPC factor to the estimation of sample size requirements in the case of a mean given a standard deviation of 1.0 and desired error interval of 0.10 at the 95% confidence interval, we arrive at the following *assuming a population size (N) of 1000*. Note that we must first calculate the sample size requirement in the absence of a finite population ($n_1 = 384$) in order to apply the FPC factor.

$$\frac{((1.0^2)(1.96^2) / .10^2)}{1 + (n_1 / N_1)} = 277$$

Similarly, applying the FPC factor to the calculation of sample size requirements in the case of a proportion results in a parallel reduction in the number of required interviews as shown here.

$$\frac{((1.0^2)(1.96^2) / .10^2)}{1 + (n_1 / N_1)} = 277$$

In the case of sample sizes, the FPC factor is applied to the estimate under the infinite population assumption. In this case, a sample size of 384 was prescribed. Applying the FPC factor reduced this to 277 based on a population of 1000. Clearly, in the case of sample size estimates, application of the FPC factor is not directly aimed at the variance component of the equation. Rather, it is used to deflate the sample size under the infinite population assumption. In other cases, however, the FPC factor is directly applied to the variance or standard error portions of equations, as will be demonstrated below.

FPC and Hypothesis Testing

It should be clear that the finite population correction (FPC) factor directly affects variance estimates. The extent to which variance is reduced depends on the ratio n/N. As Everitt (1998:126) demonstrated, the FPC correction term is applied to the variance term $(\bar{x})$, as shown in Equation B.7 where $(1 - n/N)$ is the FPC term.

$$\mathrm{Var}(\bar{x}) = \frac{\sigma^2}{n}\left(1 - \frac{n}{N}\right) \tag{B.7}$$

Leveraging the FPC to reduce variance estimates can be applied to a number of useful situations as described by Crow, Davis, and Maxfield (1960:38–54). For example, the normal test, which tests whether the population mean (μ) has the value a, requires a z-test, as shown in Equation B.8.

$$z = \frac{\bar{x} - a}{\sigma / \sqrt{n}} \tag{B.8}$$

It is possible to utilize the FPC in the calculation of z, which effectively increases the value of z, depending on the ratio of n/N. This is illustrated in Equation B.9 and described in greater detail by Crow et al. (1960:39).

$$z = \frac{\bar{x} - a}{\dfrac{\sigma}{\sqrt{n}}\sqrt{\dfrac{N - n}{N - 1}}} \tag{B.9}$$

In a similar fashion, the FPC can be used to reduce the confidence band around estimates based on the ratio of n/N. Equation B.10 presents the $100(1 - \alpha)\%$ confidence interval for an infinite population. This is reduced with the addition of the FPC factor, as shown in Equation B.11.

$$\bar{x} \pm z_{a/2}\frac{\sigma}{\sqrt{n}} \tag{B.10}$$

$$\bar{x} \pm z_{a/2}\frac{\sigma}{\sqrt{n}}\sqrt{\frac{N - n}{N - 1}} \tag{B.11}$$

An area that is seldom the beneficiary of FPC-based variance deflation involves tests for two independent samples. The standard approach assumes an infinite population (see Equation B.12).

$$z = \frac{\bar{x}_1 - \bar{x}_2 - d}{\left(\dfrac{\sigma_1^2}{n_1} + \dfrac{\sigma_2^2}{n_2} \right)} \qquad (\text{B.12})$$

Crow et al. (1960:53) suggest that when N_1 and/or N_2 are finite, the FPC can be used to reduce r^2, as shown in Equation B.13.

$$z = \frac{\bar{x}_1 - \bar{x}_2 - d}{\left(\dfrac{\sigma_1^2 \left((N_1 - n_1) / (N_1 - 1) \right)}{n_1} + \dfrac{\sigma_2^2 \left((N_2 - n_2) / (N_2 - 1) \right)}{n_2} \right)} \qquad (\text{B.13})$$

This approach is rarely leveraged in applied customer satisfaction research. Clearly, it offers the opportunity to demonstrate statistically significant differences that would otherwise be overlooked. When incentive systems rely on the demonstration of statistical significance, the implication of using the FPC can be substantive.

Glossary

ACSI Study—The American Customer Satisfaction Index is sponsored by ASQ and the University of Michigan's National Quality Research Center. It relies on a 100-point scale and benchmarks performance across more than 160 companies. Over 50,000 interviews are conducted annually as part of the ongoing study.

affective loyalty component—When loyalty is considered an attitude with behavioral outcomes, we can identify two components: affective and cognitive. The affective component of loyalty is presumed to reflect emotional ties to the service or product supplier. See also *cognitive loyalty component.*

attrition risk—This number is frequently assigned to individual customers based on the possibility of relationship termination. Survival analysis is often used to calculate the probability of a given customer's mortality—that is, the probability that the customer will sever his or her relationship with the product or service provider.

Baldrige Award—National award related to service and product quality. Customer satisfaction plays a large role, as do quality and operational results, leadership, process quality, and human resources management.

best in class—Typically refers to a specific competitor considered to provide optimal service or product offerings. Comparisons to these competitors are the basis for *competitive benchmarking.*

beta coefficient—Optimized weight encountered in dependence models, such as regression analysis, that indicates the magnitude of effect a given predictor variable has on the outcome variable.

bivariate statistics—Any measure used to summarize the relationship between two variables regardless of their measurement level (i.e., nominal, ordinal, interval, or ratio).

canonical correlation—The correlation between two sets of variables. One is generally considered the predictor set and the other the outcome set. A single coefficient represents the extent to which the two sets of variables are linearly dependent.

causal modeling—Family of analytical techniques (e.g., path analysis) that employ cross-sectional data and make inferences concerning the causal relations among variables. Although causality is not proven, researchers can conclude that the relations in the data are consistent with the causal hypotheses.

census—As opposed to a *sample,* a census involves gathering data from the entire population of interest. Occasionally, this is possible in customer satisfaction research when the population is composed of a relatively small number of businesses or customers. A true census is very difficult to achieve because it is rarely possible to obtain data from every customer.

cognitive loyalty component—When loyalty is considered an attitude with behavioral outcomes, we can identify two components: affective and cognitive. The cognitive component of loyalty is believed to reflect rational considerations with respect to a service or product supplier. These might include justifications such as price and proximity. See also *affective loyalty component.*

collinearity—Mathematical problem especially troublesome in dependence models. It occurs when the relationships among predictor variables are strong, resulting in a very unstable model. Manifestations of this condition include sign reversals associated with beta coefficients and large standard errors around beta estimates.

competitive benchmarking—Customer satisfaction data gain additional value when considered vis-à-vis the performance levels of competitors. An index of *best in class* competitors or key individual competitors permits customer satisfaction data to be exploited for competitive strategy development.

condition index—Means of diagnosing the extent to which collinearity may be degrading a dependence model. Levels greater than 90 indicate substantive problems.

confirmatory analysis—Any analysis that requires the researcher to specify a priori the hypothesized outcome. Factor analysis, for example, can be exploratory or confirmatory. In the latter case, the researcher specifies which variables are expected to load on which factor(s).

control chart (Six Sigma)—Control charts track processes by plotting data over time. Deviations from the center line (CL) are of special importance because they can reflect process irregularities. When deviations exceed the upper control limit (UCL) or lower control limit (LCL), a statistically significant deviation has occurred.

correlation—A wide variety of correlations exist for different data situations. All bivariate correlations reflect the extent to which two variables covary. Correlation does not, by any means, imply or demonstrate causality.

covariance—Extent to which two variables vary simultaneously across the observations in a data set. Covariance is exploited in key-driver analyses that seek to establish an implied cause-and-effect relationship between a specific service or product quality variable and an outcome measure like overall satisfaction or loyalty. Covariance relies on *variance* in both the dependent and predictor measures.

cross-sectional analysis—Typically, survey research is cross-sectional. This means the data were collected at one point in time. It can be differentiated from longitudinal or time series data analysis, which involves data collected over a period of time at equal intervals, like months. See also *longitudinal data analysis.*

customer experience management (CEM)—Approach to managing customer relationships that focuses on the customers' experiences and interactions with the company. See also *customer relationship management.*

customer relationship management (CRM)—Promised as a revolutionary paradigm shift with respect to how companies interact with customers. CRM has not fully delivered the bidirectional flow of benefits it was supposed to. Many companies gather substantial amounts of customer data, but do little with it. True CRM programs utilize the customer data to improve the relationship.

customer satisfaction—Quantification of customer satisfaction, which typically involves a score on a multipoint scale, ostensibly reflects a summary of the extent to which the customer's expectations are being met.

customer value management—Approach to understanding why consumers buy certain products. It assumes that consumers weigh the price and quality of competing products or services and make summary conclusions about the value each presents. Rational consumers presumably purchase the choice that offers the greatest value.

data matrix—Composed of both rows and columns, a data matrix contains all of the information used in statistical analyses. The rows typically correspond to individual respondents, and the columns represent the variables. An individual cell in a data matrix is the score provided by a given respondent on a single variable.

dependence model—Dependence models involve the extent to which a single variable or set of variables depends on a set of one or more predictor variables.

dependent variable—In dependence models, the dependent variable is the outcome variable. It is considered dependent on one or more predictor variables. See also *endogenous variable.*

derived importance—Derived importance is based on leveraging the covariation between a critical outcome variable like overall satisfaction and specific, actionable predictor variables. Typically, derived importance implies the use of multiple regression analysis, but this need not be the case. Derived importance should be differentiated from stated importance measures in which respondents are asked to indicate how important various product and service issues are to them.

earnings per share—One of the most familiar financial metrics used to evaluate a company's performance, earnings per share is equal to net income divided by the number of shares outstanding.

eigenanalysis—Means of decomposing a symetric matrix like the correlation or covariance matrix. This technique is used in *principal components analysis.*

employee satisfaction—Typically a summary metric that ostensibly reflects the degree to which an employee is satisfied with his or her job. This is frequently referred to as job satisfaction. A variety of inputs affect employee satisfaction. These range from pay and benefits to upward mobility, coworkers, and role ambiguity.

endogenous variable—Endogenous variables are outcome or dependent variables. Overall customer satisfaction is frequently an endogenous variable: it depends on a variety of service and product quality variables.

EQS—Computer program for developing structural equations models.

exogenous variable—Exogenous variables are predictor or independent variables. Service and product quality are typically used as exogenous variables in dependence models characterized by some measure of overall satisfaction as the outcome variable.

finite population correction factor (FPC)—When a sample exceeds about 10% of the population, FPC can be implemented to reduce the variance estimate when calculating confidence intervals or applied when comparing two means or proportions.

gap analysis—Typically refers to the difference between stated satisfaction and stated importance. This approach to resource allocation is outdated and tends to be exhausting for respondents because they must rate each service or product quality attribute in terms of both importance and performance.

geographic information system (GIS)—Not frequently used in customer satisfaction and loyalty research but potentially useful in helping understand patterns of satisfaction across geographic regions.

goodness-of-fit statistic—Used in confirmatory analyses such as confirmatory factor analysis or path analysis to assess the extent to which the data are consistent with the hypothesized structural or measurement models.

heteroscedasticity—In regression analysis, this condition reflects an undesirable distribution of the residuals. For example, as values of one or more of the predictor variables increase, the residual value (i.e., error in prediction) increases. This violates one of the fundamental assumptions of regression analysis.

hierarchical linear model (HLM)—Analytical approach designed for situations in which the independent variables differ among themselves in terms of the organizational level being referenced. For example, a situation in which some variables pertain to the managers of retail outlets while other variables pertain to individual employees within those retail outlets.

Hierarchical Bayes Regression (HBR)—Novel approach to dependence modeling, HBR is hierarchical because it has two conceptual and mathematical levels. One key benefit of the approach is that it yields respondent-level importance weights. As a result, it is possible to reveal latent segments of respondents who share similar driver profiles.

hierarchy of needs—Originally formulated by Maslow, this hierarchy provided a framework for psychologists to understand human motivation and behavior.

house of quality—Quality functional deployment (QFD) is a set of quality management tools that is very customer oriented. It is frequently referred to as the "house of quality" because the primary diagram used by this approach resembles a house subsuming input areas like customer ratings, design requirements, and importance ratings.

identification—Term frequently used in structural equation modeling, identification refers to the relation between the number of available observations and parameters to be estimated. A just-identified (saturated) model has as many observations as parameters. More problematic is the underidentified model in which there are more parameters than observations, making estimation impossible.

ill conditioning—Mathematical problem especially troublesome in dependence models. It occurs when the relationships among predictor variables are very strong, resulting in an unstable model. Manifestations of this condition include sign reversals associated with beta coefficients and large standard errors around beta estimates.

imputation—Process conducted to rectify problems associated with missing values in multivariate data. A variety of approaches to imputing missing values are available. These range from rather simplistic mean substitution techniques to more sophisticated regression-based procedures.

independent variable—Typically in dependence models, the independent variable(s) are presumed to affect one (or more) outcome variables.

inferential statistics—Inferential statistics is based on estimates one makes based on samples from a broader population. The word *inferential* technically refers to the inferences made about the overall population based on the smaller sample.

influential observation—With respect to multiple regression analysis, an influential observation is one that exerts excessive influence over the beta coefficients. Removal of such influential observations can sometimes substantively change the regression equation.

interaction effect—In a dependence model context (e.g., regression analysis), an interaction effect involves the product of two (or more) variables on the dependent measure. The implication of a significant interaction effect is that "the sum of the parts is greater than the whole."

interval data—Endpoint anchored Likert scale data that employ five or more points are typically treated as interval-level data. The characteristics that distinguish interval-level data include valid inferences concerning the distance between each scale point. With interval data one can reasonably conclude that a score of 4 represents twice the level of a given attribute than does a score of 2. Interval (or ratio)-level data are assumed on the dependent side of a multiple regression equation.

job descriptive index (JDI)—Developed in the 1970s, a popular standardized employee satisfaction questionnaire containing 72 items fall into five categories: work, pay, promotion, supervision, and coworkers.

key-driver analysis—Generally any dependence model designed to assess the effect of various predictor variables on a single outcome variable. Examples include regression analysis, logistic regression analysis, and discriminant analysis.

Kruskal's relative importance—Dependence model technique known to be robust with respect to collinearity. The technique produces a metric that represents the average, squared partial correlation over all permutations of independent variables.

latent variable—A latent variable is inherently unobservable. Factor analysis and other similar procedures are frequently used to facilitate the understanding of latent variable structure. Examples of latent variables include intelligence and motivation. These are typically measured using test instruments in the form of questionnaires with predetermined scales that ostensibly reflect the underlying latent constructs.

level of analysis—Refers to the level at which an analysis is conducted. For example, employee satisfaction data may be considered at a variety of levels including the organization, department, work group, or individual.

Likert scale—Attitudinal scales employed in applied customer satisfaction research are typically referred to as Likert scales. These may be endpoint anchored (i.e., very dissatisfied to very satisfied) or fully anchored, in which case each point on the scale has a label. It may be argued that the fully anchored Likert scale yields ordinal level data and the endpoint anchored Likert scale yields interval-level data.

linkage research—In customer satisfaction and loyalty research, this refers to the effort to relate psychometric survey data to business outcome data such as profitability, revenue, or market share.

LISREL—Software application developed by Jöreskog and Sörbom, specifically for latent variable path model applications.

logistic regression analysis—Logistic regression analysis is a dependence model appropriate for binary outcome variables. Such cases violate a fundamental assumption of OLS regression—that the dependent variable is normally distributed. Logistic regression employs a nonlinear link that permits more robust model development using binary outcome variables.

longitudinal data analysis—Longitudinal data analysis involves examining relationships among variables across time. Data are typically recorded in terms of uniform periods of time like months, quarters, or years. Of concern is how variables and their relationships with one another vary over time. See also *cross-sectional data analysis.*

lower confidence level (LCL)—In a Six Sigma control chart, the lower control limit (LCL) reflects a level of a given process parameter that is outside (below) the center line (CL), which is the desired level. See also *upper control limit (UCL).*

loyalty—Construct that is frequently and erroneously confused with its behavioral manifestations. Loyalty is an attitudinal state focused on an organization, service, or product that results in desirable behaviors such as repurchase or tenure as a customer. Measuring the behaviors is not the same as measuring the attitude.

manifest variable—Whereas a latent variable is unobservable (e.g., intelligence), a manifest variable is more tangible. The actual questions in survey instruments represent manifest variables. Techniques such as factor analysis permit us to understand the latent dimensions underlying sets of manifest variables.

matrix—Block of numbers characterized by n rows and r columns. In customer satisfaction research, a matrix is typified by n rows (where n = number of observations) and k columns, each of which relates to a specific variable. Using matrix algebra, complex analyses can be conducted and communicated in an especially parsimonious fashion. OLS regression, for example, is represented as $b = (X'X)^{-1}X'Y$, which produces a vector of beta weights.

matrix algebra—Matrix algebra is used extensively in modern statistical analysis and applied customer satisfaction research. It is a very convenient way to express complex statistical formulas.

measurement model—In SEM with latent variables, the measurement model represents the confirmatory factor analytic portion of the architecture. The measurement model specifies the relationships between the manifest and latent variables.

Minnesota Satisfaction Questionnaire (MSQ)—Standardized test relating to employee satisfaction. The test was available in two forms, containing either 20 or 100 questions.

missing values—Missing data are especially problematic in multivariate analyses because most statistical packages exclude any observation that does not have valid data for every variable in a given multivariate procedure. Missing values occur when respondents fail to answer a question, skip patterns force a respondent to not answer certain questions, key punching errors occur, and a variety of other reasons.

motivation theories—Family of theories with roots in psychology seeking to explain human behavior. Motivation theories provide rational explanations for the emotional, physiological, and other determinants of human behaior.

motivator-hygiene theory—The motivator-hygiene theory posited that two separate continua affected human work behavior. Motivators were positive reinforcers and hygienes were considered to have negative connotations. The theory considers pay to be a hygiene, intrinsic rewards like pride are motivators.

multicollinearity—See collinearity.

multiple correlation coefficient—Represented with an uppercase R to differentiate it from the simple bivariate correlation coefficient, the squared multiple correlation coefficient plays a pivotal role in assessing the efficacy of multiple regression analyses. The multiple correlation coefficient is analogous to the simple bivariate correlation, but it reflects the extent to which a series of variables covaries with a single outcome measure.

multivariate data analysis—A dataset is considered multivariate if each observation (row) has more than two variables. Multivariate data analysis subsumes all statistical techniques that operate on more than two variables per observations simultaneously. Thus factor analysis, multiple regression analysis, and path analysis all represent multivariate statistical techniques despite their rather divergent objectives.

nominal data—Nominal data are categorical. There is no inherent ordering associated with values of a nominal level variable. Examples of nominal variables include eye color or body type.

nonlinear regression—Form of multiple regression analysis that accommodates nonlinear relationships between the predictor and dependent variables.

nonparametric statistics—Body of statistical estimation and inference techniques that are free from distributional assumptions.

nonrecursive causal model—In structural equation modeling, causality is typically assumed to have a unidirectional flow. This is known as a *recursive model*. Reciprocal causation is permitted in the case of nonrecursive causal models. In this case, we may permit two variables to cause one another. Assumes that product and service quality affect overall satisfaction (y_1), which in turn causes customer loyalty (y_2), which would represent a simple recursive causal model. To make this a nonrecursive model, we would estimate an additional path from loyalty to satisfaction. The implication of this is that satisfaction causes loyalty and loyalty also causes satisfaction. Such reciprocal causal relationships are not uncommon when modeling psychological phenomena. Nonrecursive structural equation models are somewhat problematic from an identification perspective (see *identification*).

operationalize—In marketing research, we attempt to define a concept by constructing questionnaire items that purportedly measure it. How a construct is operationalized refers to how it is measured in (typically) a questionnaire context.

ordinary least squares (OLS)—Ordinary least squares is the most frequently encountered form of estimation used in simple linear or multiple linear regression analysis. It involves the estimation of a regression line that minimizes the sum of squared deviations between the observed and predicted values of a dependent measure.

ordinal data—Ordinal data are ordered. Inferences may be made concerning the order of ordinal data values but not their relative position. For example, if all students in a class were assigned a rank with respect to their height, this would be ordinal data. We could conclude that one student was taller than another but not how much taller.

overidentified model—In confirmatory analyses where goodness of fit must be assessed, model identification plays a pivotal role. An overidentified model permits parameter estimation and is desirable, as is the just identified model.

path analysis—This technique was developed in the early 1900s by Sewall Wright and represents the structural foundation for latent variable path modeling. It is included in the broad class of techniques known generally as causal modeling.

path coefficient—A path coefficient in path analysis is equivalent to a standardized beta coefficient and reflects the extent to which one variable influences another.

PCA—See *principal components analysis.*

PCR—See *principal components regression.*

principal components analysis—A dimension-reducing technique used frequently in customer satisfaction research to reduce collinearity attributable to too many variables or variables that are too highly intercorrelated. The technique is conceptually and mathematically similar to factor analysis but does not assume variables can be decomposed into their unique and common variance. As a result, PCA does not suffer from the factor indeterminacy problem associated with the estimation of communalities in common factor analysis. Component scores are frequently used subsequently in regression analysis due to their orthogonality (see entry under *principal components regression*).

principal component regression—Involves the use of PCA to reduce a set of predictor variables into a more manageable, smaller group of orthogonal component scores. With orthogonal components on the predictor side of the regression equation, there is no concern that collinearity will degrade the model. This approach is frequently used to circumvent the degrading effects of ill-conditioned data and, less commonly, to reduce a predictor variable set to more manageable numbers. The latter usually implies the former problem, of course.

profit margin on sales—Profitability metric equal to net income divided by net sales for a given period.

proportional hazards regression—Survival analysis technique that models the hazard function based on a set of predictor variables.

psychometric—Relating to the science of measuring attitudes.

quadrant chart—Used extensively in customer satisfaction research, the quadrant chart typically has as a *y*-axis (vertical) that indicates importance (derived or stated) and an *x*-axis (horizontal) that reflects performance level in terms of respondent satisfaction. Thus four quadrants based on the integrated importance–performance data are possible. Each represents a different combination of importance and performance (e.g., high importance and low importance). The strategic implications with respect to the product or service quality issues that fall into each quadrant can help organizations maximize their customer satisfaction.

quality functional deployment (QFD)—Set of quality management tools that is very customer oriented. It is frequently referred to as the "house of quality" because the primary diagram used by this approach resembles a house. QFD helps organizations convert customer needs into process or product designs.

rate of return on assets—Combines the profit margin on sales with asset turnover. The rate of return on assets is equal to net income divided by net sales (profit margin on sales) times net sales divided by total average assets (asset turnover).

rate of return on common stock equity—Is equal to net income after preferred dividends are divided by average common stockholders' equity.

ratio data—Ratio data represent the richest data from an analytical standpoint. They are ordered, inferences can be made about the relative magnitude of different values, and, perhaps most importantly, there is a natural zero. Income represents a ratio-level variable.

recursive causal model—In a recursive structural equation model, causal flow is assumed to be unidirectional. For example, consider a simple path model with two independent and two dependent variables. The independent variables, product and service quality, are assumed to affect the first dependent variable (overall satisfaction), which, in turn, affects the second dependent variable (loyalty). In the recursive model environment, we cannot permit the second dependent variable to loop back and affect the first. To do so would be to posit a nonrecursive causal model.

regression analysis—Dependency model used to assess the extent to which a set of predictor variables affect a single interval- or ratio-level outcome variable.

relationship survey—Broad class of customer satisfaction survey instruments that does not focus on specific transaction interactions. Instead, relationship surveys attempt to provide more holistic measurements of the customer's perceptions of the service/product producing organization. See also *transaction survey*.

relative importance—In the realm of key driver (multiple regression), relative importance implies a metric that will permit interval- or ratio-level inferences concerning the relative effects of two predictor variables. Note that when evaluating beta weights, it is only possible to make ordinal (rank order) level judgments about how two competing variables affect an outcome variable.

return on investment (ROI)—Financial term that has been exploited increasingly by researchers and business management consultants to define the presumably positive outcome of a management program, research endeavor, or other activity.

return on quality (ROQ)—Program that focuses on the financial returns associated with quality improvement initiatives. The approach emphasizes the link among quality, customer satisfaction, customer retention, and profitability.

ridge regression—Special form of multiple regression analysis employed when collinear data are especially problematic. Ridge regression involves using a *ridge estimator* value (usually between zero and one), which is added to the data matrix. The resulting regression equation generally is more stable.

R-square statistic—In regression analysis, the squared multiple correlation coefficient represents the proportion of dependent variable variance accounted for by the set of predictor variables. In applied customer satisfaction research, it is not uncommon to encounter R^2 greater than 0.80. R^2 is the multivariate equivalent of the bivariate correlation coefficient squared (r_{ij}^2).

sample—Refers to a subset of a population. Survey samples refer to psychometric data obtained randomly from a population.

SAS—Statistical analysis system. A comprehensive programming and statistical software package used extensively in marketing research generally and customer satisfaction research specifically.

saturated model—In causal modeling, a saturated model is one in which all possible paths are estimated. No exogenous variables are constrained to zero with respect to any of the dependent variables. A saturated model is able to replicate exactly the original data covariance of matrix and therefore has perfect goodness of fit.

SERVQUAL scale—The multi-item SERVQUAL scale is considered one of the first attempts to operationalize the customer satisfaction construct. The SERVQUAL scale focused on the performance component of the service quality model in which quality was defined as the disparity between expectations and performance. The battery of items used in the SERVQUAL multi-item scale is still used today as a foundation for instrument development.

simple linear regression—Regression equation characterized by a numeric outcome variable and a single predictor variable. This is differentiated from multiple regression analysis, which includes more than one predictor variable.

Six Sigma—The Six Sigma system is empirically driven, placing emphasis on root cause analysis and closed-loop business processes. The primary objective of the Six Sigma process is to reduce variance around critical business measures relating to service or product quality. Reducing process variation yields improved products and services. Services or products that are produced at the optimum Six Sigma level yield a mere four defects per million.

SPSS—Statistical Package for the Social Sciences. An advanced statistical analysis program used extensively in marketing research and customer satisfaction research.

stakeholder scorecard—A term coopted from the balanced scorecard concept in which a variety of business performance metrics are summarized and consolidated in a single management report. The stakeholder scorecard can involve performance data relating to customers, employees, suppliers, and distributors.

stated importance—Stated importance relies on the respondent's introspective capacity to communicate which product and service quality issues are important. This is typically achieved through the use of survey instruments that ask respondents to indicate how important various issues are to them. Stated importance has been criticized on several grounds. Among these are respondents' tendency to indicate all issues are important, thus minimizing the variance of responses across items.

stepwise selection—Used extensively in multiple regression analysis when collinearity is problematic. This is a purely mechanical procedure that checks the residual sum of squares as each variable is entered into the equation. Variables that fail to meet the entry criterion (frequently referred to as the *F-to-enter*) are dropped from the model because their unique contribution to accounting for variance in the dependent variable is trivial. Stepwise selection can be forward or backward. The latter refers to a reversal of the procedure in which an F-to-remove is calculated for each variable and those that do not exceed the criterion are dropped. It is possible for a variable to be included initially in the model selection process and subsequently dropped as other variables are added.

structural equation model—Structural equation modeling is a family of techniques that includes an integrated confirmatory factor analysis and path analysis in a causal model that demonstrates the linkages between latent constructs.

structural model—In SEM with latent variables, the structural model depicts the causal relationships among latent variables. The structural model is rooted in path analysis, developed in the early 1900s by Sewall Wright.

survival analysis—Survival analysis, a longitudinal statistical technique, focuses on variables that are predictive of mortality. When applied to human mortality, key predictor variables might include smoking, age, cholesterol level, and weight. When applied to customer relationships, survival analysis might suggest that tenure, complaints, and purchase patterns are indicative of risk level. See also *proportional hazards regression.*

top-box score—The top-box and top-two box scores are metrics frequently employed when presenting univariate customer satisfaction data. Many organizations track the proportion of respondents who rate their product or service on a Likert scale's top one or two numeric categories. The top-box score when using a 5-point Likert scale is the proportion of respondents who indicated their satisfaction level was a 5.

transaction survey—Type of customer satisfaction survey focused on a specific interaction and its various components. The transaction survey attempts to decompose the transaction into its components and identify subprocesses that may be problematic. Transaction surveys must be administered within 24 to 72 hours of the interaction, generally, because consumer recall of transaction satisfaction tends to decay rapidly.

underidentified model—In confirmatory analyses where goodness of fit must be assessed, model identification is critical. An underidentified model is characterized by too many estimable parameters in relation to the number of observations. This situation precludes model estimation and must be reexamined.

unit of analysis—The level at which an analysis is conducted. The unit of analysis in most customer satisfaction research is the individual customer. However, customers may be aggregated at a district, state, or country level and treated statistically at a level. Data combined to a district level, for example, imply that the unit of analysis is the district.

univariate statistics—Focuses on individual variables and their distributions. Univariate profiles derived through the systematic examination prescribed in EDA approaches represents an excellent idea prior to undertaking more complex multivariate analyses. Univariate examination will reveal any pathological conditions at this level and can lead to correction through various transformations.

upper confidence level (UCL)—In a Six Sigma control chart, the upper control limit (UCL) reflects a level of a given process parameter outside (above) the center line (CL), which is the desired level. See also *lower control limit (LCL)*.

variance—Statistical term relating to the extent to which a distribution is spread around the average (or proportion). In customer satisfaction research, variance in service or product quality issues is exploited in key-driver models aimed at establishing *covariance* between predictor and outcome variables. Variance associated with a specific variable may reflect real or perceived variations in service or product quality.

variance inflation factor—An indicator of the extent to which collinearity in a regression model is degrading. Variance inflation factors help statisticians diagnose the collinearity problem and assess the extent to which different variables contribute to the condition. See also *condition index*.

References

Adams, B. 2001. Customer relationship management uncovers revenue from loyal guests. *Hotel & Motel Management, 216,* 9:36–37.

Adams, J. 1975. Inequity in social exchange. In R. M. Steers and L. W. Porter (Eds.), *Motivation and work behavior.* New York: McGraw-Hill.

Agresti, A. 1990. *Categorical data analysis.* New York: John Wiley & Sons.

Alderfer, C. 1972. *Existence, relatedness, and growth.* New York: Free Press.

Allen, D., and Rao, T. 2000. *Analysis of customer satisfaction data.* Milwaukee: ASQ Quality Press.

Allen, D., and Wilburn, M. 2002. *Linking customer and employee satisfaction to the bottom line.* Milwaukee: ASQ Quality Press.

Allison P. 1995. *Survival analysis.* Cary, NC: SAS Institute.

Almquist, E., Heaton, C., and Hall, N. 2002. Making CRM make money. *Marketing Management, 11,* 3:17–23.

Anderson, E., and Fornell, C. 1994. Customer satisfaction, market share, and profitability. *Journal of Marketing, 58,* 53–67.

Anderson, E., and Fornell, C. 2000. Foundations of the American Customer Satisfaction Index. *Journal of Total Quality Management,* 11:7, S869–S882.

Anderson, E., Fornell, C., and Rust, R. 1997. Customer satisfaction, productivity, and profitability: Differences between goods and services. *Marketing Science,* 16:129–45.

Atkinson, J. 1958. *Motives in fantasy, action, and society.* New York: D. Van Nostrand.

Atkinson, J. 1964. *An introduction to motivation.* New York: D. Van Nostrand.

Atkinson, J., and Litwin, G. 1960. Achievement motive and test anxiety conceived as motive to approach success and motive to avoid failure. *Journal of Abnormal and Social Psychology, 60,* 52–63.

Auh, S., and Johnson, M. 1997. The complex relationship between customer satisfaction and loyalty for automobiles. In M. D. Johnson, A. Herrmann, F. Huber, and A. Gustafsson (Eds.), *Customer retention in the automotive industry: quality, satisfaction, and loyalty.* Wiesbaden, Germany: Gabler. 141–66.

233

Barsky, J. 1999. *Finding the profit in customer satisfaction.* Chicago: Contemporary Books.

Bearden, W., and Teel, J. 1983. Selected determinants of consumer satisfaction and complaint reports. *Journal of Marketing Research, 20,* 21–28.

Beck, R. 2000. *Motivation: Theories and principles.* Upper Saddle River, NJ: Prentice Hall.

Belsley, D. 1991. *Conditioning diagnostics: Collinearity and weak data in regression.* New York: John Wiley & Sons.

Belsley, D., Kuh, E., and Welsch, R. 1980. *Regression diagnostics.* New York: John Wiley & Sons.

Bergeron, B. 2002. *Essentials of CRM: A guide to customer relationship management.* New York: John Wiley & Sons.

Bernstel, J. 2001. Strained relationship. *Bank Marketing, 33,* 10:14–19.

Bhalla, G., and Lin, L. 1987. Cross-cultural marketing research: A discussion of equivalence issues and measurement strategies. *Psychology & Marketing, 4,* 4:275–85.

Birkes, D., and Dodge, Y. 1993. *Alternative methods of regression.* New York: John Wiley & Sons.

Blanchard, K. 1994. Punished by poor management. *Incentive, 168,* 1:168.

Bollen, K. A. 1989. *Structural equations with latent variables.* New York: John Wiley & Sons.

Boulding, W., Kalra, A., Staelin, R., and Zeithaml, V. 1993. A dynamic process model of service quality: From expectations to behavioral intentions. *Journal of Marketing Research, 30,* 7–27.

Bryant, B., and Cha, J. 1996. Crossing the threshold: Some customers are harder to please than others. *Marketing Research, 8,* 4.

Budescu, D. 1993. Dominance analysis: A new approach to the problem of relative importance of predictors in multiple regression. *Psychological Bulletin, 114,* 542–51.

Buzzell, R., and Gale, B. 1987. *The PIMS principles.* New York: Free Press.

Churchill, G., and Surprenant, C. 1982. An investigation into the determinants of customer satisfaction. *Journal of Marketing Research, 19,* 491–504.

Cirillo, R., and Silverstein, D. 2002. Can CRM be saved? *VARBusiness, 18,* 3:53–56.

Cronin, J., and Taylor, S. 1992. Measuring service quality: A reexamination and extension. *Journal of Marketing, 56:*55–68.

Crosby, L. 1992. Toward a common verbal scale of perceived quality. In *The race against expectations* (45th ESOMAR Congress, Joint Session on Customer Satisfaction and Quality Management), Amsterdam.

Crosby, L., and Johnson, S. 2002a. Building CRM strategies. *Marketing Management, 11,* 1:10–11.

Crosby, L., and Johnson, S. 2002b. The globalization of relationship marketing. *Marketing Management, 11,* 2:10–11.

Crosby, L., Johnson, S., and Quinn, R. 2002. Is survey research dead? *Marketing Management, 11,* 3:24–30.

Crow, E., Davis, F., and Maxfield, M. 1960. *Statistics manual.* New York: Dover.

Council on Financial Competition. 1987. *Service quality.*

Danaher, P., and Rust, R. 1996. Indirect financial benefits from service quality. *Quality Management Journal, 3,* 63–75.

Davenport, T., Harris, J., and Kohli, A. 2001. How do they know their customers so well? *MIT Sloan Management Review, 42,* 2:63–73.

Deci, E., and Ryan, R. 1985. *Intrinsic motivation and self-determination in human behavior.* New York: Plenum Press.

Dillon, W. R., and Goldstein, M. 1984. *Multivariate analysis: Methods and applications.* New York: John Wiley & Sons.

Draper, N. R., and Smith, H. 1998. *Applied regression analysis.* New York: John Wiley & Sons.

Dyche, J. 2001. *The CRM handbook: A business guide to customer relationship management.* Reading, MA: Addison-Wesley.

Elandt-Johnson, R. C., and Johnson, N. L. 1980. *Survival models and data analysis.* New York: John Wiley & Sons.

England, G., and Harpaz, I. 1983. Some methodological and analytic considerations in cross-national comparative research. *Journal of International Business Studies,* 14:2, 49–59.

Everitt, B. 1998. *The Cambridge dictionary of statistics.* Cambridge: Cambridge University Press.

Fornell, C. 1995. The quality of economic output: Empirical generalizations about its distribution and relationship to market share. *Marketing Science, 14,* 203–11.

Fornell, C., Johnson, E., Anderson, W., Cha, J., and Bryant, B. 1996. The American Customer Satisfaction Index: Nature, purpose and findings. *Marketing Research, 8, 4.*

Galimi, J. 2001. Beef up the business value of CRM by getting back to basics. *Managed Healthcare Executive, 11,* 10:44.

Goldenberg. B. 2002. *CRM automation.* Upper Saddle River, NJ: Prentice Hall.

Gordon, I. 2001. CRM is a strategy, not a tactic. *Ivey Business Journal, 66,* 1:6–8.

Gronholdt, L., and Martensen, A. 2002. Customer satisfaction and loyalty modelling: A comparison of regression and artificial neural networks. Unpublished paper, Department of Marketing, Copenhagen Business School.

Gulycz, M., and Brown, S. 2002. *Performance-driven CRM: How to make your customer relationship management vision a reality.* New York: John Wiley & Sons.

Gupta, K. 2002. How customer-focused programs differ. *Marketing News, 36,* 10:19–20.

Herzberg, F. 1968. One more time: How do you motivate employees? *Harvard Business Review, 46,* 53–62.

Herzberg, F., Maunser, B., and Snyderman, B. 1959. *The motivation to work.* New York: John Wiley & Sons.

Heskett, J., Sasser, E., and Schlesinger, L. 1997. *The service profit chain.* New York: Free Press.

Hosmer, D. W., and Lemeshow, S. 1989. *Applied logistic regression.* New York: John Wiley & Sons.

Ilieva, J., Baron, S., and Healey, N. 2002. Online surveys in marketing research: Pros and cons. *International Journal of Market Research, 44,* 3:361–76.

Ingold, C. 2002. CRM systems allow agents to customize service. *National Underwriter, 106,* 4:4–5.

Jackson, J. E. 1991. *A user's guide to principal components.* New York: John Wiley & Sons.

Jain, S. 1990. *Marketing planning and strategy.* Cincinnati: South-Western.

James, D. 2002. Better together: MR and CRM combined get companies closer to ROI. *Marketing News, 36,* 10:15–16.

Johnson, M., Herrmann, F., Huber, G., and Gustafsson, A. 1997. An introduction to quality, satisfaction, and retention: Implications for the automotive industry. In M. Johnson, A. Herrmann, and A. Gustafsson (Eds.), *Customer retention in the automotive industry: Quality, satisfaction, and loyalty.* Wiesbaden, Germany: Gabler. 1–17.

Jolliffe, I. T. 1986. *Principal component analysis.* New York: Springer-Verlag.

Kadet, A. 2002. "I can't believe they treat people like this." *Smart Money, 11,* 11:118–22.

Kerr, S. 1975. On the folly of rewarding A, while hoping for B. *Academy of Management Journal, 18,* 4:769–83.

Kieso, D., and Weygandt, J. 1977. *Intermediate accounting.* New York: John Wiley & Sons.

Kleinbaum, D., and Kupper, L. 1978. *Applied regression analysis and other multivariable methods.* Boston: Prindle, Weber, and Schmidt.

Kohn, A. 1993a. Why incentive plans cannot work. *Harvard Business Review, 71,* 5:54–61.

Kohn, A. 1993b. *Punished by Rewards: The trouble with gold stars, incentive plans, A's, praise, and other bribes.* Boston: Houghton Mifflin.

Kohn, A. 1994. Why incentives fail. *CFO, 10,* 9:15–17.

Kruskal, W. 1987. Relative importance by averaging over orderings. *The American Statistician, 41,* 6–10.

Lee, E. T. 1992. *Statistical methods for survival data analysis.* New York: Wiley.

Li, S. 1995. Survival analysis. *Marketing Research, 7,* 17–25.

Mahajan, V., and Wind, Y. 2002. Got emotional product positioning? *Marketing Management, 11,* 3:36–42.

Maslow, A. 1954. *Motivation and personality.* New York: Harper & Row.

Maslow, A. 1968. *Towards a psychology of being.* Princeton, NJ: Van Nostrand Reinhold.

McArdle, J., and Hamagami, F. 1996. Multilevel models from a multiple group structural equation perspective. In G. Marcoulides and R. Schumacker (Eds.), *Advanced structural equation modeling.* Mahwah, NJ: Erlbaum.

McCauley, D., and Colberg, M. 1983. Transportability of deductive measurement across cultures. *Journal of Economic Measurement, 20,* 3:267–98.

McClelland, D. 1985. *Human motivation.* New York: Scott-Foresman.

McClelland, D., Atkinson, J., Clark, R., and Lowell, E. 1953. *The achievement motive.* New York: Appleton-Century-Crofts.

McCullagh, P., and Nelder, J. 1983. *Generalized linear models.* London: Chapman Hall.

McKenzie, R. 2001. *The relationship-based enterprise.* Toronto: McGraw-Hill Ryerson.

Nadler, D., and Lawler, E. 1977. Motivation: A diagnostic approach. In J. Hackman, E. Lawler, & L. Porter (Eds.), *Perspectives on behavior in organizations.* New York: McGraw-Hill. Reprinted in B. Straw (Ed.), *Psychological dimensions of organizational behavior.* 1995. Englewood Cliffs, NJ: Prentice Hall.

Naes, T., and Martens, H. 1985. Comparison of prediction methods for multicollinear data. *Communications in Statistics–Simulation and Computation, 14,* 545–76.

Naumann, E., and Giel, K. 1995. *Customer satisfaction measurement and management.* Milwaukee: ASQ Quality Press.

Nichols, C. 2000. CRM systems provide excellent source for research. *Marketing News, 34,* 19:28–29.

Nunnally, J. C. 1978. *Psychometric theory* (2nd ed.). New York: McGraw-Hill.

Oliver, R. 1980. A cognitive model of the antecedents and consequences of satisfaction decisions. *Journal of Marketing Research, 42,* 460–69.

Orme, B. 2000. Hierarchical Bayes: Why all the attention? *Quirk's Marketing Research Review, 14,* 3:16–63.

Parasuraman, A., Berry, L., and Zeithaml, V. 1985. A conceptual model of service quality and its implications for future research. *Journal of Marketing, 14,* 41–50.

Parasuraman, A., Berry, L., and Zeithaml, V. 1988. SERVQUAL: A multiple-item scale for measuring customer perceptions of service quality. *Journal of Retailing, 16,* 12–40.

Pettit, R. 2002. The state of CRM: Addressing deficiencies and the Achilles' heel of CRM. *Business Intelligence Advisory Service Executive Report, 2,* 3:1–30.

Reichheld, F. 1996. *The loyalty effect.* Boston: Harvard Business School Press.

Reichheld, F. and Sasser, W. 1990. Zero defections: Quality comes to services. *Harvard Business Review, 68,* 105–11.

Rust, R., and Zahorik, A. 1993. Customer satisfaction, customer retention, and market share. *Journal of Retailing, 69,* 193–215.

Rust, R., and Zahorik, A. 1995. Return on quality (ROQ): Making service quality financially accountable. *Journal of Marketing, 59,* 2:58–71.

Rust, R., Zahorik, A., and Keiningham, T. 1994. *Return on quality (ROQ): Making service quality financially accountable.* Cambridge, MA: Marketing Science Institute.

Schumacker, R. E., and Lomax, R. G. 1996. *A beginner's guide to structural equation modeling.* Mahwah, NJ: Erlbaum.

Songini, M. 2001. Fleet expands CRM tool to hundreds of banks. *Computerworld, 35,* 11:35.

Spence, J., and Helmreich, R. 1983. Achievement-related motives and behavior. In J. A. Spence (Ed.), *Achievement and achievement motives.* San Francisco: W. H. Freeman. 7–74.

Stewart, G., et al. 1993. Rethinking rewards. *Harvard Business Review, 71,* 6:37–46.

Storbacka, K., and Lehtinen, J. 2001. *Customer relationship management.* New York: McGraw-Hill.

Van de Vijver, F., and Poortinga, Y. 1982. Cross-cultural generalization and universality. *Journal of Cross-Cultural Psychology, 13,* 4:387–408.

Vavra, T. 1997. *Improving your measurement of customer satisfaction.* Milwaukee: ASQ Quality Press.

Vroom, V. 1964. *Work and motivation.* New York: John Wiley & Sons.

Weiner, B. 1985. An attributional theory of achievement motivation and emotion. *Psychological Review, 92,* 548–73.

Willet, J., and Sayer, A. 1996. Cross-domain analyses of change over time: Combining growth modeling and covariance structure analysis. In G. Marcoulides and R. Schumacker (Eds.), *Advanced structural equation modeling.* Mahwah, NJ: Erlbaum.

Yu, L. 2001. Successful customer-relationship management. *MIT Sloan Management Review, 42,* 4:18–19.

Zeithaml, V., Berry, L., and Parasuraman, A. 1996. The behavioral consequences of service quality. *Journal of Marketing, 60,* 31–46.

Index

A

B